How She Really Does It

How She Really Does It

{ Secrets of Successful
Stay-at-Work Moms }

Wendy Sachs

Da Capo
LIFE
LONG
A Member of the
Perseus Books Group

Many of the designations used by manufacturers and sellers to distinguish their products are claimed as trademarks. Where those designations appear in this book and Da Capo Press was aware of a trademark claim, those designations have been printed with initial capital letters.

Designed by Jeff Williams
Set in 11-point New Caledonia by the Perseus Books Group

Library of Congress Cataloging-in-Publication Data

Sachs, Wendy.
    How she really does it : secrets of successful stay-at-work moms / Wendy Sachs. 1st ed.
        p. cm.
    Includes index.
    ISBN 0-7382-1017-X (hardcover : alk. paper) 1. Working mothers. I. Title.
    HQ759.48.S23 2005
    306.874'3—dc22

                                        2005002360

First Da Capo Press edition 2005

Published by Da Capo Press
A Member of the Perseus Books Group
http://www.dacapopress.com

Da Capo Press books are available at special discounts for bulk purchases in the U.S. by corporations, institutions, and other organizations. For more information, please contact the Special Markets Department at the Perseus Books Group, 11 Cambridge Center, Cambridge, MA 02142, or call (800) 255–1514 or (617) 252–5298, or email special.markets@perseusbooks.com.

1 2 3 4 5 6 7 8 9—09 08 07 06 05

Contents

Preface   *ix*

{ 1 }

Why Work Is Good from Our Heads to Our Souls:
The Power of Staying at Work   *1*

{ 2 }

The Shelf Life of Eggs:
Biology Confronts Reality   *21*

{ 3 }

The Breast Pump in the Briefcase:
The Art of Juggling   *43*

{ 4 }

Giving Up the Guilt:
The Pressures, the Expectations, the Myths   *69*

{ 5 }

Something's Got to Give:

How to Switch Gears and Careers   93

{ 6 }

Moms at the Helm:

A Business Boom Explosion   115

{ 7 }

Making It Work for You:

Life Goes in Cycles   139

{ 8 }

Finding the Holy Grail:

What Moms Really Want   161

Acknowledgments   189

Notes   193

Index   197

For Michael

My loving husband,

I don't know how he really does it

Preface

Identity Crisis: Diapers Versus Briefs

Upon giving birth to my son three and a half years ago, I was quickly initiated into the cult of mommyhood. Part of the rite of passage in this postpartum society is to enter a parallel universe, a highly social and active world where moms and babies spend their days hustling around to a wide array of classes, lunches, and playgroups. When my son was six weeks old, we joined organized "New Mommy" lunches that took place at various New York City restaurants. For $20, moms bonded over sore nipples and poopy diapers, swapped dramatic tales of labor and delivery, and shared tips on which infant gas remedy worked best. As we sat around the tables, feeding and burping our crying newborns, guest speakers would talk to us about important matters such as the benefits of baby massage and the surprising fat-burning efficiency of Strollercize.

It was here where I met my first mommy friends—a lactating sorority of out-of-shape, exhausted women who were, like me, simply looking for sisterly support as we all struggled to survive those brutal first few months of motherhood. The women at these lunches had an impressive collective résumé. They were lawyers, psychologists, engineers, financial analysts, social workers, and marketing and advertising executives. Many had graduated from some of the elite universities in this country. So when talk turned to life after maternity leave, I was surprised to discover that only two women were returning to work. One was going back to her full-time job as a credit analyst at a Wall Street financial institution, and my friend Sue, a school psychologist, planned to return part-time after taking a year of maternity leave from the school system where she worked. Some of the other women initially agonized about whether or not to return to their careers. One mom even saw a therapist to hash out her anxieties. She has since had another baby and has decided to stay home—at least for now.

At that time, I had recently left my job as an associate producer at *Dateline NBC* to work at an Internet start-up. I had been wooed by stock options and the ability to work from home. But my company was on the verge of imploding as the dot com bubble was bursting, and I was itching to go back into television, a career I had truly adored. I had thrived on the rip of adrenaline breaking news gave me—the chase, the conquest, the addictive feeling of being a part of history.

On September 11, 2001, when two planes crashed into the World Trade Center, my infant son, Jonah, was sleeping soundly on me, molded to my chest. While I watched the towers crumble on TV and smelled my delicious baby on top of me, I suddenly felt conflicted. I wanted desperately to be covering the story, the biggest news event of our generation. As the story evolved over the next few weeks, I started speaking to former colleagues about freelancing for NBC. They needed additional bodies, and I wanted to sign up. But how could I leave my infant for what would have been long days, if not weeks on end?

For the next few months I continued to grapple with how I could go back into television. I was on the outskirts of this historic event, and I couldn't stand it. Instead of field producing in Afghanistan, I was breastfeeding at Starbucks. For the first time ever my clear career path was suddenly as opaque as the Calvin Klein tights I used to wear to work. Had motherhood permanently obstructed my Big Career plans?

Many of the moms I initially met truly couldn't relate to my growing restlessness. They had made peace with their decision to stay home and were getting settled into their routines of full-time, at-home mommyhood. As I became more antsy, they seemed more content. Part of me envied them for being so thrilled with motherhood and not appearing to need more. And part of me was simply bothered by their satisfaction. I just didn't get it. I found myself getting sucked into traditional stereo-types of what defines a "Good Mother," and I began fearing that I sim-ply wasn't good enough. If I were good enough, I figured, I should be relishing motherhood, not feeling a relentless churning for something more.

It was at this time that the inspiration for this book evolved. I was shocked to discover that so many smart, talented women were dropping out of the workforce, or "opting out" as *New York Times* reporter Lisa Belkin called it. We're the women who were raised in an environment where anything was supposed to be possible. We're the ones who had the doors to advancement jimmied open for us to waltz through, so why were so many women turning on their heels and leaving once they became mothers? Had all of these women embraced their inner Marthas and dis-covered domestic bliss and fulfillment in baking the perfect linzer tortes, as some headlines suggest? I felt desperate to find moms who weren't dropping out but who were staying in—and I was equally desperate to discover how they were doing it all.

As I wrestled with what to do, I looked for support—beyond the "New Mommy" group—and asked other women about how they handled this tricky work-family quandary. When I shared my concerns about how to still have a fantastic career and be a great mommy, I found that I wasn't alone. Whereas some moms seemed genuinely happy to take a mid-career sabbatical because they both wanted to and could afford to stay at home, many more women I met were, like myself, feeling anxious because they wanted to work and were trying to figure out how to merge their career with motherhood. The "balance" everyone talks about, that Holy Grail for working moms, was much more nuanced and complicated than we had ever anticipated. The dirty truth that no one wants to admit is that the world works against the Stay-at-Work mom. We have been led to believe that career women can gracefully maneuver motherhood into already bustling lives. But ask any new mom, and we're simply stumbling along blindly trying to stay afoot, to please everyone, and to make sense of our suddenly conflicted identities. Every mother I met seemed desperate to hear about how other women strike that precarious balance in their lives be-tween motherhood and career. How do they do it? What are the trade-offs?

How do they handle the inevitable conflicts? How do they reconcile the guilt? How do they come to terms with their own ambition? Are they happy? Is there anything they regret? What are the options out there?

Despite growing up at a time when more and more women worked, we had few examples showing us how we were going to succeed at being both great moms and women with fabulous careers. Ours was the generation who grew up and came of age watching *The Cosby Show*'s smiling Claire Huxtable, the witty, tough mother of five who allegedly worked full-time as a lawyer but was always around for dinner and endless chitchat. She never seemed stressed or fried from work. She never bitched about clients or mentioned that she couldn't make it to Rudy's ballet recital or Theo's soccer game because of a grueling caseload. But as we've all now learned, *The Cosby Show* epitomized the idyllic family sitcom, not reality TV. So how are real women doing it?

What We Really Want

The debate over Stay-at-Work moms versus Stay-at-Home moms is explosive. It strikes at the core of who we are as women and as mothers. It taps into our personal insecurities and unfairly forces us to respond to society's expectations of us both in the workforce and at home. It challenges our priorities and identities, and it sometimes leaves us feeling as if we simply can't win. Even though much has been made about our generation expecting and wanting to "have it all," women today are redefining what "all" means. Definitions of "success" have more to do with job satisfaction and flexibility than with prestige and position. Women want to be respected and compensated fairly in our jobs even if we work three or four days a week at the office. We want flextime, part-time, and job-share to be viewed not as a privilege but as an integral part of the work culture. We want the freedom to amp up when we are ready and to cut back if we need to slow things down.

Because we often learn best through the prism of other women's experiences, I've chosen to share the stories of dozens of Stay-at-Work mothers, both ordinary and well known, who can inspire us and teach us the lessons they have learned along their journey of motherhood. The famous moms I have profiled each have life experiences that make them role models for the rest of us. Yes, many of their lives are privileged and undeniably made easier because they are financially able to afford more help. But all of these women have something special to contribute that makes them real and relevant to regular women. And perhaps what's most important about the "celebrity" mothers is that while they can afford *not* to work, they *choose* to work. We will hear from moms about how to deal with the crunch of work and family; how to assuage the inevitable guilt; how to find the courage to switch careers; how to get what you need, even in an unfriendly family work environment; and how ultimately to find that comfortable work-life ratio we are all hoping to achieve.

For two years I have interviewed and surveyed more than one hundred women. My interviews do not represent a scientific sampling. It's what sociologists call the "snowball" method. I spoke to my friends and friends of friends. I met with working mother groups, and I sent out surveys across the country. I spoke to women on playgrounds and at preschool and even in my pediatrician's office. I talked to women in coffee shops, at dog runs, and at birthday parties. The women I met crossed ethnic, racial, religious, and regional lines. Most are married, and all have college degrees. Author Peggy Orenstein says that "having a college education is crucial to the architecture of the female self." It makes sense that a college education is instrumental in giving women the ability to create opportunities for themselves. So I wanted to talk to the generation of women who grew up believing that they had a lot of options and that if they went to school, did well, and worked hard enough, anything was possible.

The women whom I interviewed grew up all over the country, but at the time I spoke to them they lived in Portland, Los Angeles, Phoenix, Austin, Minneapolis, Miami, New York and its suburbs, and the Washington, D.C., area. In some instances, at the request of the women I interviewed, I have changed names and major identifying details about their lives. Although my research was not scientific, it yielded thematic results. It is in using these themes that I have structured this book.

For me, this project began as a rather selfish journey. When I started, my son was a toddler. Having endured four months of colic with a baby who sapped all of my energy and missing life in TV news, I was anxious to resume my broadcasting career and to do some interesting work again. I was prepared to work full-time. I was even ready to travel. But two years after I began this project, my son is three and a half, and I also now have an eighteen-month-old daughter. I've found that as my family has grown, my priorities keep shifting. The thought of traveling for work is no longer appealing. The hours of most network TV jobs are equally daunting. I now feel that dropping my son off at preschool and watching him learn how to kick a goal on the soccer field on a Monday afternoon is as important to me as producing a story with NBC's Stone Phillips. I see time racing by, and I want to be able to savor more of those precious early moments. This does not mean that I don't want to work. It just means that I want to redefine what it is that I'm doing and how I can do it.

I walk away from this book realizing that there is no right or wrong way of satisfying the dual desires of career and motherhood. Similarly, there is no perfect formula and no one-size-fits-all solution because our needs as mothers are not static—they change over time and vary considerably among women. But what I've found is that all of us want more options— various ways to integrate our families with our careers. Women don't have to feel stuck at the intersection of career and motherhood. We need to continue demanding change in the workforce while creating even more opportunities for ourselves. I use the term Stay-at-Work moms because this book is about women who have chosen to stay in the workforce. Yes, most Stay-at-Work moms also financially need their income to pay their bills and afford their lifestyles, but everyone in this book is also working because they *want* to have a career. Our careers help define us; they make us feel complete; they enhance our well being and our relationships and give us a more secure financial future. It is my hope that by reading the stories and experiences in this book, moms will find solutions and options for themselves to inspire and empower them in their quest to have at least some of it all—all of the time.

How She Really Does It

Chapter 1

Why Work Is Good from Our Heads to Our Souls

The Power of Staying at Work

Last year my 2-year-old son Jonah attended preschool in a leafy, New Jersey suburb, where most moms spend their days tethered to their SUVs shuttling between the gym, the mall, and their children's music classes. In this town, a mom who works is about as fashionable as a woman who wears *fake* Prada. When I mentioned to my son's teacher that I was starting work full time as a CNN freelance news producer, now that my youngest child was six months old, the teacher didn't even pretend to mask her horror. "You're working in the city, *every day*?" she asked me incredulously. "Then who is going to watch your kids?" she sniffed. I smiled sweetly and cheerfully answered that I had a fabulous babysitter who would watch my children while I worked. Moments later as I pulled out of the carpool lane, it occurred to me that I was apologizing for the fact that I had a job. Sadly, I felt I needed to prove to Jonah's teacher, a woman who only teaches a couple hours a week, that working full time does not mean I'm a selfish mom who is abandoning her offspring. I didn't bother to explain that returning to my career in television is not just a choice but also a financial necessity. But as secure as I had felt in my decisions, the teacher's look of indignation cut through my Superwoman exterior like kryptonite.

For more than twenty years, women have earned more college degrees than men. In 2004, for the first time ever, more women entered Harvard than men. In 2003, 63 percent of the graduating class at Berkeley Law School was female; Harvard was 46 percent; Columbia was 51 percent.[1] Today, nearly 47 percent of medical students are women. Ironically, now that women have broken through the barriers of higher education and are arguably achieving equal status in the workplace, our biggest adversary is not always the great, white male of *The Feminine Mystique* era but rather sometimes our fellow sisters—those women who sat next to us taking the LSATs, studying for GMATs, and heading student governments.

Remarkably, even in the postfeminist era, when women are performing in professions at nearly the same rate as men, many moms who have the so-called option to stay at home feel they must justify to other women their decision for working, especially when their children are young. It doesn't start out this way. In fact, multiple studies show that the vast majority of college-aged women plan on working after they have kids. So what happens between college and motherhood that causes such a seismic shift in women's expectations and attitudes toward work and motherhood?

Popular culture is certainly one of the culprits. Today motherhood is literally in vogue. The March 2003 cover of *Vogue* celebrated motherhood with a very sexy and pregnant picture of Brooke Shields, her long, damp hair brushing against a playfully see-through, body-hugging sheath. Entertainment magazines are also capitalizing on motherhood by regularly printing photos of celebrity moms from Gwyneth Paltrow and Madonna to Kate Hudson, Reese Witherspoon, and Sarah Jessica Parker pushing strollers and toting babies. Even couture has embraced "mommy chic." A recent Gucci ad campaign had rail-thin model moms draped in Gucci clutching their surprisingly plump, naked babies. The good news for mothers these days is that having a baby no longer represents the dowdy and oppressed condition our feminist foresisters griped about; it's now the must-have accessory of a sexy, successful woman.

But the progressive look of motherhood still has a regressive feel. We are bombarded with images of seemingly selfless mothers catering to every aspect of their children's lives. The controversial 1980s "supermom" who worked seventy-five-hour weeks and broke her high heels racing to PTA meetings has been replaced by the socially palatable "soccer mom" who is readily available to accommodate her children's hectic schedules in between her own yoga classes.

Even the best-selling baby tome *What to Expect, The First Year*, in its section on returning to work, asks women, "Will you feel saddened if the sitter is the one your baby runs to when hurt?. . . Do you feel you can tune in to your baby's unspoken needs by just spending evenings and week-ends together?" The loaded questions it poses are enough to make a post-partum woman cry. The book clearly implies that staying at home is the ideal situation for both mother and child. It explains that putting one's ca-reer on hold only "sometimes" sets you back professionally and asks women if "they are willing to make this sacrifice." You might expect that given this anachronistic tone, *What to Expect* was written by men, but you would be wrong. Three women wrote this popular baby bible.

The Good-Enough Mother

There's no doubt that the bar has been raised to increasingly difficult standards. From the pressure to breastfeed and the expectation that mother and child must participate in a myriad of stimulating classes from music and movement, to gymnastics, karate, and cooking, the pendulum has swung back again. The modern message mothers hear today still car-ries a disturbingly old-fashioned tone: "good moms" don't work; at least they don't work full time.

"The judgment we face from other women is brutal," says *Cosmo Girl* New York manager Lauren Lerman and mother of a three-year-old. "I think it really comes from insecurity. The stay-at-home moms are a little insecure that they have given up their careers, and working moms feel uneasy that they're not spending enough time with their kids. I think the insecurity on both sides breeds resentment. As women and as moms I think we're hurting our cause by not supporting each other."

But did our generation ever have a cause in the first place? We inher-ited one, but it was never really our own. The images of those hairy-legged, bra-defying feminists of the 1960s feel as remote to us as the

8mm reel of the Kennedy assassination. Yes, it's a part of our collective history, but we did not grow up with it defining our identity. We took it for granted that we could have both, careers and children. In a society where almost half of all Americans agree that one parent should stay at home with their children, working moms understandably feel in conflict.[2]

The irony, of course, is that our female "liberation" has boomeranged and brought us right back to the place we were fifty years ago when women often had no other choice but to be headquartered at home. The only difference is that today the president of the PTA is more likely to have an MBA. And the "problem with no name," as Betty Friedan famously described in *The Feminine Mystique*, can now be treated with Prozac.

Wherever you look these days it does seem as if something alarmingly retro is going on—a celebration of women who are hanging up their careers to stay at home with their children. A *New York Times Magazine* article in October 2003 reported that many super-educated women are happily opting out of their stressful careers to return home where duty calls and are diving into motherhood with Olympian gusto. *Business Week, Time,* and *Fortune* have also recently reported on the exodus of mothers from the workplace. The conclusion—career and motherhood cannot peacefully coexist.

Even the protagonist, Kate Reddy, from the best-selling novel *I Don't Know How She Does It*, ultimately quits her high-flying financial career because it was devastating her home life. Although most women I've met agree that Kate's job and motherhood didn't mix well, and many felt she was actually a terrible role model because she seemed completely out of touch with her kids, nearly everyone said that they felt disappointed with the ending of the book because she leaves her career. So if Kate Reddy isn't our heroine, who is?

Working It Out

For almost two years I have been interviewing a multicultural mix of mothers, from politicians and fashion designers to psychologists, publicists, journalists, teachers, lawyers, doctors, marketing managers, bankers, entrepreneurs, advertising and publishing executives, and celebrities. I've talked to women who work part-time and women who work eighty hours per week. Many women have to work, and others choose to work, but the theme remains the same: having a career is not only good for women; it's good for mothers. Yes, there is always ambivalence, sacrifices, and sometimes agonizing choices to be made. But overall, what I've learned from these women is that having a career not only makes them feel better about themselves but also better about their relationships with their spouses and with their children.

In fact, several studies support my findings that working is not only good for your self-esteem, but it can also actually buffer depression. One reason for this is that when women are satisfied in one area of their lives, they can handle the disappointments and stress in another. These studies showed that the more dissatisfied a woman was with her home life, the more depressed she tended to be. Working women, on the other hand, felt less depressed about problems at home than housewives did.[3] They are proud of their roles as breadwinners and feel that their work is an essential contribution to their family's standard of living.[4] And even though women feel the crunch between career and kids, they say that they are happy to be working.

Waking Up with a Purpose

We work for the money, to massage our brains, because we have to, because we like to, and sometimes because it's easier to be at work than it is to be at home with our kids. Our personal ambition often drives us to continue working after we have children. It can be a demon that gnaws at us, forcing us to prove something, to make a mark in the world.

For NBC's *Today* show news anchor Ann Curry, her passion for news and personal drive is why she continues to wake up at 4:00 A.M. every day and go to the office. Financially Ann doesn't *need* to work, but emotionally she relishes the jolt that her job gives her and the feeling of satisfaction that comes with her career.

On an unseasonably warm October morning, I wait to meet Ann in the *Today* show studio's "Green Room." A spread of Danish, mini-bagels, and underripe melon sits virtually untouched for the *Today* guests when I arrive.

At a few minutes past 10:00, after the show wraps up, Ann breezes inside. She's a bit breathless as she greets me with a huge smile and a strong handshake.

At 47 years old, Ann Curry is a remarkably beautiful woman. Her exquisite features come courtesy of a Japanese mother and a Caucasian father of Scotch-Irish descent. Ann has been *Today's* news anchor since 1997.

As a mother to son Walker, 9, and daughter McKenzie, 12, Ann understands the conflicts a Stay-at-Work mom can face, albeit one with the salary of a seasoned network newscaster. Before I can even ask Ann a question, she leans back on the green sofa and launches into her own thoughts on motherhood.

"I think a lot of women are unprepared for the life change that motherhood forces upon them. It's almost frightening how many women have derailed their hopes and dreams and the work that they want to accomplish because they become mothers," Ann says matter-of-factly. "I think that the challenge is figuring out how to make motherhood fit into their lives without forcing them to lose what it is they feel they're supposed to do with their lives.

"If motherhood has always been your dream and your ultimate greatest achievement, it is laudable," Ann says, taking a sip of bottled water. "But for so many women, it's not the end zone. It's part of the journey, but many women have other things that they want to feel they've accomplished. I would not recommend you give up your job completely if you love it, if it's meaningful to you. I don't want to go back to a time when women could only focus on becoming mothers and raising their family's children."

As the oldest of five, growing up in a working class community in Oregon, Ann was more focused on establishing a career for herself than she was about starting a family.

"Being the oldest, I knew how demanding it was to have children," Ann says. "I had a sense early on that if I was ever going to do what I wanted to do with my life, then I had to do it before I had kids."

Ann has a strong sense of purpose and drive in her professional life. She went into journalism because she believed it was a career where people could make a difference.

"My father raised me with an idea that the best course of action would be to do something of service so that at the end of your day you knew that it mattered you were here," Ann says. "I fell into television because I grew up during Watergate and Vietnam and the women's rights and civil rights movements and came to realize that knowledge was power and that by providing information to people I was doing something good."

Ann says that becoming a mother has actually made her more ambitious because now she strives to be a role model for her own children. Whether it's reporting on the 9/11 terrorist attacks or the Indian Ocean tsunami devastation, Ann feels her work sends an important message to her children. She tells me of a conversation she had with her son Walker via satellite phone while she was covering the Kosovo refugee crisis in 1999.

"I said, 'Hi, it's Mommy,' and Walker said, 'Mom, I saw what those bad guys did to those poor people, that's wrong isn't it?'" she says, imitating her then-4-year-old son's voice. "And I said, 'Yes, that's wrong, Walker, those guys were being bad guys by not letting those people have their food.' 'They made them go out of their homes, didn't they?' he asked. 'Yes, they did, Walker, that was wrong.' 'Did you get them back their homes?'" he asked her. "I said, 'No, Walker, I didn't get them back their homes.' 'Well, did you get them some help?' he implored. I said 'Well, I think I got them some food, and maybe I let everybody else know that what happened was wrong, and maybe something right will happen,'" she told him sweetly. "'Well, that's good, Mom, that's good.'"

"That's what I want my children to know of me," Ann says. "I want them to look at my life and say, well, it mattered that she was here. And I know now that they can already say that Mom is trying to do good with her work."

As one of the four faces of *Today*, Ann Curry undoubtedly has one of the most enviable and relatively flexible jobs in television—a gig few people would consider giving up even after having children. Life is different for those who work behind the scenes in TV production. Stationed

throughout the beige corridors of NBC News, toil the scores of producers who often work punishing hours with generally inflexible schedules.
One floor above Ann, tucked away in a small office, sits *Dateline NBC*
producer and mother of three Soraya Gage. Money is only part of the
reason Soraya works. Like Ann, she is driven by ambition and addicted
to her job.

At 43, Soraya is a pretty, petite, unassuming, powerhouse of a producer. With straight, light brown hair barely brushing her shoulders; big,
hazel eyes; and a warm smile, she brings to mind Holly Hunter in *Broad-
cast News*.

When I talk to Soraya over lunch, she is eight months pregnant with her
third child. That night, she and a few chosen producers are invited to have
margaritas with NBC News anchor Tom Brokaw. It's Brokaw's way of saying thank you to the producers with whom he has recently worked. But Soraya was agonizing about the evening. She debated whether she should
leave her boys, George, 8 and David, 6. When she weighed the value of
the night out, even though she was pregnant and wouldn't be drinking, she
knew it was important for her career to go. But even one night away, and
Soraya says she feels out of sync with her kids the next day.

"One thing I think people don't realize: if you are a working person and
you've been working your whole life, the ambition doesn't just go away,"
she says as she digs into her salad.

"You still want to achieve, you still want to be the best, that stuff stays
with you. It would be great if you had children and then the ambition
kind of went away. And you thought, well, my family's the most important
thing, and I want to just stay home, or I won't put work on the front
burner. But it's not like that; you always have this nagging thought that
you could be achieving more, or you could be doing better.

"My problem is that I'm an overachiever, and I want to be one of the
best producers at NBC and a great mom, and I think why can't I do it all?
It would be much easier if I didn't want so much."

I agree with Soraya. It *would* be much easier if we didn't want so
much, but so many of us do crave it all, or at least a little bit of it, all of
the time. And there's nothing wrong with that. Why do women feel so
greedy and guilty about simultaneously wanting a fantastic job and a ful-

filling home life? Why do women feel they must apologize for having what men take for granted?

Nine Months of Style

Liz Lange, 37, makes no apologies for what she wants. She is living an entrepreneurial dream come true. In 1997, the former *Vogue* assistant began a fashion maternity clothing line at a time when the market was virtually void of stylish clothes for expectant mothers.

Her inspiration came from her friends who were all getting pregnant and complaining that maternity clothes were impractical and ugly—baby doll dresses and pastel colors, hardly clothes one would want to wear arguing a case before a jury or pitching an ad campaign to a client.

So for about a year Liz researched the maternity market, and without exception every retailer with whom she spoke told her fashionable maternity wouldn't fly; it would fail because pregnant women wouldn't spend money on clothes. Liz believed differently and went out on her own to prove that women would spend money on high-end maternity clothes if she gave them stylish and well-made clothes to wear.

Newly married, but not yet pregnant, Liz designed an edited line of maternity clothes—six items in three different colors of high-quality, stretchy fabric. She found a factory that would make her clothes one piece at a time for her by-appointment-only clients. The response from women was tremendous. Not long after Liz started selling the clothes, she became pregnant with her first child, and she quickly discovered that her limited line of maternity wear needed to be expanded.

"I realized this could be much bigger. I could have bathing suits, skirts and dresses, and more than just three colors. Nine months is a long time, and when you work as I did, you need plenty of clothes. My best customers are working women. They have to get up every day, and they can't get away with anything less than total professionalism. As a professional woman myself, I realized it's not crazy to spend money when you're pregnant. It's a long time when nothing else in your closet works, and you're seeing people every day, and you're putting yourself out there, and your image is important."

Today, Liz Lange is one of the biggest names in maternity fashion and a major player in the $1.2 billion industry. With a store on Madison Avenue, in Beverly Hills, and on Long Island, Liz has clothed the bulging bellies of celebrities from Cindy Crawford to Catherine Zeta-Jones. Once an exclusive label with revenues of $8 million, her line continues to expand thanks to licensing and distribution deals with Nike and Target.

Liz is a tall, svelte, attractive woman who smiles easily. Her energy is contagious and barely contained as she talks about her passion for her growing business. We meet in her airy, Madison Avenue office on a Friday afternoon. She has just raced back from picking up her 4-year-old son, Gus, from preschool a dozen blocks away. After spending a few minutes with him and her 2-year-old daughter, Alice, Liz drops them off with the nanny to get back to the office. Growing up in the tony, Upper East Side of New York City, where none of the mothers she knew had careers, Liz never aspired to be a business woman, let alone a CEO of her own business. The guilt of leaving her children tugs at her constantly, but her other baby, her young business, needs her constant attention too.

"Something that's been interesting to me over the past few years is discovering in myself a drive and an ambition and a competitiveness that I didn't even know was there. It feels like I had a little bit of a metamorphosis," she says. "I was a good student, and I cared about my grades. But I didn't think about myself career-wise in that way. When I look back now, I think, how the hell did I think my life was going to play out? Did I think I was going to be sitting at home while my husband worked? It's scary, but maybe that is what I was thinking," Liz says.

"I really feel like I'm the luckiest person in the world because I'm doing something that I feel so passionately about and that gives me such a personal gratification. When you're an entrepreneur, it's almost like a cult. It's hard to understand if you're not in it. It's so stressful every single day, but there's something so unbelievably rewarding about it. I feel fabulous when I get emails from customers who tell me that I made them feel better about themselves or changed their lives or magazines want to talk to me. I know it's not brain surgery, I'm making maternity clothing, but I feel like I'm doing something that does make a difference and is also employing other people."

Liz, Soraya, and Ann each love their careers and are unabashedly ambitious. They may be pleased to know that a byproduct of having career ambition is a happier marriage and a more satisfying family life. A *Working Women* magazine study found ambitious women report happier marriages than their less ambitious counterparts even when factoring in their stressful professional lives and family responsibilities.[5] The ambitious women were also more likely to characterize themselves as good mothers than those who described themselves as less ambitious. Why these results? The study's authors say that successful women with well-rounded lives are more positive and have more energy to begin with. It seems everything works better when women are feeling good about themselves. Many women also believe that having a career helps keep their marriage equal.

"There's no feeling in our household that something is my responsibility and not his or vice versa," says Liz Lange. "If a child gets up in the middle of the night, it's about who got up last, it's not that I get up because I'm the mom. In my mind, I can't imagine it any other way. You're both two people, you each need sleep, no one enjoys some of this stuff."

Soraya says that even if she could afford to stop working, she wouldn't for fear that it would alter the dynamics in her marriage. She believes that her career is good for her marriage.

"Our household is very equal. Bob and the kids respect me. There's no sense that Mommy is the servant. Mommy is as important as Daddy is, and Mommy has an important job too."

Sex, the City . . . and Nursing Bras

It makes sense that working is a great boost to a woman's self-esteem and all-around fulfillment. Just the routine of getting ready for work by showering, blow drying hair, and putting on lipstick does miracles for the mom who is used to schlepping around in sweatpants stained with the sticky remnants of her child's breakfast. The social aspects of a job should also not be underestimated. In our pre-motherhood days, lingering over a latte is no big deal, but after having a baby, the simple act of going out to lunch or getting coffee can feel like being furloughed. Working also helps women untangle their former identity from the mother role into which they have morphed, serving as a refreshing and important reminder of who they are. Ironically, working can feel liberating.

Thirty-eight-year-old actress Cynthia Nixon, who played the scarlet-haired, sharp-tongued working mother/attorney Miranda Hobbes on HBO's *Sex and the City*, and who is a renowned figure in the Manhattan theater community, remembers what it was like to star in the Broadway play *Last Night of Ballyhoo* when her daughter Samantha was one year old. Seven months pregnant with her second child when we meet, Cynthia tells me this story over lunch on New York's Upper West Side, a few blocks from where she lives.

"Theater actors like to pamper themselves," she says as she pierces a piece of her chicken teriyaki lunch special. "They stay in bed a lot. Some don't even speak during the day. The hard thing about being a mother and being in a play is that you have your whole day, and when you get to the theater, you've already been up for twelve or fourteen hours running around. I remember going to the theater and getting into my wig and makeup and costume and sitting offstage waiting to come on for an entrance and thinking to myself many times, well, thank God I can finally sit down and take a little rest now," she says with a laugh. "This, of course, is not the best frame of mind to be in when you're about to go on stage."

When I met Cynthia, she has just returned from Los Angeles where she was nominated for an Emmy award. While *Sex and the City* has recently catapulted her to fame, Cynthia's impressive career in TV, film, and on Broadway began when she was 12 years old. While attending Barnard College in New York City, she even starred in two Broadway plays simultaneously, running between theaters in between acts. For such a prolific actress, it's strange to hear Cynthia say that she's not a particularly goal-oriented person. In fact, just about the only thing Cynthia says she knew for sure growing up was that she wanted to be a mom. But having children hasn't dulled her desire to continue acting.

"When I had my daughter, I took two months off. I thought I would actually take off much more time, but I belonged to a theater company, and they were having trouble casting this one role, and I didn't see any reason why I shouldn't do it. I would pump right before going onstage. I was really surprised by how soon I was ready to go back."

The "Who Am I?" Moment

A woman used to be judged by her tuna casserole. Or by what her husband did for a living. But for the Gen X girl who grew up singing along to "Free to Be You and Me," a professional identity is as much a part of her as her gender.

When I was pregnant with my second child and working from home on a proposal for this book, my husband and I were trying to buy our first house. We met with a mortgage broker, and I had to explain to him my income from my various careers over the past decade. I was a Capitol Hill press secretary, a network TV producer, a public relations director, and now a so-called writer working on a yet-to-be-sold book. Like many career women, I wrapped myself around my professional identity. It defined me, it validated me, it made me feel, well, important.

But the bank and my mortgage broker apparently did not see me that way. When our mortgage papers came back, next to my name and my occupation was typed in obnoxious, bold letters "HOMEMAKER." I stared incredulously at the ink.

A homemaker? I was stunned and frankly terrified by being labeled with such a retro and sexist identity. I realized that my reaction to the label "homemaker" stemmed more from my fear of losing my identity, the woman with the Big Career Plans, the girl who was supposed to take on the world, than from the old-fashioned label itself.

For me to have no other occupation aside from raising my kids, noble as motherhood is, frankly makes me break out in a cold sweat. For many reasons, ranging from the rational to the paranoid, I know I must work.

Dateline NBC producer Soraya Gage says she realized how much her career was intertwined with her personal identity when she was taking an extended leave of absence from NBC after her second child was born. She tells me about a conversation she had at a dinner party when she on maternity leave:

"A group of women asked me what I did for a living, and when I told them I was a TV producer, they said, 'Wow, that's a really cool job, how could you give that up?' I think it's hard to be an at-home mom, I really do because I think there is a lot of pressure in society to have a job and to talk about a job."

Because our culture gives little prestige and no compensation to a career in parenthood, it comes as no surprise that Stay-at-Home dad is not a job that most men want or can usually afford to embrace. Yet, historically women were supposed to be prepared for dedicating their lives to motherhood. At a time when women are blazing ahead in exciting careers and achieving financial independence that was unheard of in their own mother's day, it's no wonder that surrendering to motherhood can feel complicated and bittersweet.

On the one hand, we are besieged by images of seemingly perfect moms from models and actresses to supercharged career women who all appear to be bathing in the bliss of motherhood. These images so inundate popular culture these days that if you're not looking adorable with your pregnant bump poking out underneath a tight T-shirt and you're not feeling particularly giddy about maternity, you wonder if there's something defective in your own chemistry. But on the other hand, as the first generation of girls who were encouraged to delay marriage, go to grad school, and make partner, giving it all up for motherhood sounds frankly hypocritical.

Our Mothers, Our Role Models

Research points to an overwhelming correlation between a mother's working and her daughter's desire to work when she has children of her own.[6] About three quarters of the Stay-at-Home moms I interviewed had mothers who never worked outside of the home. Although they speak of appreciating their mothers' constant presence and availability, many also remember looking down on their moms because unlike their dads, their moms didn't have "real jobs." On the other hand, all of the women whom I have interviewed whose mothers worked knew that they too would work when they had children. And most of these women felt little ambivalence or angst in this decision.

Actress Cynthia Nixon always knew she would be a working mother. Her own mother was the primary breadwinner of the family for most of her parents' fifteen-year marriage. Cynthia's father was a struggling radio journalist who was often unemployed while her mom took on various jobs in New York City TV production companies.

"It's hard for me to understand women who don't want to work. In my own family women have always worked and had children," she says. "It's only the upper classes that now think, isn't it incredible that I have a child and a job? My mother was gone every weekday from 8:00 in the morning until 6:00 at night, and I don't remember feeling resentful about it, it was just the way it was. She just presented it that way. I think I spent a lot of time calling my mother at the office," Cynthia says. "But I didn't feel like she was inaccessible. All of the switchboard ladies knew me when I called or would visit."

New York City internist Dr. Laura Fisher, a mother to three girls under the age of 4, was practically predestined to become a doctor. Laura comes from a family of seven children. Incredibly, the entire Fisher family are doctors, including her parents. Laura's mother was on an advanced academic track in biophysics at Columbia University back in the 1950s at a time when most women were forgoing careers to have children. Her mother continued to work while Laura was young but eventually gave up her position at New York's Columbia University to raise her growing brood. She tried to resume her career when her kids were older but found her academic track stalled. So she moved into other work, teaching biostatistics, programming some of the first computer software, and becoming active in politics.

"Mom is the one who said you can have it all," Laura says. "She was very important for why the women in our family all became physicians."

Laura hopes to be a similar model for her own daughters. "As they get older, I want them to respect me that I'm smart, I work, I'm proud of what I do, and I help other people. I want them to see that they have a mom whom they may want to be like."

Makeup mogul Bobbi Brown, who began her cosmetics company from a bunch of lipsticks and her last $5000, credits a conversation she had with her mother for laying the foundation for her career. Growing up in suburban Chicago, Bobbi says she was an average student with a laid-back attitude who had no real plans for herself other than getting married, having children, and possibly teaching.

"I wasn't into anything," Bobbi tells me as we sit in a Starbucks in Bridgehampton, Long Island, where she is spending most of her summer. After Bobbi's profoundly uninspiring first year at the University of Arizona, her mother sat her down to discuss Bobbi's future.

"My mom asked me what I wanted to do with my life, and I said I didn't know. I thought school was boring. So she said, 'Forget about what you want to do with your life, what do you want to do today?' And I thought, I'd like to go to the department store Marshall Fields and play in the makeup department. And my mom said, 'Well, why don't you become a makeup artist?' I didn't want to go to beauty school because, well, even back then that seemed rather lame. So my mom said, 'I'm sure that there's a college somewhere that will let you study makeup.' There wasn't. But I convinced Emerson College in Boston to let me."

Sitting cross-legged in her gym clothes without a trace of her namesake makeup, Bobbi tells me that it was her mom who gave her the confidence to transfer schools and create an untraditional college major.

Less than a decade after graduating from Emerson College, Bobbi found a chemist to create her vision of ten lipsticks that could mix and blend to create any color a woman needs—and Bobbi Brown Cosmetics was born.

Money Matters

Fifty-five percent of all new mothers return to work.[7] Many have to, and others choose to. For me there is no choice. It is not just financially necessary for me to make money to help pay our bills, but also psychologically it's crucial for me to get a paycheck. My mother's two divorces created crushing financial blows; at one time we were homeless, and for most of my childhood anxiety about money consumed us.

As a daughter of divorce, I feel I have an obligation to myself and to my children to protect myself financially. Even though I have faith in my marriage, the depressing statistics speak for themselves. Nearly half of all marriages dissolve, and in the year following divorce a woman's standard of living plummets 45 percent while a man's rises 15 percent.[8] This is the grim reality. Yet when the pop cultural conversation turns to motherhood, work, and "choices," it usually leaves out the very real and scary possibility that women may have to support themselves and their children. The latest census shows that there are ten million single moms in this country, and the whopping majority of them must work to support their children.

Studies show that the longer you take yourself out of the workforce, the harder it is to reenter. Certainly by delaying motherhood and establishing a career first, we have already put ourselves in a better position than most of our own mothers when they had us. But leaving work entirely, even for a few years, could be a risky move. As more time passes, it gets harder to reestablish yourself and regain your former income level. In fact, one study shows that women who work continuously until the age of 40 earn about 40 percent more than those who leave and reenter the work force.[9]

In Ann Crittenden's book *The Price of Motherhood: Why the Most Important Job in the World Is Still the Least Valued*, she writes that motherhood is the single biggest risk factor for poverty in old age. She calculates the "mommy tax" for a college-educated woman who gives up work to raise her kids can easily be $1 million over a lifetime.[10] That figure is so ghastly it will probably make most moms fall over their strollers just to hear it. In fact, she says, motherhood has become the single biggest risk factor for poverty in the United States.

Some Stay-at-Home moms talk about their educational backgrounds as their insurance policies for the future. Kimberly Morris, a mother of two toddlers, graduated from Stanford University and Harvard Law School. She quit her legal job with the city of Los Angeles when her first daughter was born nearly three years ago. Kimberly plans on taking at least five years off from work, and then she says she will return to a legal career.

"I do think I'll be able to go back into law in some capacity," Kimberly says. "At this point I just don't know what I'll do exactly."

Most career experts would agree that a Harvard law degree is usually more valuable than one from a less prestigious university, at least initially.

But is it still a sure ticket to get back into the workforce after an extended absence? And what about all of the other female law school graduates who didn't attend Harvard? Do you think they have any hope of returning to a legal career after a five-year sabbatical at home?

Ours is the first generation that is truly testing the unchartered waters of trying to weave in and out of a career. According to economist and author Sylvia Ann Hewlett, the news at this point does not look promising. Hewlett, who studies work-family issues, says that at any given time two-thirds of all women who quit their careers to raise their children are looking to reenter the work force and are finding it extremely difficult to do so. She says that women may not be able to rest on their old résumés and think they could just pick up their careers five or ten years down the road. But Hewlett says women who continue working in some capacity while their children are young are having an easier time amping up their careers when they are ready.

"The only real insurance policy is to not leave the workforce entirely," Hewlett says. "Staying in the workforce in some capacity helps protect your options down the road."

What We Didn't Expect When Expecting

I doubt that most girls of our generation ever bought into Prince Charming as our rescue hero. Most of us understood that the handsome prince could turn into a loathsome frog. We had watched our own parents abandon their marriages, or we saw divorce through the eyes of our friends. And even for those who were fortunate enough never to know divorce firsthand and whose parents stayed put, reality meant that even the best-looking marriages often had warts—though many parents valiantly tried to hide them. Of course, no one walks down the aisle expecting her marriage to turn rancid or lose luster. We all still hold on to a sexy, romantic picture of what a fabulous relationship should and could look like. But because we marry later and have had years of relationship experience before saying "I do," we're aware that the sizzle can fizzle over time, and we accept this reality—especially after children enter the picture. At least in my house, the passionate, spontaneous sex we used to have on the kitchen floor followed by feeding each other Chinese food leftovers has unfortunately been replaced by a rote semi-monthly ritual in between commercial breaks while watching *American Idol.*

Even though, like most women I know, I swore I would *never become* one of *those* couples after having kids, everyone I know *has become* one of *those* couples. The sheer exhaustion of getting through the daily grind of life with two kids makes it hard to keep relations civil, let alone steamy. When given the option of a full night of delicious sleep versus a few minutes of passion and the possibility of an orgasm, I would bet my book deal that most women would choose sleep.

The point here is that just as we entered into matrimony with our eyes pretty wide open to the reality of marriage, we entered into motherhood largely blindfolded. We had no clue about the cocktail of maternal hormones that would surge through our bodies, transforming us forever— wreaking havoc with our short-term memories and causing us to spontaneously weep during Hallmark commercials. We had no sense about the instinctual tug toward our babies that would make it physically painful to be apart from them and would break our hearts if we miss out on events like the first day of school. We weren't prepared for the conflicting feelings of rage, passion, love, and even indifference we would feel toward these creatures who grew inside of us. We didn't understand how our sense of identity would forever be altered, starting with when the labor and delivery nurses start referring to you immediately after you deliver only as "Mommy" rather than by your first name. And we certainly were never prepared for how this major life-altering, mind-numbing, body-changing event would affect our careers.

Despite growing up at a time when more and more women worked, we had few examples showing us how we were going to succeed at being both great moms and women with amazing careers. The vast majority of Stay-at-Work moms whom I met during my research had mothers who worked. But the jobs their mothers had were overwhelmingly of the more traditional and flexible "female" variety—teachers, nurses, librarians, interior decorators, legal secretaries, and the like. There are women with mothers, like my own, who are professionals and became doctors and lawyers and PhDs and businesswomen, but that usually happened after the children were school age. (My mom went to law school when I was in high school.) So the crunch years, as *Today* show host Ann Curry will later describe, those years between the birth of a child and first grade, were not nearly as difficult for our mothers who either had relatively flexible careers or hadn't even entered that phase of their life yet.

What's happening when women are trying to do it all at the same time—have babies and have a Big Career? I have found that many are succeeding and are happy, others are struggling and trying to make personal and professional changes, and many more are altering the paradigm of what success, career, and having it all now looks like.

Chapter 2

The Shelf Life of Eggs

Biology Confronts Reality

" **J'll never get pregnant** because I'm never home to have sex,"
Jenny said, taking a swig of sugar-free Snapple iced tea and popping a
prenatal vitamin. "I know this sounds crazy, but I just rescheduled my
prison shoot next month because it conflicts with when I'm ovulating."

"Can you do that?" I asked.

"The prison will still be there. My eggs won't."

Hunkered down in Jenny's windowless office on the fourth floor of
Dateline NBC news, we were two married women on the precipice of 30
with babies on our minds and a work schedule that wouldn't budge.

When I started my job at *Dateline NBC* as an associate booking producer the day before my 25th birthday, babies were the furthest thing
from my mind. As a *Dateline* booker my job was to snag the high-profile
and competitive interviews, beat out the other news shows, and get the
big "get."

The life of a booker is a life in limbo. You're at the whim of your pager;
one buzz and a phone call later, and you're scrambling to catch the next
plane to cover the latest story, which in my experience was usually located
deep in the belly of nowhere America, where dinner meant a Surf-n-Turf
special at the local Ponderosa. Even with all of the depressing motel

rooms, stale coffee, and frustrating lack of reliable cell service I experienced, I loved my job. In my four years at NBC I shamelessly chased jurors during the O.J. trial and camped out at the Santa Monica courthouse for nearly a month. I toured strip clubs looking for women who claimed they were seduced and sodomized by a South East Asian prince. I investigated hardcore news stories involving prosecutorial misconduct and first-degree murder. I reported on weapons of mass destruction, and I even chartered a private plane to Oklahoma at 3:00 A.M. to interview tornado survivors while the storm was still whipping its way across Kansas. I did interviews in prisons, trailer parks, courtrooms, and at the United Nations. And I got to work with some of the best in the business. It was an exciting job that made me feel important and made for riveting cocktail banter. But what it didn't make for was a good time to start a family.

Although many young career women won't even consider the issue of having children until after they have crossed the threshold of the big 3–0, I couldn't ignore the biological reality of what delayed motherhood could look like because sadly I saw it all around me.

The media, like most industries these days, is swarming with smart, talented women. Amid the ample estrogen in the news business, I've found that many of the most senior and powerful women in television were either unhappily still single ("News Hags" are how some of the older, saltier gals refer to themselves) or married, but suffering from infertility. These women were at the apex of their big careers, they had collected fistfuls of Emmys, they were financially secure and professionally fulfilled, but many I met were personally struggling.

Some women, longing to conceive, were undergoing intensive infertility treatments, experiencing multiple miscarriages, and incurring massive debt. I had even heard about one network correspondent desperate to get pregnant who would run to the lavatory while flying on Air Force One to shoot herself in the thigh with her fertility drugs in between chatting with President Bush. Oddly enough, these women seemed to be the lucky ones. Other women who had nourished their careers but had neglected their personal lives discovered that they might have run out of time to both find a partner and to create a family.

In 2002, Sylvia Ann Hewlett made headlines when, in her book *Creating a Life: Professional Women and Their Quest for Children*, she declared that career women are suffering a "crisis of childlessness" by squandering their fertility for their jobs. Hewlett reported that many professional women have delayed motherhood to such a point that their only hope for conception lies in the hands of a petri dish and a good fertility doctor. Hewlett's findings landed her on *Oprah*, the *Today* show, and *60 Minutes* and terrified millions of women. But all around me it seemed many women, not just those in the news business, had figured all this out long before.

In some ways I now realize I was fortunate. I had married young, and at 29 biology was still on my side—my ovaries had plenty of plump, spry eggs happily nesting inside. But I faced a double whammy of my own. I was in a demanding job but at a junior level, which meant I had no control over my travel schedule and not enough seniority to consider a part-time option. Out of a staff of several hundred, no one in my position at the time had children. To have more flexibility I needed to be promoted to producer. But chances for promotion were slim to none. There were too many associate producers and too few producer positions available, bottlenecking the route for advancement. In fact, eight years later, several of the people whom I started with at *Dateline* still haven't been promoted.

So I did what virtually no one at *Dateline* was doing. I left. I had always dreamed of a big career in TV news, but now I felt forewarned about the precarious nature of fertility and was determined to move ahead with motherhood even if it temporarily took me off my intended career track. (I did always plan to somehow return.) So at the tail end of the dot com boom, wooed by lucrative stock options and the ability to work from home, I took a job as the media director at a start-up Internet company. Two months after I left NBC, I was pregnant.

For many reasons, I am glad that I had not waited to start a family. But soon after having my son, Jonah, I found myself in flux, wondering if I had permanently derailed what was supposed to be my Big Career because I hopped off the ladder before I had ascended high enough.

The Girls in the Boys Room

The lecture room inside the stodgy Cornell Club in midtown Manhattan is buzzing. More than 200 super-educated women, all with MBAs, who are in their 20s and 30s, have gathered to hear about a new book and how they can avert a potential "Midlife Crisis at 30," a problem that seems to be afflicting a lot of young women. I am here in support of the authors, one of whom is a dear friend of mine. The crowd, consisting mostly of women working at investment banks or in finance, seems desperate to know how they are going to be able to have it all—a lucrative and fulfilling career, a loving partner, and well-adjusted children.

As the Q&A session gets rolling a woman with mocha-colored skin and regulation-length dark hair stands up in the back of the room and announces what seems like a confession into the microphone, "I just turned 30 and I have a baby," she says, her voice giving away a slight Caribbean accent. In this room chock-full of women wearing pumps and pearls, Donna is a rarified breed—she's a mom. In the culture of investment banking and finance the old boys club still rings true. Even though women have busted through the glass ceilings of most once male-dominated professions, the financial world still has dangerously low levels of estrogen. Yes, women have climbed the ranks to vice presidents and managing directors, but the environment is hardly a family friendly one, and few women under 35, let alone under 40, have children.

"When I was pregnant, people looked at me like I had two heads," Donna tells me after the lecture as we're chatting with her two friends, also young, newly minted investment bankers. "It was sort of like, how could you get knocked up and do this to your career? You're not high enough up the ladder to have a baby. And I realize that's going to hurt me. I don't have seniority, so I can't have any flexibility. And it's a very demanding job," Donna says. "People don't do this work and have children. I sort of blame myself for not having it all figured out before I got pregnant, but I don't regret having a baby."

"Women are very defensive about getting pregnant in our office," says Donna's friend Ann, an Asian American sporting a stylish suit. "There is a woman who is eight months pregnant on my team at work, and she's turning into a total bitch, I think because she's stressed out, and she feels she needs to prove herself even more than before, and she's working herself so hard and treating the rest of us terribly."

Donna nods her head. "It's really hard being pregnant and having a baby in an environment that is so completely unfriendly to mothers. But we're in a service industry that requires you to be available to clients 24/7. You really can't do that if you're a mom," Donna says. "I don't want nannies raising my children, and frankly I can't afford a staff to take care of my son for the amount of hours that I have to work to get ahead. When I came back from maternity leave, I was moved out of investment banking, which I really liked, into a less prestigious division, which I'm really not enjoying. But there was this sense that now that I had a baby I couldn't travel and do what investment banking required. It makes me upset when I think about the men in my office who really can have it all and as women we can't."

For all of the women I interviewed who seamlessly moved from maternity leave back into their careers, there are others who find it very difficult if not impossible to reenter their jobs as they knew them. There are still work structures that have stayed stubbornly male probably because their inherent design leaves no room for having a life. I found that most women in such areas as investment banking hang in for a few years and then leave after they have children. Donna gets frustrated because she sees her male colleagues as being able to "have it all." But young, male investment bankers also aren't seeing their babies even if their wives are home having them. That's the bargain they've struck to get ahead professionally, but for women that deal is often not acceptable. Maybe it's biology, maybe it's society, but when it comes to work-life issues, women more so than men seem to constantly reevaluate their options.

Breaking the Mold

At least once a day Susan Miller thinks about quitting her job. It's not that she doesn't enjoy her career; she actually loves it. But since she was promoted a few months ago and is heading up the biggest launch her company has ever undertaken, she's feeling anxious about her professional direction. For the first time in her career she doesn't know if she wants to move ahead and that is also making her feel uneasy. That's because Susan is the kind of woman who is always setting goals for herself, raising the bar a little bit higher each time. There was the year she spent abroad in the Middle East when she was in college and the year she lived in India after she graduated. She ran the New York Marathon not just once but twice even after injuring her foot a few days before the race. And at 28 years old, Susan decided to go back to school and get her MBA, just because it was one of those things she felt she needed to do.

"I had a lot of goals and I was constantly needing to prove myself. I don't come from a successful, networked family. I'm from a community in Seattle where everyone knows everyone. So being the one who moved to New York with no job and no money and got an MBA from Columbia is pretty outstanding."

At 34, Susan is a spunky, athletic woman with tight platinum curls; big, bright blue eyes; and a baby face. She is pounding cups of green tea at a sushi restaurant near her home in Philadelphia trying to decompress after a stressful week at work. Now the mother of an 18-month-old, Susan is used to breaking the mold and doing things her own way. After graduating from business school a few months shy of turning 31, and a few years older than most people in her class, Susan took the prestigious, lucrative route into consulting. She quickly realized that she was miserable. She hated the long hours, and with children now on her mind, she was uneasy in an environment where having children before making partner was clearly a no-no. So when the company downsized a year later and laid her off, she was relieved. Soon after, she found a job in brand marketing, an area that in graduate school she says was positioned as the more "family friendly" alternative to investment banking or consulting. On the cusp of taking her new job, Susan suffered a surprise miscarriage. She hadn't even known she was pregnant, but the miscarriage triggered an urgency to get pregnant and a fear that perhaps it would be more of a challenge than she had imagined. So even though Susan was just starting a new position at a global marketing company and was sitting at the bottom rung of the corporate ladder, she and her husband decided to actively move ahead with parenthood. A few months after starting her job, Susan was thrilled to discover that she was pregnant.

"At my level it was unheard of to have kids. I felt like people here were going to think it's ridiculous that I'm going to have kids and come back as an associate. My peers were shocked that I decided to get pregnant, and I think they were actually quite jealous because it was so out of the realm of what everyone did," she says. "There was a set promotion track of how you would do things and the timing of it all. It's a real corporate ladder. So for me to jump on real quick and then jump off, was like, wow! They absolutely didn't think I was going to come back. But I knew I was going to, financially I needed to, and I also knew it was going to be hard."

The first challenge for Susan after maternity leave was figuring out how she was going to be able to relieve her nanny at 6:00 P.M. when she routinely used to work until at least 7:30 P.M.

"I was scared to come back and tell people that I was going to have to leave at 6:00. I had always worked in industries where people worked really late, and I didn't feel like I was doing my best if I was leaving before 7:00 P.M., especially at a junior level. I knew I was going to have to be one of those people who left early, and I couldn't imagine how it was going to happen."

But Susan came back and made it work. She says that her boss was genuinely surprised that she actually returned to work after maternity leave, and he was supportive of her leaving work earlier than she used to. The difference now is that instead of staying at the office until everything is completely done, she winds up taking work home every night.

Less than one year after coming back from maternity leave, Susan was promoted and is now in charge of one of the biggest new accounts in the company. She says it's the combination of working her tail off and the push from a female mentor (who is also a mother) that helped Susan catch up to her other colleagues and get promoted.

Ironically, Susan is now facing a similar dilemma she encountered when she first started her job a few years ago—she wants to have another baby.

"I wish I wasn't turning 35 in a couple of weeks because again it doesn't feel like the right time to have a baby, but I don't want to wait. I don't feel comfortable waiting. But it feels weird," Susan says, as she shoves an oversize piece of tuna sashimi into her mouth. "I'm doing this major project, and I could potentially in a few months have to say, 'Oh by the way, I'm pregnant.' They're going to say, 'What is she doing? We just gave her the biggest assignment in the company!'

"But they have no idea that I'm 35. I'm sure they think that I'm 28 because I look so young. And they probably think that I'm a kid from the Midwest who couldn't wait to have a family, a kid who couldn't wait to have kids. They don't know that I've been married for a thousand years. So I keep saying to my husband, let me just wait a couple of months, and I will have traveled and done all of the things I need to do, and he says no! He's going to be 36. We just keep getting older and older, so if I wait, maybe I'll have another six months' work experience, but it's never going to be ideal."

For many working women it feels like there's never a good time to have a baby, especially for women who are still on The Climb, reaching for the brass ring, hoping that if they just work hard enough and long enough, they will get to that cushy point where it all neatly comes together. Whereas some Baby Boomer women had children in their early 20s and then moved into careers, or had careers first and then had children just in the nick of time, many women today find themselves stuck at the intersection of career and motherhood and don't know which way to turn.

Some women I spoke to tried to plot their pregnancies with military precision. Some delayed telling their bosses they were pregnant even as their bellies were noticeably bulging because they were due for a promotion and feared pregnancy would derail their advancement. But just as Susan bucked the system the first time she got pregnant, she knows she will figure something out the next time. She realizes she's getting tremendous experience in her new position and believes that she needs to really step up now, finish her project so she'll be able to take her skills elsewhere if she discovers her current job becomes too intense for her family life.

Reality TV

A demanding career and a full family life is something Soledad O'Brien, the 37-year-old co-anchor of CNN's *American Morning*, can appreciate. I meet Soledad on one of those weirdly, windy summer afternoons in New York City—the kind when the swirling air is smacking you in the face with street debris before it gracefully flutters to the ground. Seven and a half months pregnant with twin boys, Soledad is running a few minutes late. She's been stuck at a New York hospital for two and a half hours waiting to get a sonogram. She apologizes for being behind schedule as she settles into her chair and shows me the pictures of her two amorphous baby boy blobs.

"You'd hope the picture would be better than this after waiting for so long," she says in her typical good humor as we sit down for iced tea at a café around the corner from her downtown Manhattan apartment.

Soledad is known in the TV business as one of the smartest, nicest, and most talented female anchors on the air today. She is also arguably the most well-known journalist to be a member of both the National Association of Black Journalists and the National Association of Hispanic Journalists, to have been named one of *People Magazine*'s "50 most beautiful people," and to be listed among *Irish American Magazine*'s top 100 Irish Americans in 1998 and 2004.

Her exotic mix of caramel skin, a generous sprinkling of freckles, and doe-shaped eyes come from her black Cuban mother and Australian father. Soledad's parents met in the pre–civil rights era when they were students at John Hopkins University in Baltimore. When they married in 1959, they went to Washington, D.C., because interracial marriage was still illegal in Baltimore.

The fifth of six children, Soledad grew up on New York's Long Island, where her father worked as a university professor and her mother taught French and Spanish at the local high school. The O'Brien kids stood out in the predominantly white community of Smithtown. But Soledad says that even though she knew she was different and probably wouldn't date anyone in her town, she never struggled with her identity.

"My parents made it very clear that I'm black, my dad is white, but I'm a light-skinned black girl. I never had a lot of the racial angst that I think some people sometimes have. I never felt like people didn't accept me for who I was. I think people take the cue from what you do. I was very comfortable in my own skin, and my brothers and sisters were too, and I think people felt that."

Like all of her siblings, Soledad attended Harvard. She's been in the TV business since she graduated from college. After working at local affiliates in Boston and San Francisco and field producing for NBC News, Soledad landed an anchor job at MSNBC and then the prestigious co-anchor position at NBC's *Weekend Today*, where she worked for four years. She also found time to meet, date, and marry investment banker Brad Raymond. Having grown up in a large, close-knit family, Soledad always hoped to have a lot of kids of her own. So when she got pregnant with her first daughter a year into her tenure at *Weekend Today*, she was thrilled. But after having her baby, Soledad says she felt unprepared for the intensity and difficulty of motherhood.

"I remember saying to my sisters, 'I'm so miserable.' And they said, 'Of course you're miserable. You have stitches, your breasts are leaking, and you've gained thirty pounds and it's not going to come off any time soon. You also have a screaming baby in the other room, and you don't know what the hell you're doing. You would be weird if you weren't miserable.' My sisters were really great. Having someone tell you when you have a newborn that the first four months were going to be hellacious—it's so nice to hear that. You're not crazy, and it's not going to last forever."

Soledad took a five-week maternity leave after her first daughter was born and a four-week leave after the second. When we spoke two months before the birth of her boys in August 2004, she said she would be back to work in time to cover the presidential election. In that regard, things went as planned. Still, she admits that figuring out the rhythm of handling her work schedule with her baby's needs was extremely hard in the beginning.

"What used to really bother me after having Sofia was not being good at something. I felt like I wasn't really good at managing having a child. I didn't know what I was doing, and I couldn't quite figure out how to make it work with work," Soledad says. "I was trying to pump and do a show that would go for two hours and sometimes more. You have to pump every four hours, so it was very hard logistically and hard to juggle. But then I figured it out.

"One of the things I like about being a working mother, being a mother period, is that suddenly you get it. You think, damn, I'm good. Look at this, I pump, I can get my hair done, put on my makeup, go do a show, come back, and I have fifteen minutes before I have to pump again. I get so much more done. My husband was saying that one of his colleagues at work could not believe that I was overseeing the renovation on our apartment; that I'm working full time, crazy hours; and that I'm pregnant with twins. He said, 'My wife is a stay-at-home mom with a nanny full time and she doesn't do any of that.' It's not because I'm Superwoman," Soledad says matter-of-factly. "It's just that I have very limited time, so I just plot things all of the time."

Soledad's day begins when she wakes up at 3:30 in the morning. She's in the office an hour later and preparing for three hours of live, hard-core TV news. On some days after the show, if she doesn't have stories to shoot, speaking engagements, or other CNN or philanthropic obligations, she's able to pick up her oldest daughter from school and spend the afternoons with her.

"There aren't too many jobs where you can technically be off by noon," Soledad says, acknowledging that the morning news anchor job is a particularly good gig for mothers.

Agreeing that the pressure and expectations for mothers to be perfect is unfair, Soledad says she would never measure herself against a celebrity magazine-cover mom because she knows it's an illusion and an unattainable image with which to compete. She talks about her own experience when she returned to *Weekend Today* after having her first daughter.

"When I came back from maternity leave, other women who worked at NBC who were pregnant or who had babies would say to me, 'Oh my God, you look so good.' And I would say, 'Of course I do, I have three people upstairs who will push me into this outfit, or take me in and make me up. If you had a staff of people who would come over to your house, you would look damn great.' I never compare myself to those people [celebrities] because I don't have a personal yoga instructor who is going to come to my house, and I'm not on a vegan, macrobiotic diet, and I don't have a trainer. That's their job to get back into their clothes, and they get a little extra publicity if they lose weight fast, and they get ragged on if they don't, which I think is unfortunate. But it never would occur to me to look at Sarah Jessica Parker and think, how come I'm not her."

Soledad believes strongly that women, especially mothers, need to have a support system of people with whom they can confide in and be honest.

"Talk to other people and share your frustrations. Avoid people who make it all seem like it's easy because it's not," Soledad says. "It's like people in TV land who like to pretend that they got their careers so easily. It's not easy. I busted my ass to get where I got. And I don't feel like I need to tell people it's so simple because it wasn't easy. It was really, really hard. And having children is really, really hard. And juggling having children and going to work is really, really hard, but there are huge, huge upsides, and those upsides make it worth it."

Crediting her positive attitude for getting through the challenges of negotiating the demands of work and motherhood, Soledad sums it up this way, "I think the biggest aspect I got going for me is that I have a really good sense of humor about it. I'm not the worrying kind. Even in my work, I'm not a panicker. I learned a million years ago that worrying is not going to help. It's a matter of flexibility. If a trip to the zoo is going great, we'll stay an extra half hour and get lunch. If the trip to the zoo is a nightmare then we're going to leave. I never really try to be perfect in anything. I take my work seriously but I'm the first person to say I dropped the ball."

Clearly if any woman seems to have it all, Soledad O'Brien is that person. She has two daughters, a killer career, a nine-year marriage, and at the time we talk, two boys on the way. When I ask her if she believes she "has it all," she lobs the question back at me.

"What is your definition of all? I work and I have kids and thank God everybody is healthy. But that's all that I do. I don't go out. I don't go to parties. I don't really cook. I don't really entertain. I don't do much. And that's okay," she says. "My kids come home, and we hang out and play. I make dinner, and then we go to bed. I wouldn't say I have it all because I think that's the kind of thing that makes women feel inadequate."

Soledad says she doesn't feel like she's sacrificing anything except for probably her sleep, which she admits is always lacking; she's usually tired. But life, Soledad believes, is all about your choices and your perspective.

"My mom used to always say, you get twenty-four hours in a day, and you get to use it as you're going to use it, but everyone gets the same twenty-four hours. But you can't have your cake and eat it too. You can work and be a mom, it's possible to fit that in. It's a little harder to be a mom and travel a lot. It's a little harder to be a mom and travel a lot and go out to parties every night. You can only do so much. You just need to pick what you want to do."

For Soledad that means spending as many afternoons and evenings at home with her family as possible. After dinner, she reads her daughters a couple of books, sings their favorite songs, and puts them to sleep. She goes to bed soon after. Soledad says that even though she has many friends who have left their careers to stay at home, she feels no ambivalence about working—especially in a job that she's passionate about and that energizes her.

"I feel like I'm being a good role model for my kids in both showing them that you can juggle stuff but that your family can clearly be your priority. I think I'm doing a good thing for my kids, not a bad thing to them, by working. I'm sure of it. I don't have a moment's doubt about it."

Across the River, a World Apart

Fifteen miles across the Hudson River in New Jersey, 29-year-old sales manager Kimberly Cooper does find herself getting riddled with doubt. She, like Soledad, is the daughter of a Stay-at-Work mom. And also like Soledad, Kimberly always knew she would continue working after having children. But after having her first child a year ago, she was surprised to discover how torn she feels between wanting to work and wanting to stay at home.

A pretty woman with almond shaped, hazel eyes and shoulder length, highlighted blonde hair, Kimberly grew up in Hong Kong and came to the United States when she was 17 years old to attend college. At 25, she received an MBA from Columbia University. Kimberly says she feels both burdened and blessed by the tug of tradition and success from her matriarchal, Filipino family in which women and mothers have always worked.

Her family's entrepreneurial spirit and history helps motivate Kimberly to thrive in her career, but she also feels saddled with expectations. In her family the idea of a woman not supporting herself would be simply unacceptable and foolish.

"My mother comes from a very wealthy family in the Philippines, and during the war, they lost everything," Kimberly says as we eat muffins and drink coffee in a New Jersey bakery on a Saturday morning. "My grandmother had to sell water and bread at the train station to support her family. She then remarried an American, and they started the first Filipino radio and TV station. She actually turned everything around," Kimberly says proudly. "So that was the kind of environment my mom grew up in. And when she was an adult, she moved to Hong Kong where she met my dad, an Australian photographer. He didn't make much money, but she would take his income and invest it in real estate—that was her job. My mom has always had her own business."

Kimberly says that when she was growing up in Hong Kong, her mother worked but many of her mother's friends did not. They had left their careers after marrying wealthy men, but their charmed lives became cautionary tales when their marriages fell apart.

"In Hong Kong they are called 'Tai Tai wives,'" Kimberly says. "Some of the women were doctors who gave up their careers to be the wife, to run the household, to have a beautiful home, and to look after their husbands. Some of the husbands had affairs, and the wives were sort of left hanging. In some cases they are still financially supported. But it wasn't even the money; it was the 'What will I do? I was a doctor once, fifteen or twenty years ago, but what can I do now?' They don't know how to help themselves. My mother always said, 'Don't let this happen to you. You could have all of the money in the world, but if you can't earn it yourself, it can all go away.'

"There are many times when I want to quit my job," Kimberly says. But until I have the next thing in line, I just can't do that. I fear that if I quit, I'm going to be at home and I won't know what to do next. I know that the days are going to pass and I'm not going to have a plan, and years could pass and I will have lost the drive that makes me feel confident that I can provide for my family. It's a weird thing to look at, but I saw it with my mom's friends. The years have passed and they haven't gotten anything to hold onto. They haven't gotten any confidence that they can do anything, and that's really sad."

Kimberly took a thirteen-week maternity leave when her daughter was born. She says she could have taken longer, but she was eager to get back to work before she became too entrenched in the at-home mom routine—a lifestyle that she admits she romanticizes but nonetheless finds seductive. For months she had dreaded returning to work and says the first day back tops her list as the worst day of her life.

"I was afraid that I couldn't even make it to work. I almost had to stop on the highway because I turned around and I saw an empty car seat and I thought, oh my God, I can't do it," Kimberly says. "When I got to work, I couldn't get upstairs. I couldn't get past the lobby bathroom. I was crying and I thought, I am never going to get through this. I saw a colleague in the bathroom who I didn't know very well, and she had to help me get out of the door. When I got in the elevator, I couldn't press the number. I finally got the number pressed, but then I had to go back downstairs to the bathroom. It took me forty-five minutes to get upstairs. But the funny part is that as soon as I was upstairs, it was like I had never left. And I didn't cry again the whole day. I was not the wreck I thought I was going to be. By 9:00 A.M. I went straight into a staff meeting like nothing had ever happened, and I've never cried since. I knew that if I didn't go back, I might never go back. I proved it to myself that I could do it, and I'm so glad that I did."

Kimberly brings in half of her family's income, and like the overwhelming majority of Stay-at-Work moms I've surveyed, she falls onto the spectrum of working both because she has to and because she wants to. But her ratio of what she needs professionally and emotionally is dynamic. She was thrilled to land a promotion two months after her maternity leave but ultimately believes her position is unsustainable for when she has more children.

In fact, Kimberly has found that since having her daughter, Carly, her paradigm for success has shifted. A few years ago she says her goal was to be a company vice president in corporate America. But now she hopes to create a business for herself that will still give her financial security but also the flexibility to be with her children in the afternoon. She says she looks to the women above her at work and realizes that she doesn't want their lives. Instead, as proud as she is of herself in her career and as a provider for her family, she is jealous of a seemingly unlikely group, Stay-at-Home moms.

"The people I envy at work are not the directors, but the wives of the people who I work with who are at home all day with the kids. I'm not sure how they afford it because I make the same money that the husbands do, but I guess they've figured something out. So I don't think the wives have a really charmed life, but I envy them because they have their book clubs and they can spend all day at the pool and playground. When I get home, there is no time to do any of that."

For Kimberly, as for many Stay-at-Work moms, the tension is figuring out what she really wants and needs both financially and emotionally. It's the persistent ping-ponging of emotions that tugs at the gut and wages battle with a woman's desires to be both a career woman and a present mother.

"I think it all comes from where you start," Kimberly says. "If you're used to a certain level of stimulation and interaction and learning new things and getting satisfaction from your paycheck, it's very difficult to just turn that all off. But if you're not used to that kind of environment and all of your life you've wanted to have kids and you don't earn a whole lot, then it's a different situation.

"I'm not working to put food on the table, I'm working to put Whole Foods on the table," Kimberly says with a laugh as she describes the guilty pleasure she has in shopping at an upscale grocery store known for its organic produce and prepared foods.

"I think that if I didn't work and if I was with the kids all day, my husband and I would be in trouble because when we met we had a certain lifestyle. And I just don't want to dump all of that pressure on him."

Even with her conflicting emotions, overall, Kimberly feels balanced.

"I know that every day when I go to work I'm learning a lot for the next thing that I do. So I look at this as my own preparation for when I really start my own business. I'm with adults all day, and when I come home, I have Carly, so I do feel balance. And I can definitely see that not happening if I were home all day."

But ironically Kimberly sees her ability to make money as her golden handcuffs. She realizes she's fortunate to be highly educated and able to support herself, but she sometimes feels stuck because ironically she cannot afford to stop working.

"Sometimes I curse the day I got an MBA because all of a sudden I make too much money for the choice of just staying at home. If what I earned didn't make sense to be able to afford a nanny or daycare, then there would be no choice. It's the curse of just having the choice. I never in a million years thought I would say that. But having an MBA makes it difficult because I make half of our family income. And we set up our life, not to the extent that we need both of us working, but the stress of having our house would be too much."

Too Many Choices or Not Enough?

Today's moms have it easier than our own mothers in so many ways. Yet moms today seem much more overwhelmed. Whatever decision we make we feel guilty and conflicted. With a smorgasbord of choices available to us, motherhood has become much more complicated. Our mothers had fewer options, lower expectations, often a simpler life. For the most part they had children in their 20s and then moved into their careers, or didn't. They did things serially; we do them simultaneously. We have delayed motherhood to nurture our careers just as our mothers advised us. But instead of feeling liberated by the many paths available to us, new moms can feel paralyzed by their choices.

An earlier generation of feminists would probably want to strangle Kimberly with their bras if they heard her moaning over having a valuable MBA. In 1968 only 609 women received MBAs.[1] Today more than 40,000 women earn MBAs each year. We've come a long way, baby. So why do so many women feel that they really don't have a choice? Probably because 48 percent of working wives provide at least half of their family's income and they simply make too much money not to work.[2]

According to the Bureau of Labor Statistics, nearly one out of three married women makes more money than her spouse. And it's not just high-earning women whose paychecks trump their husbands. In fact, only 3 percent of the cases where women make more than the men have salaries greater than $75,000.[3] Life with children has gotten so expensive that most families in the United States today require two incomes just to survive, and often that is still barely enough, according to Elizabeth Warren and Amelia Warren Tyagi in their book *The Two-Income Trap: Why Middle Class Parents Are Going Broke.* They write that "having a child is now the biggest predictor that a woman will end up in financial collapse." Consider these depressing facts: This year more women will file for bankruptcy than graduate from college. Seventy percent of all Americans (roughly 140 million people) say they are carrying so much debt that it's making their home lives unhappy. This year more children will live through their parents' bankruptcy than their parents' divorce.[4] There is no doubt we're living in fragile economic times. Housing, childcare, and education are all so expensive that they're gobbling up most of the income even in homes where both parents work.

Even though more women around the world today are making more money than ever before, we are also working longer hours than our parents and grandparents did. The average American workweek has crept up to forty-eight hours for professionals and managers, and even so-called part-time work is edging toward forty hours a week.[5] For dual-career American couples, the combined work hours have grown from eighty-one hours a week in 1977 to ninety-one hours in 2002, according to the Families and Work Institute. *Time* magazine reports that the reality of the time crunch is as globalized as business itself. Although France has instituted a thirty-five-hour workweek, for European executives, the average is still fifty hours a week for women and fifty-five for men.[6] When it comes to the obstacles female business executives face in Europe and in the United States, says Meredith Moore—the director of research at Catalyst, a research and consulting group that focuses on women in business—"we were surprised by how little variation there was."[7]

As Soledad O'Brien says, we're each given twenty-four hours to do with as we choose. But somehow our twenty-four hours seems to have shrunk. As suburbs have sprawled into what was once swampland, more people are living farther away from work than ever before. It takes longer for us to get to work, and we stay at work longer than any previous generation. A family dinner at 6:00 P.M. seems as quaint as a green bean casserole. So if you're a regular mom working a typical nine-hour-a-day schedule, you're bound to feel the squeeze.

Executive Moms

When Marisa Thalberg, 35, an advertising and marketing executive, was home on maternity leave four years ago, she was eager to meet and bond with other moms who were successfully merging their careers with motherhood. So she, like I did, went to organized mommy luncheons in New York City where women gathered with their newborns.

"I really felt like this was my first day of school all over again," says Marisa, a petite woman with a head full of chaotic blonde curls. "It was positioned like these are going to be your new life-long friends."

"At the lunch, they made us all go around and say four things about ourselves: our name, our baby's name, how old they were, and whether or not you were going back to work. And when all of these women said, 'No, I'm not going back to work,' I thought, well, God bless them that *they* can afford to do that, but wow! This is New York, and you sort of assume that if you're living here, part of the reason is because you work, and New York is the kind of place that attracts that kind of person.

"I never thought in terms of this being about the great divide between working mothers and not-working mothers. It's more about the practicality of the fact that these women weren't going to be interested in waiting until Fridays at 5:00 P.M., and I mean that literally, to have a play date," Marisa says.

"As soon as I went back to work the common ground really was diverging. I was really hungry to meet other working women whom I could admire and relate to and who were also moms. I thought there must be some group like that to join, and I was really shocked to find that there wasn't. The more that I mentioned it to other women, I got a real 'head-slapping' reaction. Every woman I met said, 'Why doesn't something like that exist?' I had no vision then of creating a new business—but this idea became something I and enough other women felt was necessary, that I wound up starting an organization around it."

And so Marisa gave birth again, this time in 2002 to Executive Moms, an organization and website devoted to women who are both mothers and professionals. Executive Moms now boasts more than 2,000 members nationwide.

One of the reasons Marisa wanted to start a group of like-minded mothers with careers was because she found that being a mother, let alone a Stay-at-Work mother, was more complicated, stressful, and lonely than she anticipated. Like many new moms, she also struggled then with feelings that at times felt socially unacceptable.

"I wasn't totally comfortable at the start of motherhood, and I really thought that made me less of a mother," Marisa says. "Having a child was actually much harder and scarier than I thought. Plus I was used to excelling at things, and I say that sort of in a funny way and sort of in a serious way. I always got As in school and so I couldn't accept the possibility that on the most important thing of all I was going to be middling to average or subpar. I don't want to make it seem like mothering is a competitive sport, but I just wanted to be really good at it for myself. So that's what's been one of the nicest things about Executive Moms. A majority of people we've surveyed said that being a working mom helped make them a better mom, a piece of data that I love, and I think that is very affirmational. If it's in your character that you need stimulation and if that's going to help make you feel a little more whole, how can that not be good for your child?"

Marisa jokes that she was ready to go back to work before she even returned home from the hospital. In fact, she says, she wishes she could have flipped her maternity leave and taken off months four to seven—a more fun and rewarding time than the exhausting newborn period. Many moms have shared similar feelings with me, saying that they couldn't wait to get back to work because maternity leave is ironically more exhausting and demanding than working. However, research shows that taking a long maternity leave is healthy for moms and helps stave off postpartum depression.

A study by the National Bureau of Economic Research in Cambridge, Massachusetts, a private nonprofit research organization, found that mothers who take at least three months of maternity leave show 15 percent fewer symptoms of depression after they come back to work compared with women who take six weeks or less.[8]

Interestingly, Marisa says that according to a survey she did of 150 mothers in her Executive Moms network, the length and quality of maternity leave has been shrinking. She discovered that it's common for many women actually to be working during their maternity leaves.

"I found that women, whether they want to, choose to, or have to, are not exactly off when they are on maternity leave. I think if you're conscientious about your career, there is something a little scary about being out of sight for three months. I remember feeling that way. You don't want to feel that they are getting along fine without you."

It is perhaps fitting that many of the women Marisa has surveyed have said they didn't feel comfortable completely disengaging from the office even though they were recovering from childbirth and taking on the hardest job of all—learning how to parent. It's as if even from the get-go, women feel the need to prove to their employers that motherhood isn't going to interfere with their careers. Are women more insecure about their job security than men, or are we simply being pragmatic? Maybe a bit of both. Shockingly, the United States doesn't legally recognize maternity leave. In fact, the United States and Australia are the only countries in the industrialized world that don't give compulsory maternity leave compensation; 163 other countries offer guaranteed paid leave in connection with childbirth.[9] Sweden has the most generous maternity provisions, with new mothers getting ninety-six weeks off and receiving 80 percent of their salary for more than half of that time, whereas women in Britain get twelve months of leave with new moms receiving up to full pay for the first six.[10] The Family Medical Leave Act, enacted in 1993 in the United States, made it legal for parents to take twelve weeks of unpaid leave for the birth or adoption of a child as well as to take time off for a sickness in the family. But this only applies to people working for companies with fifty or more employees, and only 11 percent of private sector companies in the United States fall into this category. Maternity leave compensation in the United States is not federally mandated but usually comes in the form of short-term disability cobbled together with sick days and vacation days.

On average, American women appear to be taking some of the short-est maternity leaves in the world. In my own research, I found that pro-fessional women took between two and twelve weeks of maternity leave. And many actually continued to work in some capacity from home. Com-pared to European policies and those in the former Czech Republic and Russia where women get twenty-eight weeks and twenty weeks of leave respectively, the American average of twelve weeks of maternity leave seems awfully skimpy. Yet short maternity leaves are what most American women have come to expect. And it is often when we are on maternity leave, nursing our babies, up to our armpits in stinky diapers and dirty bottles, that is dawns on us: being the mom is a heck of a lot harder than being the dad. And although most men's lives resume to normal shortly after a baby is born, for women, their lives can feel utterly unfamiliar. From your body hair to your pelvic floor, motherhood profoundly changes everything.

"People say, 'Why isn't there an Executive Dads?' Well, there could be," Marisa says. "But I do think at the end of the day, there are particu-lar aspects of this that are a woman's issue because the major emotional tugs are uniquely felt by women. Those emotions are complex, and that's why for Executive Moms it will never be about, 'here are the five steps to do it better.' I don't know if there is a 'solution.' But there is clearly some-thing in seeing other people who are struggling, surviving, and thriving that fundamentally helps you to become better equipped to do it all too."

Chapter 3

The Breast Pump in the Briefcase

The Art of Juggling

The day I started working at CNN was the day I stopped nursing my daughter. It's not that I wanted to stop. It simply seemed impossible to pump at my new job. At CNN, the vast majority of people work in a newsroom-style mosh pit or in shared offices. As a new producer, working on a show dominated by men and women without children, I felt uncomfortable about drawing attention to my needs as a mom, let alone the needs of my breasts. As I surveyed the office space I assumed that there was no place to plug in and pump. It wasn't until weeks later, after my milk supply dried up and I was feeling guilty and a bit depressed about giving up nursing, that I realized a "Lactation Room" did actually exist.

It turns out that a few women at CNN had fought to make a room dedicated for pumping possible. At first, CNN executives resisted giving up precious real estate for a few nursing moms. But these brave women continued to push the issue. They investigated precedents in the company and discovered that CNN headquarters in Atlanta had a room to pump. It was their collective perseverance that made executives at CNN in New York reconsider and create a designated lactation room, around the corner from the copy machine and complete with its own nameplate on the wall. Senior producer Karen Palmer is one of the women who has bene-fited from a private place to pump.

"This is not a frill," says Karen, 41, a no-nonsense African-American woman with short cropped hair and a huge, toothpaste commercial–like smile. "It's a process that we shouldn't be made to feel ashamed of, and I think that's what happens in a lot of places. I think because of the fact that breasts happened to be attached to your body, people sort of go, uggh! But they have a place for us to go to the bathroom and that's an equally natural process.

"It's a question of getting people to look at it not as if you're asking a favor but that you're fulfilling part of a natural process. Women aren't going to stop having babies. They are not going to stop nursing kids. If anything, the more we hear about the health benefits, the more women will nurse," she says matter-of-factly.

In 1997 the American Academy of Pediatrics recommended that all mothers nurse their babies for one full year. But as of writing, only five states—California, Connecticut, Illinois, Minnesota, and Tennessee—have legislation requiring employers to "take specific actions in accom-modating breastfeeding employees . . . and to provide a private place that is not a bathroom stall to do so."[1] Seventy-one percent of all new moms nurse their newborns. The number drops to 50 percent at three months and 36 percent at six months when most women have returned to work.[2] And because so many jobs require travel, out of office meetings, and non-traditional settings, juggling the logistics of breast-feeding with work is clearly one of the first dilemmas a new mom can face.

"I had only been back from maternity leave for three weeks, and I found out that the social event for our big sales presentation was going to be on a boat," says Kimberly Cooper, sales manager. "Everyone was stressing about getting our presentations together and worrying about all of these other things, and my entire focus became, Oh my God, I'm going to have to figure out how I'm going to pump on a boat. And I did. I put my handheld breast pump in my bag, and I pumped in a tiny bathroom stall. And I thought, 'Oh, the things I'm going to do to make sure my lit-tle girl gets what she needs.'"

The Battle to Breast-Feed

Wendy Bellissimo calls from the stroller department of a Los Angeles baby store to say she's running a bit behind schedule. Things are taking longer than expected on a shopping expedition with actress and model Brooke Shields. She is decorating Brooke's baby nursery and helping her register for her upcoming baby shower. Wendy is best known as the woman behind a wildly successful baby and child bedding business bearing her name and is also the hottest and most sought after decorator for celebrity baby nurseries. Her nursery creations are seen in such magazines as *InStyle* and *Child*, and her bedding designs, once sold in hundreds of boutiques across the country, are now available at Babies R Us. What few people know is that Wendy also made her mark in a legal "battle of the boob" when she challenged breast-feeding rules, ironically, at a trade show convention for juvenile products.

Wendy was preparing to travel to Texas for the annual trade show with her 4-month-old-daughter when she learned that she would be prohibited from breast-feeding her baby in her showroom. The convention officials said that her baby gave her an unfair competitive advantage (because people like babies) and having the baby in the showroom could be dangerous. Wendy was incredulous. She hired an attorney and discovered that there is a Texas law that says the baby is entitled to be with the mother at all times. As the battle to breast-feed got heated, Wendy recruited her friend and fellow mom, Camryn Manheim, the star of ABC's *The Practice*, to help wage a media war against the banning of her baby. *Entertainment Tonight* came to the set of *The Practice* and interviewed Wendy and Camryn about a mother's right to nurse. The day after the *ET* segment aired, the directors of the trade show capitulated—Wendy could bring her infant daughter after all.

"It was a huge fight," says Wendy, a beautiful, statuesque woman with long, highlighted, blonde hair, a Julia Roberts–like smile, and a big bulge in her belly holding her fourth daughter-to-be. "What I learned from this and other women should learn from this is that you still need to fight for these rights. The officials didn't care whatsoever. And this year I'm going to have a new baby. I can't tell you how many moms came up to me who said they were forced to make the choice [between working and nursing]."

Seventy-six countries protect a woman's right to breast-feed; the United States does not. Even though the majority of new moms nurse, only 7 percent of big corporations have lactation rooms. But you don't see women's rights groups storming Washington demanding national legislation to provide pumping facilities for lactating women. Aside from La Leche League, the pioneering nursing organization that still brings to mind a brigade of earthy moms who don't shave their armpits, and a smattering of other pro–breast-feeding groups advocating that breast is best, lactating rights are not exactly on the top of the agenda for most women.

Many new moms accept that they will have to make do with inconvenient accommodations, and they don't complain because frankly who wants to remind their boss that they are disappearing for chunks of time several times a day to attach a mechanical contraption to their nipples. And let's face it, when you return from maternity leave, you're hoping to stay below the radar so you can duck out as early as possible to get home to your baby. The last thing you want to spotlight is the fact that you now have mommy needs that could interrupt your work. As CNN senior producer Karen Palmer says, there still is a "yuck factor" associated with nursing, if not for nursing women themselves, then for the society that observes them doing it; understandably many women in the workforce feel uncomfortable about dealing with pumping, let alone lobbying for lactation facilities if their company isn't particularly accommodating. But Karen says we shouldn't be afraid to stand up for ourselves.

"Business hasn't thought that it's their role to accommodate nursing moms and that it's always the individual's role to make it work. I'm puzzled by that because nobody expects individuals to not have families, and if we agree that somebody needs to take time to give birth and to recover, you would think that you would want to accommodate another process that allows them to make sure that their kid is a little bit healthier and a little bit stronger so you ultimately take fewer sick days away from the office and that whatever anxiety you might be feeling is sort of minimized knowing that you're doing everything you can for your kids.

"I look at this from a cost-benefit perspective. Even if only one person is using a lactation room at a time, it's going to get used constantly, and people know it's there and they don't feel bad about asking to use it," Karen says. "It brought me back to work happier. I wasn't going to take a six-month leave because I didn't want to be a drain on the rest of the staff. Women should remember that when it comes to getting what they need, there is power in numbers. And this isn't just about nursing, it's about many of the issues that working moms face."

For Jordana Well, 32, a producer of documentaries at the Discovery Network in Silver Spring, Maryland, and mother of a 4-month-old, the progressive attitude at her company has helped make life as a working new mother much easier. In fact, Discovery has an employee program called "Life Works" that includes pregnancy and life management courses. The company gives pregnant women care packages with videos and books about pregnancy and childcare. They provide a week's worth of emergency home childcare. They subsidize the purchase of a breast pump and even offer lactation consultant services free of charge. Discovery also has several comfortable lactation rooms with cushiony chairs, phones, a refrigerator, and a place to hang pictures of your children. These accoutrements are small—and some might say silly—but they show commitment in the workplace culture to making women feel comfortable when it comes to taking care of themselves not just as employees but also as mothers.

"I've skipped out of meetings early because I need to pump, but I don't get any nasty looks. No one makes jokes about it," Jordana says. "It's like, go do your thing, and managers are really sensitive to your needs. I think it's really a combination of policy and the personnel they hire. I always wanted to come back to work, but what Discovery did was make the transition easier."

Surviving the Crunch

NBC's *Today* news anchor Ann Curry intimately knows the issues a Stay-at-Work mom confronts. For years she was simply exhausted as she raised her babies and held on to a demanding job that required her to start her day in the middle of the night.

"For several years I never slept, I only napped," Ann tells me as we sit on a sofa in the show's Green Room, where interview guests wait to debut on morning television. Before Ann landed her gig in 1997 at *Today*, she worked as the anchor of *NBC News at Sunrise*, which aired at 5:00 A.M. each weekday. It was during her five-year stint at *Sunrise* that Ann gave birth to her two children, daughter McKenzie and son Walker.

"When I found out that I was pregnant with my second child, I wept. It wasn't that I didn't want him that I wept; it was for myself because I knew what was ahead of me. I knew it was going to be the most physically draining and most challenging job one can ever have," Ann says softly. "But I am so proud now that I got through it; I'm just so proud now of what I've done to raise these kids and what they've become so far. I would not have it any other way, but oh my goodness," she says, letting out a deep sigh as if realizing she can exhale again.

"At one point I had two babies waking me up at all hours of the night and then I had to get up at 2:45 in the morning and go do some television and that was really hard," Ann says. "So my coping mechanism of choice was chocolate. I'd eat Hershey kisses for breakfast and get up on TV and be totally wired."

During those early years in the trenches with two small children at home, no family nearby, and a job that began before dawn, Ann says she was just barely holding on.

"There was a breathlessness, an inability to do very much more than do my job and take care of my children. I didn't do bills. I didn't work out. I didn't really lose the weight I had gained being pregnant until my son was finally five years old. My number-one goal was to take care of my kids and to be a great mother. But I couldn't drop the ball on my job."

Ann's unforgiving work schedule took its toll on her physically. She says she remembers trying to exercise and feeling her heart beating so fast that she thought she was having a heart attack. But she fought to stay focused on both her work and her family, not wanting to give up the tremendous professional opportunity of a network anchor job.

"When I went to work, I forced myself not to think about my children, and I gave 100 percent to my job. And when I was at home with my children, I refused to think about work, I refused to answer calls, to obsess about my job, my boss, or any of that. I focused completely 100 percent on my children. I carved out as much time as I could with my kids and still kept my job."

Ann discovered that the balancing quandary so many working mothers face does not have a simple solution. She got through the early years by convincing herself that this difficult period—the physically brutal, dangerously sleep deprived stage—would ultimately end as her children grew.

"In the early years of life your baby really needs you all of the time. If you're a working mother you can't give your child all of your time and that's the dilemma. Men aren't required to have this sort of struggle. It's part because of biology and part because of society. The peace I made was that it's impossible to really balance both work and babies and that having it all was really a lie and that this idea of multitasking was really self-abusive. I concluded that there is a crunch period. The time basically from the birth of a child until when the child goes to first grade requires you to almost be an athlete, to really step up. The question is, how do you get through that time? That's not to say that when they are in first grade they don't need you, they do, but they're in school, and so being at work is easier."

Now that Ann's children are 9 and 11 years old, she happily reports that the juggle is more manageable. If she isn't shooting or traveling for a story, Ann is usually able to pick up her children after school. She and her kids camp out at the school library doing homework for about an hour and then pile into a cab and head home. She throws together a quick dinner so the entire family can sit down and eat at 6:00 P.M. Ann's husband, Brian Ross, a businessman, also makes it a point to come home early so he can join his family for dinner. Family dinners are very important to Ann: "I almost require it," she says. "Last year we were unsuccessful at making that happen, and this year we've made it a priority."

Like many successful Stay-at-Work moms, Ann says the help she gets from her husband is critical to her being able to manage both of her full-time jobs—mom and *Today* news anchor. Brian is home in the morning with the kids, getting them off to school while Ann is at work. In the evenings, she and her husband are with their children for dinner, baths, reading time, and bedtime.

"After dinner there's still homework to be done, so my husband takes one child and I take the other. We go into separate rooms, work on the homework, then we switch children and bring each other up to speed," Ann says.

After homework, it's bath time, and everyone except for Brian is in bed usually by 8:30 P.M. If Ann has homework, which she often does to prepare for the next day's interviews, she takes it into bed with her too. Ann still gets up hours before the sun rises to arrive at the NBC studio by 5:30 A.M.—but she says life these days is considerably easier than when her children were younger.

I have been talking to Ann for more than an hour when her cheerful assistant comes into the Green Room to tell us that we need to wrap up. She has an interview with Maya Angelou to do before she picks up her kids that afternoon. As we finish up I ask Ann what advice she has for new moms wondering how to juggle it all: work, family, and the inevitable conflicts that arise. Without hesitation she begins: "I would say that the overwhelming feeling of being a brand new mom and trying to hold down a job, that feeling will go. You will get it eventually, and it may feel awful at first, but you have to figure out the system that works for you. I think if you love your job and you feel it's a part of what you need to do with your life, then I would recommend that you don't give it up, that you keep it, that you give it 100 percent when you're at work, and then when you're with your family you really give them 100 percent.

"Try in the first four to five years of your child's life to structure yourself so you can give as much time to your children as you can without losing your job, and if it means taking a shorter work schedule for a period of time, then do that. If you love your job, if it's meaningful to you, if it's purposeful to you, then you shouldn't give it up."

Clearly having a career that inspires and motivates you is perhaps the most critical factor in surviving those "crunch" years as Ann describes. She had an extraordinary opportunity as an early morning news anchor on NBC's *Sunrise* and felt that if she could get through those years and if she worked hard enough, she could move ahead in her industry. One of Ann's strategies was compartmentalizing her life and being able to focus with laser beam precision on what was in front of her—making sure that she kept work and family separate.

Ann's words often ring in my ears. As I work at a manic pace to meet my aggressive deadline for this book, writing all day and only catching my children for an hour or so at night, feelings of guilt regularly consume me. When I'm with my kids, I valiantly try to immerse myself in their activities and not let the white noise of the world, whether it's my book, house chores, or anything else invade my mental and emotional concentration on them. I confess: I rarely succeed. I'm easily distracted and before I know it, I'm recomposing paragraphs in my head or thinking of research I need rather than concentrating on the Play-Doh caterpillars I'm creating with my kids. But I think Ann's advice makes sense, and I'm trying to get better at keeping my work from overlapping into my home life. I realize now that if you feel fully present when you're with your children, you feel less guilty about the time you spend away from them.

Making Partner

Brooke Horman, 35 and mother of two, is one of those lucky women who never lets herself feel guilty about leaving her children when she goes to work. And like Ann Curry, she says that one of her secrets to having a satisfying career and a fulfilling home life is by creating emotional boundaries between work and family. A lawyer by training and a senior vice president at a boutique private banking firm in New York, Brooke believes that the trifecta of fabulous childcare, daily organization, and a hands-on husband helps make her hectic life run relatively smoothly.

"I think a large part of it is that I don't worry about my kids during the day, which is a really big issue and perhaps the biggest piece of the puzzle. Not that you can't worry about your children. But you can't worry about the childcare options you've chosen," Brooke, a tall brunette with bright green eyes and an easy laugh, tells me as we sit in her office overlooking midtown Manhattan. "I think once you have those issues settled it makes working a lot easier. I am so comfortable where my kids are, for me that's the key to everything."

Brooke has been juggling a busy schedule since before she even had children. For four years she went to law school at night while working a full-time job. Efficiency and organization helped her manage her stress over the years, and these skills have clearly prepared her for motherhood. Now she's the mother of a 3-year-old daughter and a 7-month-old son. She works four days a week, and Fridays she's home with her kids. She and her husband, Matt Bromberg, a securities firm attorney who practices in New York, have perhaps the most egalitarian marriage that I've come across.

Matt takes his children to daycare each morning while Brooke commutes to the city from New Jersey. Brooke does the after-work pickup as Matt, who gets home around 6:30 P.M., prepares dinner. Both Matt and Brooke feed and bathe their kids together and alternate on who puts whom to sleep. The only nagging guilt they feel is the length of time their children spend in daycare—eleven hours. But the rhythm of their life, consistency of their joint schedules, confidence in their daycare provider, and equal partnership when it comes to childcare makes it work for them. They are also unbelievably organized people.

"In terms of daily routine I do everything the night before," Brooke says. "It sounds really silly, but I try to be organized and get the kids' bags and bottles together for daycare before I go to sleep at night."

Brooke, who also happens to be my next-door neighbor and friend, is the kind of on-the-ball person who orders snow gear for her kids before the leaves have even changed color. Perhaps it's her work in financial planning, where looking ahead and embracing risk-adverse strategies is crucial to keeping her wealthy clients from going broke, that has actually helped her organize her personal life too. Brooke does laundry every Friday when she's home from work. And Matt goes grocery shopping at 9:00 A.M. every Sunday with his daughter Lilly, where he meticulously plots almost a week's worth of dinners days in advance. Matt and Brooke both thrive on routines and order whereas my husband and I operate in chaos. So while I'm dashing to the store to buy boots for my son as a blizzard is brewing, Matt and Brooke are prepared. They swear that makes life much easier, and I know that they're right. I'm always aspiring to become more like them even though I inherently find structure stressful. But clearly, thinking ahead and working together is what makes the Horman/Bromberg family operate so well.

Peggy Orenstein writes in *Flux: Women on Sex, Work, Love, Kids & Life in a Half-Changed World*: "Couples who share household responsibility most equally are those in which the salaries are similar and the *husband* has a flexible job . . . and that serves as a corrective to the tendency of moms to automatically do it all."[3] A couple of days after I interview Brooke, I read Matt this statement.

"Yes, well, that makes sense. I do think of Brooke as an equal partner, but I didn't really recognize that as part of the 'formula for success' until you pointed out the dynamic. But I also think some of the way I operate is a product of how I grew up. While my dad traveled a lot for work, when he was home he cooked, cleaned, and took care of all the outdoor chores. He made our Saturday morning pancakes and took us to get sneakers and stuff like that. So that's how I saw it done. I certainly realize that Brooke works just as hard as I do, and I also recognize that she can get stressed by her job, and like any normal person, gets frustrated with the kids. I simply try to do my share. I would feel guilty if I came home and just sat around, so I unload the dishwasher and start preparing dinner. The more I think about this, the more I recognize that it may very well be driven in equal part by my sense of partnership and by my internal pressure to feel productive. I feel good when I get things accomplished. I also like to think that I make Brooke's life easier. I do this not only for her but also for me in that it makes her more pleasant to be around."

While Matt may represent the postmillennial Renaissance man, the kind of New Age guy who gets as much gratification from hard wiring a light fixture as he does from whipping up a hearty, homemade Bolognese sauce, he's still a rare breed among men. The Bureau of Labor Statistics reports that women continue to take on the brunt of household and childcare responsibilities. In fact, in 2003 women reported doing about four times as much housework and twice as much childcare as men.[4]

Pushing Back and Setting Limits

Michelle Martinez could use a Matt Bromberg. She's always polling her friends about when they go grocery shopping because she feels as though she simply never has time even to buy milk. As the mother of a three-year-old and the associate publisher at a national magazine, Michelle works a brutal schedule and doesn't get a lot of help from her husband when it comes to household and childcare issues. A tiny brunette with pin straight hair, big brown eyes, and a wicked laugh, Michelle says she's often frustrated because everything falls on her shoulders—paying bills, buying her daughter's clothes, taking care of the house, and even planning her family's social life.

"I always say that I need a wife," Michelle says, half-smiling, the frustration in her voice seeping through. "My nanny is sort of like my wife. Recently I started asking her to go to the grocery store for me. She'll drop the check off for me at Kate's music class. I've started delegating more to help keep my sanity."

While Michelle constantly struggles to get her husband to help more at home, at work, she has been successful in defining boundaries and limits for herself.

Michelle is her family's breadwinner and has been working in magazine publishing for fifteen years. She says that the volatile and competitive nature of the magazine world seems to breed a culture of managers who are infamous for stressing out and even abusing their staffs. And even with more women at the top these days, the environment is still surprisingly un–family friendly.

"The magazine business is great for women until you get into management and then all bets are off," Michelle says, taking a sip of white wine at a trendy restaurant near her New York City office. "The problem is that the generation of women who are running the magazines are women who are ten years older than me and their philosophy of life is different. They believe that in order to be successful you have to give blood and sacrifice your family life, and if you want to make a million dollars a year, that's what it takes. But my generation does not wholeheartedly believe that. We think that you can be wildly successful and do a really good job and not sacrifice your home life. But when I watch my boss, I see that she works late because of how she runs her life. If she were more focused during the day she could get out earlier. Even before I had kids I wanted to have a life. I think I'm famously inflexible when it comes to defining my boundaries."

Defining boundaries doesn't mean that Michelle doesn't work hard. She typically puts in ten-hour days at the office and logs 60,000 miles of travel a year. This year she's been on the road at least one day a week.

"After I had Kate, I never thought I'd be able to juggle it all. I thought I would lose my mind and be in a straitjacket. I actually didn't want to go back into management, and I thought I would take a step down. But a woman I was working for said, 'Don't worry, you can do it.' And you can do it. It's amazing what you can do if you want to. I don't have to be in management. I could move back into sales and have a more flexible life. But then I would probably be permanently taking myself out of the publisher track. So I'm doing this partially because I want to. But what I've learned is that you can't let your boss push you around. You're entitled to your life. I know my boss; she'll keep pushing and asking. She'll have me do as much as I'll say yes to. So I have to set the boundaries. I have to decide where my limit is and say no, and ultimately I think she respects me more for that."

The Spin Cycle

Cindi Berger is dodging traffic down the Long Island Expressway, racing to get home in time for her nine-year-old daughter's championship softball game. During her commute home, she's returning phone calls, and I'm on her list that afternoon. Earlier that day I had called to see if I could set up an interview with Cindi, who is one of the most successful and best-known celebrity publicists in the country. She calls me back to confirm an interview time for the following week and tells me that coincidentally she's in the midst of a working-mother conflict of her own. It's been a particularly brutal day, Cindi says. Her client, the female recording group the Dixie Chicks, has been doing back-to-back interviews all day promoting a new album. But Cindi has a softball game to make and has to leave the city by 4:15 P.M. to factor in a sizeable commute to Long Island that runs anywhere from ninety minutes to two hours. So she has tag-teamed with a colleague to relieve her so she can get home, change into jeans, pick up her daughter, and get to the game. This is business as usual for Cindi Berger, mother to two children and publicist to many of America's most famous divas, including Sharon Stone, Bette Midler, Barbara Walters, Rosie O'Donnell, and the Dixie Chicks.

The next week I meet Cindi in her sunny, midtown Manhattan office where she's surrounded by pictures and posters of some of the celebrities she represents. Because she is such a large and prominent personality in the celebrity world, I half expect that Cindi will be a physically intimidating person herself. After all, life in publicity requires being a brazen bulldog of sorts. But instead I find myself strangely surprised that Cindi is rather petite and ultrafeminine with long, tight, curly dark hair and a very attractive, unstressed face.

Cindi tells me that she got into publicity quickly and decisively, even if mostly on a whim. It was the summer after college graduation, and she wasn't sure what she was going to do next. On a beautiful May morning she was floating on a raft in a friend's pool, drinking from a can of Tab and flipping through *Cosmopolitan* when she stumbled upon an article about celebrity publicists.

"I thought to myself, hmm, I love the theater and I love the movies, I could do this. I could really do this. So I said to my friend Robin, 'I'm going to the city.' And she said, 'What do you mean you're going into the city, it's gorgeous out, why are you leaving?' And I said, 'I know what I want to do with my life; I'm going to be a celebrity publicist.'"

So Cindi hopped out of the pool, borrowed her parents' car, and drove into New York City, depositing her résumé at a couple of publicity firms. A few weeks later she got a job as a receptionist at PMK. Twenty years later, Cindi is a managing director.

A little over a decade ago, Cindi was the first woman at her company to have a baby. Without any precedent to follow, she was determined to figure out her own way to integrate motherhood with her successful career and made a proposition to the partners at her firm.

"I came back from maternity leave, and I said to the partners, my career is really important to me but my family comes first, my family will always come first. Do you think I can turn that empty office down the hall into a nursery? There were two men that worked here and the rest of us were women. They all said OK, let's give it a shot.

"I had no idea if it would work, but it did. I converted the desk into a changing table. I put pretty things on the walls. I had a crib and lots of toys and a tape recorder that was always playing Raffi in the background. I drove my daughter and my nanny in with me from Long Island three days a week for three years.

"My company was really extraordinary. No one brought their kids into work, and to me it was a very natural thing. When my daughter was nine months old she actually went to her first press conference, a Barney press conference."

Now that her children are in school, Cindi is obviously no longer bringing them to work with her, but she is insistent that her family remain her priority, and she's proud to say that she has never missed any of her children's extracurricular events. She says that her children always come first, and she gives me some examples: "If I have a client on a television show or doing a taping and there's an event at either of my kids' schools then I'm at my kids' schools," Cindi says matter-of-factly.

"Earlier this summer it was visiting day at camp, and I had to be there at 2 o'clock for a camp show, and I had to be in New York City for a meeting in the morning. So I drove into the city to go to my meeting, and I drove out to camp to spend an hour at the visiting session, and then drove back to the city because I had work to do. It was brutal, but I did it. I thought twice about having to go back into the city, but not about missing visiting day at camp."

Cindi says that one of the secrets to her success in juggling work and family is delegating some of her commitments to others on her staff.

"My assistant is truly my right hand and my clients are well aware of my family. But I do always try to make it work. The governor was honoring Bette Midler a few weeks ago, and I was heartbroken I couldn't be there because it was the same night as my daughter's dance recital. So I had someone else be with Bette."

When it comes to managing her home life, Cindi says that the thread holding it all together is her support system, including her husband and her longtime babysitter.

"As a working mother, you have got to be extraordinarily organized, and you have to have a real solid support system, whether it's a nanny, a husband, or another partner. You really need that support. My husband is an oncologist who's on call 24/7. He also has a very demanding career. But we tag team. If I can't drop off the cookies at the school because I have to leave early and they have to be at the bake sale at a certain time, my husband will do that. There's always a tremendous amount of shared responsibility. My husband also never misses an event for my children's activities."

While I'm interviewing Cindi, her assistant pops into the office and says that Sharon Stone is on the phone. Cindi excuses herself and puts on her headset to talk to one of her favorite clients. After Cindi hangs up the phone, she tells me that midway through her phone call with Sharon, she remembered that she needed to call her children's babysitter to remind her about the birthday party her kids are going to that afternoon. Apologizing for the further interruption, she calls her sitter to make sure that all of the carpool logistics are coordinated and to alert her about which present on the mantel to take.

For Cindi, a self-described type-A personality who listens to several radio traffic reports consecutively to strategize her commute home, she credits hyper organization skills for managing the constant juggle of her career and family. Technology, she says, has blurred the boundaries between work and home, and while in some instances it's made her job easier, in other ways it's given her even less time to mentally organize.

"As a working mother who commutes, the car for me was my own private time. It was that quiet time that I had to think, 'OK, my daughter has two birthday parties, my son has a birthday party, and then he's going to a friend's house this weekend.' So I would think about activities that I need to do that was separate from work in my car. Or I would think, 'Oh my gosh, I have to order the roast because the holidays are coming,' or 'I didn't pick up the dry cleaning, I have to do that.' The car gave me that time to sort of let my mind free flow. Cell phones have taken that time away. Because when I'm in the car, my assistant will roll calls through to me, so I'm still working for another ninety minutes until I get into the house. And I'll pull into the driveway and the phone goes off, and I walk up my steps and things have to be left in my car and in my office."

As easy as she makes it all seem, Cindi acknowledges that there are dozens of times when she finds herself in conflict.

"A couple of years ago my daughter was asking me to volunteer at her school and I thought, 'OK, I don't volunteer a lot, and I wish I could.' So this time there's a bake sale, so I go to the grocery store, and I buy all of the ingredients and at the same time I am dealing with a huge problem that was happening in Europe involving an *Elle* cover shoot. Everything was changing rapidly, and I had to bake cookies for school the next morning and in between my sister called. I said to her, 'Oh my God, I'm losing my mind, I'm dealing with a problem in France, and I've got a client who is not going to get there in time, and I have a world famous photographer who's having a heart attack, and the magazine is on a deadline, and they have to shoot the couture collection before the collection leaves, and I'm baking cookies!' It was such hysteria. And out of everything I told my sister, she says, 'You're baking cookies from scratch?' And I said yes, it's a project that I have to do with Sydney [my daughter], and we're making chocolate chip cookies, and we're going to put them in a bag with a little ribbon around it and bring it for the bake sale. And she said, 'Cindi, there are shortcuts you need to take for your own sanity. Nestlé's has cookies you slice and put on a cookie sheet and bake for eight minutes and then they're done.' And I thought, Oh my God, it's an epiphany. I had no idea there was a shortcut you could take. And I thought what genius! That is the best thing Nestlé had ever invented for the working mother, and that's what we did. It was still a project that we did together. It was a shortcut, so as a working parent you have to learn some shortcuts. It doesn't jip your child but it makes your life a little easier."

Cindi also says that her secret to managing it all is to set limits between work and her home life. Although she makes it clear that she's always reachable to a client, she tries to restrict the extracurricular activities of her job.

"I don't go to nighttime screenings any more. I only go to a premiere when I have a client in it. If I need to see a film, studios will set it during the day for me. [In this business] you could go to a party and the theater every night, but I just don't do it. I only do it when I have to."

Creative Boundaries and Taking Control

When I leave Cindi's office, my first thought is that if I had met her ten years earlier, I might have altered my career path entirely and gone into publicity just like her. Or maybe I'd have wanted to work *for* her. Cindi is so impressive and empowering in her ability to put family first while being at the top of her game in her career—she's a true role model for the rest of us. Although Cindi's self-created onsite daycare is not the reality for most women, and frankly the thought of schlepping my own kids into the city during rush hour is more stressful than leaving them with a nanny or at a local daycare, Cindi's experience demonstrates that you shouldn't be afraid to ask for unorthodox work-family arrangements because they may be possible to achieve.

Creating boundaries between work and family is also a key strategy between managing work and family life. Cindi, Michelle, Brooke, and Ann have each constructed boundaries for themselves between work and family. For Ann it was a mental exercise at first. She refused to let her mind wander into work when she was with her children, and she refused to think about her kids when she was working. By compartmentalizing, she was able to completely focus on both important parts of her life. Cindi, Ann, and Brooke also rely heavily on their husbands to share in the daily childcare responsibilities.

Cindi clearly makes sure that family is always her priority, and her career has certainly not suffered because of that. In fact, she believes she's even more respected by her clients because they see how much she values her children. And Michelle, who is not senior enough to control her own schedule, has had the courage to stand up to her boss and "push back" to make sure she can still have a family life even though she is constantly pressured to work longer. Managing her time wisely at work is a key to Michelle's success and solid reputation. And because she is highly efficient and respected in her industry, she ultimately feels more confident and able to stand up for herself.

The theme of setting boundaries and creating limits has been echoed by dozens of women to whom I've spoken. Lynn Dalton, a lawyer who works part-time, in-house for an international media company, told me that she rarely takes calls or answers emails on her days off because she wants people to respect her schedule. "If people know that one time I'll take their call and then the next time I won't, then they're going to get pissed off. But by establishing the boundaries early on and saying, 'sorry, you know I don't work Tuesdays and Thursdays,' then you're controlling the situation. It can take an extra day or so for me to get information back sometimes, but my company knows that I do a good job, I'm efficient and loyal to them, and I think my work situation benefits everyone."

In an era of high-tech inundation where we can be beeped, buzzed, Instant Messaged, Text Messaged, faxed, phoned, and emailed, many women told me that their boundaries between work and home were not just psychological but technological. Some refused to accept their company's BlackBerries because they didn't want to be further tethered to their job and forced to respond to email all night and on weekends. Others thought technology freed them up to conduct business from home even as they were changing poopy diapers, nursing newborns, or supervising the installation of their backyard swing sets. Cindi stays connected to work by her cell phone when she leaves the office, but she still tries to maintain a policy of not conducting business for a couple of hours at night when she's concentrating on her kids. Placing limits, enforcing boundaries, and protecting your home life as much as possible is important in managing the juggle.

CNN senior producer Karen Palmer says that the onus is on women to figure out how to mesh their work responsibilities with their family life and to create a plan of action.

"As women we need to come up with creative solutions so we can have the things that we want. I don't think you can ever assume that men are going to work that out for you because the bottom line is to get the job done. So your job is to figure out how you can make their lives simpler by giving them a plan to get what you want that still allows them to get what they want. When I was pregnant, I actually came to the folks at CNN and said I'm pretty sure I'm going to take a certain amount of maternity leave. I'm going to take my computer home with me so if God forbid you really need me you can reach me. And even though my hours are going to be different when I come back from maternity leave, there will not be a situation where you can't get a hold of me or feel bad about calling me. You have to be willing to make the contributions, and you have to be more creative about how you make them and make sure that other people don't feel that your having the kid is entitling you to something that perhaps they want to get a piece of."

Split-Brain Strategies

It's a muggy, summer day in New York City, and Rebecca Stern can't decide what kind of frothy, coffee concoction to order. Back home in Jerusalem where the assortment of caffeinated drinks hasn't gotten as complicated as a caramel machiato, she usually just gets iced coffee. But here in the States, where she's visiting family for a few weeks, she always gets stumped.

Rebecca, 41, is the mother of three young girls spanning 2 to 7 years old. A Toronto native and educated in the United States, she now lives in Israel and works for a U.S. non-profit organization where her job is to help navigate some of the sticky political issues in the Middle East. She routinely meets with prominent players in the Israeli government, including the prime minister and defense minister. Because of the time difference between Jerusalem and Washington, D.C., where her company is based, Rebecca's workdays start early but don't end until nearly midnight when she turns off her phone and Washington knows to stop calling.

Rebecca says that the essence of Israeli society, one that is extremely kid-focused and where many families have three or more children, actually allows her extreme career to feel more manageable. Perhaps because virtually all women and mothers work, due to the astronomical costs of living, Israeli culture actually caters more to family time. Maybe the roots of this ideology come from the Kibbutznik nature of Israel where the community took responsibility for building a country and caring for its children. But these days even as the economy stays globally competitive in such aggressive industries as technology and medical research, many parents are still able to end their days in the late afternoon to pick their children up from daycare centers that all close around 4:00 P.M.

"One friend of mine is a lobbyist for the women's lobby and she says that her feminism ends at 3:30. It's just part of the pulse of a couple's day that one of the two has to drop whatever it is that they are doing at 3:30 and go get the kids," she says. "My sister-in-law is a hotshot lawyer and a mother of five, and she walks out the door at 4:00 P.M. A lot of women I know work what in America would be considered part-time and in Israeli terms it's their whole day, they work 8:00 to 3:00 or 8:00 to 4:00. And when there's a school play, it's always at 4:00 P.M. on a Wednesday afternoon, and all of the parents come, dads too."

Living in Israeli society, it's no wonder that Rebecca feels comfortable and even empowered to integrate her work and family life.

"If I need to reschedule a meeting with a government official because I have a kids' holiday party at school, and I said to them I can't make it because I have a conflict, which would be the correct way to explain the situation in America, they would give me a hard time. But if I say my conflict is my kids' holiday party, then it's no problem, and I get a new meeting."

Rebecca also credits her agility at mentally shifting between her two worlds as the key to managing her full life.

"My secret to being able to do my job and have these little kids is transitions. When I'm with my kids in the late afternoons, I want to feel like I'm really concentrated and focused on them. If I have to take a call from the prime minister's office, I just do switch off and switch on and make sure that my work dealing takes five minutes. I'm able to handle these things very quickly. I think over the years I've become very good at these transitions. I get so into my kids' projects and all of the after-school activities. When I'm driving and shuttling them around in the afternoons, I can handle the calls, that's not a problem. But when I pick up a child and walk into that room, I don't want to be on the cell phone. When I'm hearing how the class went, I don't want to be on the cell phone. In my mind the secret to doing it all is constant transitions and being able to make them without feeling guilty in either direction."

Rebecca says because of her untraditional schedule, she's constantly juggling her two jobs as political player and mother. She tells me a story about just how dramatically her two worlds can overlap.

"About a year ago I took my 2-year-old daughter to the mall on a special outing to shop for sandals and to get ice cream. As soon as I got to the mall the bureau chief from the prime minister's office called and said, 'Rebecca, where are you?' I said, 'If you really must know, I'm with my daughter buying sandals and ice cream at the mall.' Then he asked, 'Well how soon can you get here?' So I said, 'I could be at your office sooner if I bring my daughter with me rather than dropping her off at home first.' And he says, 'Bring your daughter.' So I got the sandals and the ice cream, and I zoomed over to the prime minister's office, and I deposited my daughter with the secretary, and within a minute I was whisked into the prime minister's office. Now keep in mind, in American terms this would be like going to the White House for a meeting with the President and National Security Adviser in the West Wing while your daughter waits with the president's secretary.

"That day it all happened so quickly because there was some urgent issue that needed to be handled immediately. But I'm in the meeting, and I start thinking to myself, my daughter is just getting toilet trained, oh my God, she's going to pee in the prime minister's office! Then I'm wondering, will she tell the secretary if she has to pee or will she just go? I thought maybe I should just excuse myself for a minute and go out and check on her. I actually didn't leave, and fortunately she didn't pee. But it shows that as women we are always multitasking or juggling or doing that split-brain thing that we do."

Multiple Balls in the Air

Multitasking and motherhood are inseparable. It starts when you're still in the hospital taking congratulatory phone calls while trying to success-fully burp your newborn, entertain your in-laws, and in my case, order the deli platters for my son's bris (a Jewish circumcision ceremony). Ann Crittenden speculates in her book *If You've Raised Kids, You Can Manage Anything* that a mother's ability to multitask is probably biologically rooted in survival.

"Millions of years of evolutionary selection pressures may have given the human female brain certain cognitive advantages that facilitate the survival of offspring—such as the ability to remember multiple tasks in focus simultaneously, the ability to read nonverbal danger signals and a certain fearlessness when danger threatens."[5]

Of course, a dangerous situation today no longer entails children being devoured by woolly mammoths, but rather the threat of failing to pack extra diapers or losing a special blankie or forgetting the portable DVD player for a long car ride. As all mothers can appreciate, the needs of our children usually hover near the surface of our already crowded brains. Even with all of the noise going on in our heads, moms (unlike most dads) somehow remember the birthday parties, parent-teacher conferences, and doctor's appointments. Or in Rebecca's case, the fact that her 2-year-old wasn't fully potty trained—this as she was in the midst of handling greater global concerns.

Rotating on a Tight Axis

Multitasking is something Dr. Laura Fisher knows how to do well. After all, as a physician with her own practice and as a mom to three girls under 4, spaced only twenty-six months apart, every day she undergoes an intricate juggling act that begins somewhere between 4:30 and 5:30 each morning when at least one of her early-rising girls awakes. An athletic woman with cropped blonde hair, tortoise shell glasses, and a seemingly limitless amount of energy, Laura speaks passionately about her identity as a physician, a job she's been doing for nearly two decades. Her manner is an awesome combination of efficiency and warmth. She speaks without ever seeming to take a breath. I talk to Laura in her modest New York City office surrounded by photos of her children and her own oil paintings. At 44, Laura has been a doctor for literally half her life, an identity she relishes.

It never crossed Laura's mind that she couldn't be a doctor and a mother simultaneously. In fact, she says her biggest concern was not merging motherhood with medicine, but worrying if she was *ever* going to get married. Laura didn't meet her husband until she was 37 years old. They married when she was 38 and had three girls in less than three years.

"I just love medicine, and I always wanted to work," Laura says emphatically. "I always knew I wanted to be a working mom."

Laura believes adamantly that it's important for women not to forfeit themselves entirely to motherhood when they have children.

"You have to have something going on in your head that you can think about so you're interested, so you're not bored, so you have self-esteem, so you can talk to your husband or friends or relatives about it. I don't think you can let the rest of the world stop when you have your kids."

The doctor takes her own advice well. She works Monday through Friday from 8:00 A.M. until 4:00 P.M. when she dashes out her office for a fifty-minute workout at the gym. It's here, Laura says, where she can read her medical journals or indulge in a novel. Her secret to doing it all and making her hectic life less chaotic is by having her entire universe revolve around a five-block radius—apartment, office, and gym.

Forgoing a spacious house in the suburbs for an apartment in the city that keeps her commute to a five-minute walk allows Laura to be a full-time doctor and still spend quality time with her children.

As Laura's experience demonstrates, a significant element in keeping the fragile balance between career and family is often the physical distance between the divergent universes of work and home. Many of the happiest working mothers I've met—from the West Coast to the Southwest to the Northeast—were those whose lives revolved around a tight area of concentration.

"I made a deliberate choice not to commute," Laura says. "It's not easy living and working in the city because it's so expensive. I grew up in the suburbs bicycling, playing tennis, and doing sports. In the city it's hard to raise kids with the benefits of the outdoors and sports. But without a commute I can walk to my office, which is five minutes away from my home. If I left the city, my commute would probably take about three hours a day. Instead I really treasure that time I have with my kids. Right now I feel like it's all working. My kids are happy, and I'm happy."

Letting Go of Perfect

Staying organized and efficient, setting boundaries, delegating responsibilities, and having terrific childcare and support at home is critical to the success of the Stay-at-Work mom. But time and again I've heard another piece of advice from nearly everyone to whom I've talked: We need to "let go of perfect"—both at home and in the workplace.

"I just think that's the most important thing for any working mom to know is that it's very normal to feel that no one's getting any time including yourself, your husband, your work, and your kids. It's gotten easier, more because I've let go."

"You don't always have to be perfect. When you're young and you're first starting out, everything has got to be perfect. And I've learned it just doesn't have to be that way," says cosmetics CEO Bobbi Brown.

"I think I have somehow accepted at this point that I am doing the best that I can," Liz Lange, fashion maternity designer and CEO, says. "I think that I am a good mother and a good businesswoman and probably if I just focused on one I'd be better at either one. But that actually wouldn't make me happy. If I was just a mother and I wasn't working, I don't think I would be very happy. I don't mean that judgmentally because I know there are women who really do love staying home, and I really respect that. But it's never been me. On the other hand, I would never just want to be working. I see very successful women [without children] who are kind of alone at the end of the day.

"I don't have it all because things are giving on both ends, but I'm happy with what I do have, and I feel enormously lucky. I'm thrilled that I have my husband, my two children, and that I have this business. But we all have a finite amount of energy. So I think it's about getting comfortable with that and finding the right balance."

Indiana native Christy Hubbard, 35, always wanted to be a lawyer. After graduating from Indiana University, she started law school in Iowa. During an internship, she met her husband Gene, a Native American from the Navajo Nation in Arizona. The two married and soon had a baby. Then 24 years old, Christy quit law school because she was miserable being away from her daughter. At that time, her father-in-law was terminally ill, so she and her husband moved back to the reservation in Ganado, Arizona, where Gene grew up. Christy became a teacher so her schedule could allow her to spend more time with her baby. Two years later she had another baby. But law, Christy says, was her calling, and she hated feeling financially insecure. So she went back to law school, scored the third highest on her state bar exam, and is now working at a firm in Phoenix doing trademark and copyright law.

Christy is her family's primary breadwinner. She says she is driven by both her passion for law and a fear of financial instability. She is on a partner track at her law firm, but that hasn't stopped her from expanding her family. She now has four children, 10, 8, 2, and 8 months old, and she works full-time from 6:30 A.M. to 4:30 P.M. so she can be home early enough to do homework, play, and have dinner with her kids. She says that her struggle has been learning to curb both her ambition at work and at home and accepting the fact that she can't be perfect.

"I am not going to be a superstar at work," Christy says. "They won't be writing firm-wide emails about me and about the amazing things I do. I try instead to be a solid attorney on whom my clients can rely. At home, particularly at school, I am not going to be super mom. Sometimes homework assignments will go missing, and I always send store-bought cookies, but when I am home it is all about the kids."

"I know I can't stay at home, so I don't torture myself with it anymore. I also adopted some of my husband's 'who cares what they think' attitude. If I didn't stand before God and make vows to you, if you didn't come from my womb, or I didn't come from yours, then you don't get a vote," Christy says. "I used to consciously dress down when I went to my kids' school so it wasn't obvious that I worked—much less that I was a lawyer. Now I think that's silly. This year I took them to school their first day and attended school mass in my full career costume—a suit, heels, and pearls. I guess I've just accepted who I am."

Chapter 4

Giving Up the Guilt

The Pressures, the Expectations, the Myths

Pregnancy and motherhood have become downright chic. Sexy, hot, expectant celebrity moms are all the rage. Their pregnant bosoms over-flowing in designer frocks and beautiful, un–stretch marked, bulging bel-lies radiate from magazine covers. So while a good half of the pregnant population is gagging on their prenatal vitamins, barfing before breakfast, or aching from sciatica, pop culture has done an extreme makeover on this often not-so-pretty rite of passage.

The gloriously sexed up, blissed-out image may have succeeded in making motherhood more fashionable than it used to be, but as babies have become the trendy accoutrement for the fabulous woman who has everything, the pressure to feel ecstatic, look fantastic, and be enam-ored with motherhood has ironically become another kind of burden. Perhaps it's because so many women are struggling with infertility today that the passion for motherhood has taken on almost a religious fervor. For a host of reasons, the once natural cycle of life that magically turned a woman into a mother is no longer inevitable. Given this climate, where motherhood has become not only chic but also often tricky to achieve, publicly expressing ambivalence or angst about being a mom is, well, unfashionable.

I have to admit, I breathed a sigh of relief when I successfully got pregnant the old-fashioned way. Nausea and all, I threw myself into pregnancy as if it were an activity to be mastered. I had books to read, new clothes to buy, and kegels to practice. I dutifully gave up my coffee and Merlot, avoided unpasteurized cheeses and artificial sweeteners. I took on prenatal yoga with a vengeance and tried not to laugh when my instructor asked us to visualize our vaginas and meditate to our unborn. I had been married for six years but had procrastinated on pregnancy because professionally and emotionally it never felt like the right time. But now I surprised everyone, including myself, by just how enthusiastic and sappy I had become about the whole enterprise.

So when my son debuted three years ago, I was expecting to fall in love. Instead I threw up. My body was in shock. My brain was numb. It all felt oddly anticlimactic. As I was being pushed into my recovery room, my uterus still contracting, my vagina aching, and my ice pack leaking, I thought to myself, so this is it? I kept examining my newborn's squished face waiting for my Mama Bear instinct to kick in. It didn't. I was going through the motions of what I thought a "Good Mom" was supposed to do. With military precision, every two hours I whipped out my breast and shoved it into my confused and hungry baby's face. He seemed miserable, but I was determined that he ingest that magical mammary fluid that doctors swore would protect him from all sorts of plagues and infections. Meanwhile, the exquisite mother-baby bond I anticipated and read about wasn't exactly happening, and my son was hardly helping.

At 3 weeks old, my son, who the maternity nurses all promised would be an "easy baby," started crying and didn't stop for nearly four months. I was on the verge of a breakdown. I felt depressed and defeated. I didn't blame myself the way some mothers of colicky babies often do; I just wallowed in my own misery. I hated all of the moms who had peaceful babies. I sometimes even hated my own baby. And I often hated my husband for his part in making this baby.

To add to my insecurity and ambivalence about mommyhood, one of my best friends, Gayle, gave birth to twins just three weeks after I had Jonah. She called me from her recovery room, her voice still a mixture of post-C-section, medicated, hormonal happiness, and announced that she had fallen in love with her daughter at precisely 8:10 that night. When she felt the wave of love, she looked at a clock to record the moment. "That's great," I lied as my fussy newborn fiercely sucked on my raw nipple. The fussier Jonah got, the crankier I became.

Three years and another baby later, I've learned a truth about motherhood that many women don't bother to discuss. It can, for lack of a better word, suck, especially in the beginning. This is something no one tells the pregnant woman who is more consumed with shopping for a newborn than actually caring for one. And this is, of course, something that she never reads about in *People* magazine where celebrities are always shown snuggling with their babies and proclaiming that motherhood is "the greatest thing they've ever done," better than winning that silly Golden Globe or getting a lifetime's supply of free couture.

Wouldn't it be refreshing if the celebrity on the cover confessed that motherhood could be a real drag, or at least it was harder than she thought it was going to be, and after years of undergoing IVF treatments she was sort of bummed out that her baby wasn't the easygoing, happy go-lucky guy she signed up for, and she's scared silly that her body may never quite bounce back. Brooke Shields did go public with the postpartum depression she experienced after having her daughter, Rowan, in May 2003. In fact, she has written a book about that time, but Shields is truly an anomaly among famous mothers. For some reason, celebrities are supposed to embrace motherhood perhaps even more than the rest of us, and they never publicly gripe about 3:00 A.M. feedings or changing poopy diapers because who knows, maybe they're not doing them. But when regular moms get sucked into the myth of motherhood as a perpetually erotic, backlit state of being that is always fun and completely fulfilling, they are getting set up for a major disappointment. The truth many women don't quite realize until after they give birth is that being a mom is tough. And it may not come as naturally as we were led to believe.

Mother Nature

Renowned anthropologist Sarah Blaffer Hrdy argues that far from being selfless, primate mothers have always combined nurturing with ambition, mother love with sexual needs, ambivalence with devotion. In her book *Mother Nature: Maternal Instincts and How They Shape the Human Species*, she points to the totally dependent nature of newborn human infants and their need to appeal both physically and emotionally to their mothers to survive, as evidence that moms can be fickle and therefore human newborns are sophisticated enough to win moms over, ensuring their own existence.

> Maternal ambivalence is treated today as if it were a deep secret only just being unveiled. Over thousands of years, in worlds where infant survival often depends on maternal calculations, tradeoffs, choices, and prioritizing an infant had to be appealing in order to extract more rather than less care from his mother, or in extreme cases to be cared for at all. Maternal ambivalence and infant allure are scarcely areas where many of us expect to find natural selection callously about her work. But diverse strands of evidence lead to the unavoidable, if disturbing, conclusion that natural selection has indeed operated in this realm.[1]

So when your newborn is colicky or when your toddler is throwing a tantrum, and you're feeling guilty for wanting to throw him or her out the window, you should understand that your maternal instinct is intact. As female primates, Hrdy says, we are wired to respond warmly to plump, cooing, giggling babies. Universally, our species finds scrawny, screaming infants undesirable. So a mother's love and devotion is not an unconditional constant but a fluid, temperamental one. And we shouldn't feel guilty if we're not always oozing maternal affection.

Behind the Guilt

Guilt and motherhood seem brutally intertwined—it's as if it's a biological requisite to having children. Feelings of guilt, worry, anxiety, and ambivalence crackle through many Stay-at-Work moms who wonder if they are making the right choice and fear that they are missing out both at work and at home.

In traditional societies children rarely leave their mothers' sides. They ride on their mothers' backs or are smooshed into slings or other contraptions that allow mom and child to forage in the forest, fetch water, or these days sell tzotchkies and other goods in the local market. *National Geographic* pictures often show these babes suckling on the droopy boobs of their nonchalant mothers who are doing their daily business of simply staying alive. In cultures where babies are always burrowed onto their mother's bosoms, moms are never are made to feel guilty about leaving their kids behind to go to work because mother and child are literally connected at the hip.

Women in Western societies and of the modern era aren't usually found roaming the countryside foraging for berries unless their baby is strapped into a high-tech backpack and they're out for a power trek on a Saturday afternoon. But for centuries it has not been practical for mother and child to be attached all day long, every day. So where does all of the guilt come from? Like ambivalence, is it biological? Or is it cultural? Or is it some potent combination of both?

Anthropologist and best-selling author Helen Fisher argues that women are indeed biologically predisposed to feelings of guilt when it comes to their children. Because women have high levels of estrogen and oxytocin, she tells me that we are hormonally programmed to nurture and rear our babies. In fact, our species has survived because of attentive, protective mothers, and those genes have been funneled down into our own DNA. But unlike a million years ago, when our prehistoric sisters easily commuted to the forest to gather the goods for dinner while simultaneously nursing their babies, the modern working gal faces fierce obstacles that make marrying both jobs tough to do. In the United States, the combination of a rigid non–family focused workplace, children spaced close together, and a lack of familial support stresses perhaps our most intense primordial affiliation—the mother-child bond.

As Helen Fisher puts it:

Fifteen thousand years ago, you would never have two children under four years old. We were not built to have children so close together. For millions of years, the natural spacing was four years apart; the same thing is true in gorillas and chimpanzees and even greater in orangutans (they wait five to seven years to conceive between children). The reason that the four-year birth spacing was maintained was because if you nurse a baby on demand, several times an hour, and sleep with a baby at night who keeps nursing, and combine that with a great deal of exercise and low body fat, you wouldn't conceive until you've really slowed down on the nursing. So a woman was only dealing with one child at a time, and the mother carried that child on her back while she did the gathering of vegetables; that's what she was expected to do. She left the older kids in camp in multi-age playgroups in an extremely secure, social environment with all of her relatives and friends. So there was no anxiety about daycare, and there was no anxiety about leaving the baby because she never left the baby since she was nursing around the clock. So she could do all of her basic jobs simultaneously and comfortably.

What we're lacking today is about fifteen other people around us to help care for the babies. We don't have the other adults, friends, relatives, older children, we have none of that. And women today often have more than one child under four years old, so no wonder we're suffering![2]

Fisher also tells me it's our relentless, American work ethic, which has us working on average 20 percent more hours a year than the rest of the world, that threatens the nature of family life.

"Our ancestry didn't work 80 hours a week; they often worked 30 hours a week. We know this from looking at modern hunters and gatherers. The anthropologists who lived with them literally counted the work hours. When the adults come back to camp, women are doing other work like tanning hides, and men are making bows and arrows, but their children are all around them while they are doing it so work and play are mixed together," Fisher says. "When I spent a week with one of these hunting and gathering tribes, I realized that they do an incredible amount of sitting around. When they catch a buffalo, they have three weeks of meat; there's no refrigeration, so you don't have to accumulate."

There is no doubt that women experience a guilt that is both biologically and culturally rooted. As our society idealizes the mother in a traditional at-home model, Stay-at-Work moms can feel conflicted, especially when innately they feel the tug to be with their children but financially and emotionally they need a career. Fisher says the dual desires to have babies and to work in addition to childrearing are deeply embedded in the female. So it comes as no surprise that when the two passions collide, as they often do in our culture, moms feel a kaleidoscope of emotions ranging from depression to anxiety.

"All animals have social rules and when those rules are broken the animal feels discomfort. Human guilt probably comes from that discomfort. There is nothing a mother needs to do more than raise healthy babies and when that is thwarted it's going to cause a whole host of problems. It probably arises from a host of chemical systems, from fear and anger to a sense of urgency to be with the child. We're talking about basic brain systems, and the most primitive form of guilt."

The Freud Factor

The slew of psychological research in the past fifty years has both confused and terrified us about the impact we mothers have on our children. Many of the theories, including the concept of "attachment theory" (which gave scientific legitimacy to the idea that if women work when their children are young, they risk ruining the bonds with them) caught on in the 1950s in a postwartime climate that encouraged women to stay home and have babies. Once women were mostly pushed out of the workforce, their performance as mothers was judged under a microscope. They were either too attentive and suffocating or cold and negligent. This was the era when mothers were blamed for everything from causing colic to autism.

Recent scientific research has fortunately cleared up many of the myths that moms are responsible for a whole array of neurological and physiological problems in their children. Yet the residual effects of decades of ideology that positioned mothers as virtual messianic and omnipotent beings in their child's life still linger in our collective cultural consciousness.

One thing the research did confirm was our innate suspicions that babies need their mommies. But just how much do they need us? And what do you do about the daily, inevitable separations of modern-day working mothers?

The Madonna Complex

There is a Jewish expression that says: God could not be there all of the time; therefore he created mothers. Despite women's strides and progress over the past few centuries, the antiquated notion of the "Good Mother" is still one of the most sacrosanct and persistent images in our society. The image feels grossly out of date, utterly unmodern. Yet this ideal still resonates in our culture. For a woman to be accused of being a "Bad Mother" is like sticking a scarlet letter on her child's stroller and inviting the world to criticize her choices and child-rearing.

It's an obvious double standard. Hard-working women who work long hours and are devoted to their careers are often judged to be less devoted to their children. This is where the Stay-at-Home mom can hold the moral high ground. After all, isn't it she who has sacrificed her life for her children's? Hard-working men are praised for supporting their families, whereas hard-working women are chastised for destroying them. Even when years of studies show that children of working mothers do just as well socially and academically as their friends whose moms don't work, the notion remains.

Nevertheless, in our schizophrenic society that simultaneously idealizes and devalues mothers, moms are still expected to prepare the lunches, pack the sippy cups, join the PTA, plan the play dates, make the doctors' appointments, and volunteer as class mom. The bar continues to be raised to meet the "Good Mother" standard. For working mothers, this can be especially difficult. The duality of identities, Good Mother and Good Employee, are in constant conflict.

It seems the pressure and competition to be a great mom has increased over the past few decades. More is expected of mothers today than in our own mothers' generation.

And the expectations can make even the most secure women question their choices. For all of her broadcasting awards and national recognition, TV producer Soraya Gage says simply hanging out with the Stay-at-Home crowd aggravates her own insecurities.

"It's funny, when I'm with the at-home mothers, I'm intimidated because they're really on top of their kids, and they're really great moms," Soraya says earnestly. "I actually feel better here at work than I do when I'm there because sometimes I feel like I'm not as good as a mom."

"Motherhood has become central to a woman's notion of femininity, more so than marriage," writes Peggy Orenstein in her book *Flux: Women on Sex, Work, Love, Kids, & Life in a Half-Changed World.*[3] If that's true, that would explain why so many women experience so much angst and put in so much effort to measure up to society's ideal of the Good Mother. If motherhood cuts to the core of our womanhood, then our identity as women is enmeshed with how we perceive ourselves as mothers.

Guilty Confessions

I'll admit that my own perception of how I rank as a mom is sort of flimsy. I'm easily influenced by what other mothers seem to be doing better and often wonder if I should be doing more. On one of those sticky, steamy, bad hair days in July I'm racing to drop my son off at camp before heading into New York City for work. On my drive toward the Lincoln Tunnel, I make a long overdue call to an at-home mommy friend. She says she can't talk because she's on the other line interviewing possible ballet instructors for her 3-year-old daughter for next year. "You're such a good mom," I say reflexively, knowing that I have neither the time nor inclination to research music, art, gym, yoga, or any other classes for my preschool-age son—classes that won't be starting for at least another two months. But why did I automatically think that's what "Good Moms" should be doing? Does my friend's time and interest in organizing those types of activities and her ability and desire to be the one shuttling her kids from school to classes to playdates make her a better mother than I?

The next morning as I'm paying for my morning coffee I get another reminder about how I measure up as a mom. As I hover by the espresso machines waiting for my order, I turn to a neighborhood mom next to me in line who looks frazzled. Jamie hoists her cute 2-year-old onto her hip and tells me she's exhausted from working on her business plans to start her own preschool. She wants to launch her own program because she's not thrilled with what they have to offer in town. "Really?" I ask her, more curious than offended that the school my son would be attending was less stimulating and creative than it should be. As an early childhood educator, Jamie was disappointed with the choices available and was interested in creating a preschool of her own. A motivated mom with the education and experience to start her own school is of course a great thing. But her drive seemed to highlight my own laziness. I realized I had never interviewed teachers or preschool directors. I hadn't gone to open houses or classes or inquired about school curriculum as other moms had done. In fact, because I was terribly consumed at work and so late in even trying to register my son, Jonah, I wound up pathetically begging, pleading, and nearly bribing the school director just to get Jonah to the top of the wait list. So when he ultimately landed a spot in school, I was just relieved that he was enrolled.

The combination of my slacker mom tendencies and so much kid stuff to keep up with is probably why I'm always feeling perpetually insecure in my mothering. I'm the last to get my kids signed up for everything. My daughter, Alexandra, went to her 12-month checkup at 13½ months. I haven't gotten around to getting their vitamin or fluoride prescriptions refilled even though they ran out weeks ago. In other areas of my life, like cleaning out my refrigerator, no one sees how I'm slacking off—except of course my husband, who is arguably as unmotivated in domestic activities as I. But when it comes to the maintenance of our children, it seems as if our lives are transparent, inviting judgment and criticism—and not just from grandparents and siblings. Like it or not, when it comes to motherhood, America's "Live and Let Live" society tightens its reins, and there is a definite—if more or less unspoken—idea of what a good mother looks like and how she ought to be behaving.

Naomi Wolf, author of *Misconceptions: Truth, Lies and the Unexpected on the Journey to Motherhood,* sees things this way: "I believe the myth about the ease and naturalness of mothering—the ideal of the effortlessly ever-giving mother—is propped up, polished and promoted as a way to keep women from thinking clearly and negotiating forcefully about what they need from their partners and from society at large in order to mother well, without having to sacrifice themselves in the process."[4]

I don't want to sacrifice my career for my children, but my feelings about work are often intertwined with how my children are doing. On the days when my kids seem happy, work feels good. The minute they start having problems, however, I ultimately blame myself for not being home more. Ironically the day the manuscript for this book is due, a time when I've been working nonstop and haven't had time to come up for air, let alone had quality time to spend with my children, I find a teacher's note in my son's backpack from preschool. It reads: "Jonah has been having a hard time keeping his hands to himself and sharing. We have seen an increase in shoving and pushing. Is there anything going on at home?" Uggh. My heart drops. I get a sinking feeling in the pit of my stomach. I thought Jonah was doing great. That's what the other notes have said, so what's happened? I email my husband the report from school. "Why do you think he's acting out?" my husband writes back to me. Of course, *I'm the mom* and I *should* intuitively know these things, but frankly I'm not really sure what's going on. As I start worrying about my son, horrified that I have to call and apologize to the mother of the classmate Jonah pushed into a bookshelf, I find myself thinking about ABC's show *Desperate Housewives* and the TV character Lynette. She's the former CEO who ditched her career to stay at home full time and raise four children. Even though her life's work is now dedicated to caring for her kids, her boys still eat paint and tackle children. I find this reassuring as I weirdly look for a little solace from a popular TV drama.

As I'm pondering my own new dose of guilt for the day and tinkering with my manuscript, my cell phone rings. It's my friend Brooke Horman, a senior vice president in private banking in New York City. She has called to say hi and to see how my book is coming. When I tell her I'm working on a chapter about guilt, she starts laughing and says, "Well, speaking of guilt, you're never going to believe the conversation I just had with my secretary. A few nights ago I was stuffing party favor bags for Lilly's birthday party at school and had some extra favors hanging out of my briefcase when I came to work yesterday," Brooke says. "My secretary noticed them, and I told her that tomorrow is Lilly's third birthday. So when I came into work today, my secretary asked incredulously, 'Why are you here? I thought you would be taking the day off to be with your daughter on her birthday.' I was so surprised that she assumed that. Truthfully, it would never occur to me to take off a day from work to go and have cupcakes at Lilly's school," Brooke says. "We're having a party for her next week. But when my secretary said that, it did make me pause for a moment, and it definitely made me feel a little guilty."

What is it about children's birthdays and behavior that seem to act as a measure of a mother's devotion to their kids? Many mothers, it seems, and perhaps particularly Stay-at-Work moms, feel that their child's birthday is their annual public review. Brooke didn't feel guilty about missing the school party, but after the conversation with her secretary, she wound up feeling rotten. A couple of years ago, my husband and I went to a 1-year-old's birthday party where the mother who worked full time announced to nearly everyone at the party that it took her nine hours to make the enormous Elmo birthday cake.

There are plenty of bakeries in her neighborhood, but she confided to me that she made the cake because it somehow made her feel less guilty about working full time. It was as if being up to her elbows in flour and frosting made her feel more maternal. Clearly she was proud of her gorgeous cake, but underneath the pride of baking did she feel she needed to show the other moms, a mostly at-home mother crowd, that she was just as good as they are? In the postmillennium era, it's amazing how we still cling to the old-fashioned nursery rhyme image that the baker/homemaker is the Good Mother.

Olympic Moms

Motherhood as competitive sport is a relatively new phenomenon. A half century ago, when most women were stationed at home with their kids, homemaking, not motherhood, was their personal measurement for success. A woman was measured by her apple pie or by the cleanliness of her kitchen. These days, when working outside of the home is considered a "choice," those who don't continue with their career but take on a career in motherhood often do so with the vigor and ferocity of a competitive athlete. These are the Olympic Moms, as designer Vera Wang likes to call them.

Vera Wang is having a typically busy day and apologizes for keeping me waiting. She has just gotten out of a meeting about the launch of her new fragrance and was taking calls from a celebrity bride-to-be who needed to schedule a final fitting with Vera personally. A slight wisp of a woman with waist length, pin straight, jet-black hair, Vera is perhaps best known as the world's most famous wedding dress designer. In recent years, the Vera Wang brand has expanded to include couture, fragrances, and china, among other things. Dressed today in a typical low-key black ensemble, Vera comes scurrying down the stairs and settles into a chair in the design area of her corporate office in Manhattan. Sketches and fabric swatches are littered about the table. Her custom couture designs hang unceremoniously on headless mannequins all around us.

"My life is like a reality TV show," she says with a laugh. "I think even my closest friends don't know what's going on in my life during the day. There's never a minute when there isn't something happening or a fire to be put out. The kinds of calls that come through our office and the kinds of clients that we have and the kinds of things we're asked to participate in is mind boggling."

Vera says that there is so much chaos and activity swirling around her growing business that her family motto is "We try to catch as catch can." Now 55, Vera came to motherhood later in life. She got married at 40 and tried unsuccessfully for several years to get pregnant through various infertility treatments. She even quit her job at Ralph Lauren to focus full time on getting pregnant. When she didn't conceive, she and her husband adopted two girls, Cecelia, now 14, and three years later, Josephine, 11. The adoption of her daughters coincided with the beginning of her bridal business. Balancing the birth of a business with the life transformation of having children was tough in the beginning. And as her business and brand exploded since its inception a little over a decade ago, Vera says her life is a constant whirlwind. From photo shoots, celebrity fittings, fashion shows, design sessions, business meetings, and even appearing as herself in a movie, Vera admits she never stops moving. That, she says, is what is sometimes hard to reconcile with the demands and desires of motherhood.

"You certainly can't compete with a mother who focuses on their kids 120 percent, and anyone who says you can is lying. My daughters' school is full of what I call 'Olympic Mothers' who bake the perfect cupcakes and pack the perfect lunches for the class picnic and call to tell me when I'm on security patrol. My sister-in-law is an Olympic Mother. She knows what her children's curricula are and what teacher they have for every subject and all of these other things that I don't know. I'm embarrassed to say that I don't know who the homeroom teacher for my daughter was this past year, but that doesn't mean I'm not involved, it doesn't mean that I don't check up on her homework every night. It doesn't mean that I'm not interested. But with all of the intense focus that I place on my business, I certainly can't compete with a mother who is only focused on their kids. That is their career, and I think probably nothing replaces that. My daughters will never know a mom who does that but, on the other hand, perhaps as a working mom, I'm lighting the way for them so they will feel confident to pursue their own dreams, whatever they may be."

As busy as Vera is in her career, like most working mothers, her children are always on her mind.

"I worry every day that I'm not there enough for them. Another working mother said to me that at least I'm fostering independence. And one thing my daughters really have is a certain confidence level and a sense of independence that I think is great. That comes partially because I'm not able to be there and be totally protective of them at all times. There are certainly good things about them having a working mother."

Even still, Vera admits that she wished she could have been around more when her girls were younger to get the ice cream cones after school, but she feels proud of her business and confident that she has made the right decisions for herself.

"I feel that I have a really complete life. I don't feel really cheated of anything. I'm not thinking like a career woman who has never had children, God, I missed out on raising a family. And there are mothers, particularly in my daughter's classes, who say, 'Listen, Vera, I gave up my law practice, and I sometimes envy you,' and I say, 'Don't envy me.' But they don't have that side of their life at all, and every once in awhile they feel a little forlorn about it and a little bit frustrated. And they have a law degree from Yale Law, and now they are baking cupcakes and worrying about security patrol. It's an imperfect science. It's not easy. Whatever way you choose to go in your life, it's going to affect your children somehow.

"I think to be a really good parent you have to be fairly happy with yourself, and I honestly believe that in my case it was about my career and about wanting to make a contribution in life and to leave something behind in my work and that's what meant something to me. So I hope in some way that influences my daughters for whatever they want, even if they want to be an Olympic Mom; then I want them to feel totally free to pursue that."

For Vera Wang, as for many of the other women I have interviewed, having a career and making a difference in the world—whether it is through medicine, business, journalism, or fashion—is what drives them to continue in their careers after becoming mothers.

The Myth of Our Own Mothers

On every birthday since I can remember, my mother has recited the story of my birth. When I left for college, my mom even started an annual ritual of setting her alarm at 7:40 A.M., precisely the time I was born, to call me, her voice often still thick with sleep, to recount the day I entered the world. As the story goes, my mom got to the hospital just in the knick of time to deliver me. As they rushed her down the corridors to the operating room (the days before labor and delivery rooms), she called out to my dad and announced, "I've changed my mind, I don't want to have a baby!" But after she delivered me in the pioneering style of natural childbirth, she changed her mind. One look at me, and my mother says she was smitten. She swears I was the most beautiful baby in the world, or at least the prettiest baby in Miami's Baptist Hospital nursery.

But soon after arriving, I stopped breathing. Apparently my trachea was underdeveloped and crying caused it to clamp tight, restricting my airway. My mom was told she could take me home but had to make sure

I didn't cry or I could suffocate to death. The dramatic tale of my birth is always punctuated at the end by my 22-year-old mother leaving the hospital in her Hot Pants (it was 1971), apparently her waistline contracted to its pre-pregnancy size in a matter of days. And once she was home, as she's told me at least a million times, her life's work became making sure that I didn't cry. So she held me and rocked me and didn't leave my side for more than nine months until I healed.

The utter devotion of my mom toward me and her mother-daughter love story is hard stuff with which to compete. So it is no wonder that thirty years later after I had a somewhat less enthusiastic reaction to the birth of my son, I felt that something was wrong with me. I felt guilty for not thinking Jonah was the most magnificent baby of all time. I felt guilty for not feeling a passion for motherhood. I just felt guilty that I wasn't as good as my own mother. Yes, we can compete with our peers, but competing with the image and ideal of our own mother can be even more daunting. Especially when we believe that our moms did a really good job.

Rabbi Angela Buchdahl, 30, often feels as if she's not as together as her mother—a Korean immigrant who really seemed like she could do it all. Angela's mother taught English as a second language, was president of the Korean woman's association, and founded a Korean library and a Korean school in the Seattle, Washington, area where Angela grew up.

"I always thought she was a great mom," says Angela, a bubbly woman with bobbed dark hair and freckles peppering her pretty face. "I was in awe of her. She seemed so well respected in the community and did so many great things and somehow she always managed to be home at 5:30 P.M. and put together this massive Korean meal of five or six courses. I ask her now, 'How did you do it?' And she says, 'I don't really know, I threw it together.'"

When we talk, Angela is nine months pregnant with her second son and has recently made an angst-ridden decision to cut back her hours as a rabbi and cantor at a large synagogue in Scarsdale, New York. Whereas some women may have been relieved to slow down, Angela says she felt anxious about going part-time.

"It was emotional, and I felt somehow guilty like I was disappointing my senior rabbi that I didn't want to work that much. But in some ways, the hardest person to tell was my mother because I felt like she showed me that you could be a working mom and be really successful and still be a great mom who is around a lot. And I felt like somehow I was failing because I wasn't able to do it all. Or somehow admitting that this was just too much for me at this time. My mom was actually really happy about my cutting back my hours and supported it. But I remember I was sort of scared to tell her."

Of course, regardless of whether our mothers worked while we were growing up, a mother's influence sweeps into almost every corner of her daughter's life, from career and family to a sense of self-worth and identity.

"My mother never worked," Ellie Turner, a public relations executive and mother of two young children, says. "I totally get the pressure from my mother to not work because she thinks I should be home with my kids. That's really hard because I'm stressed at work, and every day she calls me when I'm commuting on the train, and she asks, 'Are you on the train yet? When are you getting home?'"

Working Hard to Have Baby

It's a sunny, summer morning when I meet Suzanne, 38, in her neighborhood Starbucks for a snack with her 2½-year-old son. They had just finished their Friday morning gym class and have come for a treat as they do every week after class. A leggy blonde known for her infectious smile and upbeat personality, Suzanne looks drained. She's had a tough week at work and has gotten home late every night, after her son, Joshua, was asleep. She leaves for work before he wakes up, so she literally hasn't seen Joshua in four days. As an advertising executive whose job is to help attract business, Suzanne seems to have a dream job. Her evening work consists of entertaining clients at spas, Broadway shows, and concerts. She makes a comfortable six-figure salary, works four days a week, and enjoys her career, which is why she always feels terribly conflicted about complaining.

"It's just been a really hard week," Suzanne says. "Joshua was really acting out last night when I got home. I know he really missed me and that was hard. This morning, he woke up and said, 'Mommy I'm so happy to see you, you look so pretty,' and I just wanted to cry," Suzanne says, her own eyes filling with tears. "I get very emotional about this. Maybe it's because I worked so hard to have Joshua that I feel so guilty and torn."

To say Suzanne had a hard time having a baby would be an enormous understatement. Five years ago, after several attempts of artificial insemination, Suzanne became pregnant. But halfway through her pregnancy she developed a rare and dangerous autoimmune disease that threatened the life of the fetus. Her disease went into remission about a month after it began, but at thirty-eight weeks pregnant, Suzanne sensed that something was terribly wrong. She went to her doctor who reassured her that the baby was fine. But she wasn't convinced. The next day, after not feeling her baby move for several hours, she rushed to the hospital. The baby's heart had stopped beating. Two weeks shy of her due date, doctors induced labor and Suzanne delivered a stillborn baby girl. The pain of losing a full-term baby is unimaginable. For three months Suzanne could hardly function. But two years and several rounds of infertility treatment later, Suzanne was pregnant again and gave birth to Joshua.

"Josh really was a gift. For the first year of his life I was a total lunatic constantly worrying that something terrible was going to happen to him. I wanted to spend every day just protecting him. I actually felt terribly guilty about leaving him to go to work. I still feel guilty from time to time, but the intensity of the guilt has mellowed somewhat as he's gotten a bit older."

Like many of us, Suzanne's feelings about working and motherhood teeter almost weekly. She thrives on the applause she gets from work and the practical satisfaction of her paycheck, but the stress and responsibility can be overwhelming; she has the financial pressure to make a significant portion of her household income. Suzanne and her husband, Robert, a lawyer, moved to a Connecticut suburb a year ago after living in New York City for fifteen years. An intensely positive person, Suzanne has adjusted to her daily roundtrip two-and-a-half-hour commute. But for Suzanne it's the cumulative effect of consecutive long days and nights at work when she feels off balance. Now she is preparing to begin another round of fertility treatment in the hopes of getting pregnant again. A few days later I check in with her at work. She's having a good day and is feeling better than the last time I saw her.

"It's a rollercoaster; some days I feel great, other times if I'm not doing a good job at work or Joshua's not doing well at home, it doesn't feel worth it. It's a constant battle. But I really don't have a choice."

It wasn't supposed to be this way. Our generation of girls was told we could do everything and be anything. Choices meant which major you were picking, what graduate program you would enter, what birth control you would use. Choice was about liberation, not limitation. And yet, in our 30s, often the time when career and motherhood intersect, many women find themselves stuck, confused, and sometimes feeling guilty.

The Verdict: Guilty or Not Guilty

"Pleeease don't go to work Mommy," pleads my tearful son Jonah as he lunges for my legs, wrapping himself around my calves and clinging to me like a koala bear, as I head out the door to go to CNN where I'm freelance producing on the *American Morning* news show. "Mommy will be back soon," I tell Jonah in a sing-song voice dripping with sunshine, trying to mask the awful truth that I, in fact, will not be back soon, and that I won't even see Jonah until he wakes up the next morning. My then seven-month-old daughter, Alexandra, already seems to suspect this. She watches me as I reach for the door, and her face erupts into tears. Alexandra has only recently begun to realize that I leave her every day for terribly long stretches, and her new awareness has made both of us miserable. I know that a couple of minutes after walking out my door, my kids will be fine, but nonetheless the daily ritual of tears breaks my heart. I realize I have to work, but still I feel gripped with guilt for leaving.

Maternity wear designer Liz Lange also says she feels torn when it comes to leaving her children to go to work. Liz works about a dozen blocks away from her children's preschool in New York City and around the corner from her apartment so she is able to do some of the drop-offs and pickups from school.

"I picked up my son from school today, and then when I dropped him off at home with our nanny, he said, 'Mommy, stay one hundred minutes, don't just stay five minutes.' I feel terrible about that," Liz says. "There are moms out there who are staying one hundred minutes and that's hard. I tell myself that my children have never known it any other way, so this is just what they expect, and they know that their mom is very happy."

Nevertheless, Liz can't help but feel that she's constantly calculating how much time she's spending with her children. It's a daily give and take that's always hard to balance.

"This morning my nanny dropped my son off at school, and I picked him up. I try to keep a tally in my head: I didn't do drop off this morning, so I'll do pickup. I'm constantly weighing it," Liz says.

"I am lucky because I work for myself, so there is flexibility. But because of my business, which is growing so rapidly, I'm definitely a mom who has this major other thing going on that's always kind of present. I feel guilty about that on the one hand; on the other hand, I could never have it any other way."

During interviews for this book, when I approached the subject of guilt, I assumed all moms must feel guilty for working because isn't that the inevitable side effect created from the mixed messages we've been hearing—that we should go to graduate school, gun for partner, and then "stop out" of the workforce because that's what "Good Moms" do? But when I asked more than 100 Stay-at-Work moms if they felt guilty, I was completely surprised to find that most moms didn't have guilt about working. They said they didn't feel guilty because working was an economic necessity, not a luxury. They also didn't feel guilty because most had working mothers, and most felt good about their own relationships with their moms. So they believed that because they turned out okay, so would their own children. They also didn't feel guilty because they felt that having a career made them better mothers and spouses. Many women wished that they could spend more time with their kids, but most weren't wracked with guilt. In fact, instead of feeling guilt-ridden, the women felt empowered about contributing to their household income; they felt proud of their careers, fulfilled as women, and believed that by working, they in turn were acting as important role models for their own children, particularly their daughters. In fact, most women felt so confident in their dual lives that several women said to me, "I feel guilty for not feeling guilty."

Actress Cynthia Nixon, who was raised by a working mother, told me: "I feel like we've been fed a lot of stuff about a mother's supreme selfless sacrifice and how this is the supreme good. And I think there are certain sacrifices you would be wise to make for your children whether you are a man or a woman, but I feel you have to consider what's best for your family and you're part of your family. I think you need to relieve yourself of the guilt, relieve yourself of worrying that you shouldn't ever be leaving your child with someone else. Your kid is going to be fine; you don't have to endlessly anticipate what that child needs. If that child is not getting enough of you, you will be informed. Don't take your child and make an idol out of them, don't put them on a pedestal. They are a person with needs, you're a person with needs, and your husband is a person with needs."

Other women said to me that we have to learn to let go of the guilt for not being there all of the time and make the most of it when we are able to be home.

"There is so much emphasis for being there for all of the 'firsts,' says science writer and mother of two Ingrid Wickelgren. "I think it's important not to get caught up in that. So what if the baby takes a step and I'm not there right at that moment. When I see it, it will be the first time for me, and I think that's just as exciting."

Loretta Hawthorne, 29, a brand marketing manager and mother of a 1-year-old, says, "I wish I could spend more time with Billy, but I don't feel guilt because I feel like he's thriving."

This was the common theme shared by dozens of women. They work, but there is no guilt. Interestingly, the moms I met told me that they only felt guilty when they were taking time for themselves. Lack of personal time is one of the biggest issues working moms face. In fact, a survey conducted by Executive Moms, a working mom's network in New York City, found that 66 percent of 160 respondents cited their desire for more personal time as a bigger issue than the lack of good childcare or the wish for a more accommodating spouse.[5]

CNN anchor Soledad O'Brien showed me her unmanicured fingers and toes as evidence that she doesn't take the time to get them polished. Soledad says that her nails often look ratty because she would never spend an hour getting a manicure when she could be spending that time with her children. Cynthia Nixon says she doesn't feel guilty about leaving her kids for work, she only feels guilty if a babysitter is watching her kids and she's *not* working. Nicole Swanson, 33, a Mary Kay cosmetics manager and mother of two, put it this way: "I really feel the guilt when I'm out or I decide to take some time for myself on a Friday or Saturday afternoon. And after I've been gone for a while, that little voice in the back of my head says, you need to get home, you need to get home. And maybe I've only been gone for forty-five minutes, but I start to feel so guilty, thinking, oh my gosh, I shouldn't be out here doing this, I should be home with my children. That's usually when I feel the most guilty."

Lose the Guilt, Stay Connected

As Stay-at-Work moms we clearly can't be with our kids all of the time. So what are the rituals and things we can do to stay connected to our children and to their lives? In every interview I've done I've asked moms what they did to alleviate their own guilt (assuming at first they had some guilt) and what they did to stay involved. The rituals moms told me about ranged from the religious and spiritual to the mundane.

"Even though our hours are helter-skelter, we're very present parents," designer Vera Wang says. "I think we're involved in what they do. We care about what they do. I usually can be seen with the other moms on Saturday and Sunday mornings at the Chelsea Piers skating rink in New York City watching my kids skate. It's the little things that I try to do as consistently as I can, given that my schedule is constantly in flux," Vera says.

"When my older daughter was at the George Balanchine School of Ballet, I used to always make sure I picked her up at least once a week. We also always try to have our kids with us at the dining table even if they have eaten at 5:00 P.M. and we're eating at 8:00 P.M. We like them to be with us. Very often our idea of dinner parties are having our friends over for dinner with their kids. Even if it's an adult party, the kids can run off and do their own thing. Those are our happiest moments," Vera says. "And one of the best things for me is jumping into bed with my two daughters beside me and watching *American Idol* or *Murder, She Wrote* or *Colombo* where we can all be involved together. That physical proximity is wonderful too. There are many ways even though I'm not around a whole lot they feel my presence."

Reflecting back, Vera doesn't apologize for working but says that she does feel guilty that she couldn't give her girls more time when they were younger.

Soledad O'Brien says being raised in a fairly strict and religious household where her dad made a big breakfast every Sunday after the whole family went to church has influenced the way she wants to raise her children. Recently, Soledad and her husband have started a weekly ritual of taking their daughters to a nondenominational church across the street from their weekend house in upstate New York.

"It's really nice," Soledad says. "The girls go to Sunday school; for Cecilia it's really a play group, and she loves it, it's a great ritual."

Cynthia Nixon says that picking up her 6-year-old daughter, Samantha, from public school is an important part of her day.

"My mother almost never picked me up at school because she was at work. But I remember a few times when she did, and I remember how amazing that was. So I try to pick up Samantha as often as I can even if I'm doing something later that afternoon, and I have to hand her over to somebody else after an hour. I feel that somehow that moment of me being there really seems to matter to her," Cynthia says.

TV producer Soraya Gage tries to keep up with certain routines for her children as much as she can. But because her job as a news producer is so demanding and unpredictable, she finds herself sometimes playing catch-up.

"I don't work on Fridays. I have a four-day week, and my kids are very conscious of my Fridays because that's when I pick them up at the bus and that's when we do things in the afternoons and when they can have friends over. A lot of times this year I've had to work on Fridays, and that's been very hard because they like routine and predictability, and it throws them off," Soraya says.

"Last year it was a really hard work year for me. I missed a lot, and I felt really bad about that. I missed the end of school picnic for Davie, and my babysitter went with him, and it was all moms in the park. But then I tried to make it up by taking the day off and reading to Davie's class. I always want to be class mother but I feel like I can't commit myself because at the last minute something's going to happen at work. But I think it's really important for your kids to see you involved in their class work, so I try to do what I can."

Doing the Best That You Can

I have found that women are particularly proactive in how they negotiate the challenge of feeling present and involved in their children's lives. Soraya Gage started a book club with women she met while on maternity leave when her oldest son was born just so she could stay connected to other mothers in her community. "We talk about the book for a half an hour and then we spend two hours talking about our kids. It's great to get that feedback."

Another former colleague of mine who is the mother of a 4-year-old took a TV producing job where her day starts at 5:00 A.M. and is over at 2:00 P.M.—this schedule allows her to pick up her daughter from school and also be class mom. And still another woman I met lobbied her school board to change the PTA meetings to evenings rather than mid-mornings so Stay-at-Work moms could more easily participate.

"I think it's all about trying to give up the guilt," Liz Lange says. "We put so much pressure on ourselves as women. And if you want to be working, then you should work and not feel that you're doing something wrong."

Chapter 5

Something's Got to Give

How to Switch Gears and Careers

On a family farm tucked in the shadows of the meandering hills of the Berkshires in the westernmost corner of Massachusetts, Jane Swift wakes up before the sun and forces herself to do an hour of step aerobics in front of the TV. By 6:00 A.M., her twin baby girls and 3-year-old daughter wake up. After a breakfast of formula and cereal, the girls are dressed and ready for daycare. Three-year-old Elizabeth gets to wear her special green dress, a reward for successfully going on the potty.

Dad is now up, and it's time for mom to jump in the shower, throw on a suit and a strand of pearls and race off to a business meeting. So begins another morning for another working mother in Massachusetts. Except that this mommy to three girls under 3 is arguably the most powerful person in Massachusetts—Governor Jane Swift. By day's end, Governor Swift has zigzagged across the state, holding meetings and press conferences and reluctantly attending a fundraiser. And after a busy day running the Commonwealth, Swift does something none of her predecessors would have imagined—she hustles off to her monthly support group for working moms.

"It's the one personal thing I try to put in my schedule," she says.

Jane Swift's combination of extraordinary fate and fertility has made her one of the most well known politicians in the country. At 36, Swift became the first female governor of the Commonwealth and the youngest governor in the United States.

But what catapulted her from gubernatorial obscurity to international headlines was when Swift became the first governor to give birth while in office to not just one baby, but to twin girls in May 2001.

When I first met Jane Swift in 2002 in her airy, corner office of the State House in Boston, I was struck by how young, pretty, and surprisingly perky she seemed. With friendly, inquisitive green eyes and freckles sprinkled across the bridge of her nose, she seemed like a high school cheerleader all grown up. It was hard to imagine that this attractive, 30-something woman had the burdens of the Commonwealth of Massachusetts leaning on her shoulders.

For Swift, one of four kids from a close Italian/Irish Catholic family, having children was always a priority.

"The bigger surprise is that I'm governor," she says with a laugh.

In many ways, Jane Swift *was* the accidental governor. And her multiple pregnancies played out in the public eye were at once her assets and her liabilities. Swift grew up in the gritty, working class town of North Adams, Massachusetts. At 25, she became the youngest woman elected to the Massachusetts State House. In 1998, Massachusetts Governor Paul Cellucci asked Swift to run with him on the Republican ticket for Lt. Governor. Two weeks after Swift announced her candidacy for Lt. Governor, she discovered that she was pregnant. At the time, Swift says, she had no idea how hard it would be to handle a campaign and a pregnancy simultaneously.

"Only someone who was never pregnant could be as unconcerned about combining a campaign and pregnancy as I was," Swift says. "Ignorance was bliss until I started being sick everywhere."

Swift's baby was due a couple weeks before election day, and her pregnancy became the hot topic spawning endless commentary and controversy.

"My first reaction was, thank God she's not having an abortion," said Evelyn Reilly, executive director of the Christian Coalition of Massachusetts, "and my second reaction is, I hope she'll have enough time to spend with that child."[1]

Radio show callers wanted to know how Swift could serve the public and nourish a newborn. One caller even asked how she was planning to breast-feed.

"There's a thing called a pump," Swift answered sweetly.

The Cellucci/Swift ticket won, but the reality of a newborn and a new job was more difficult than Swift anticipated.

"The hardest adjustment was having our first child. I know that there is a general sense and I think it's true for lots of women, that subsequent children are what's sort of the straw that breaks the camel's back. That was actually not true for me. Things were so muddled and so difficult publicly and privately figuring out how to combine my new job as a statewide elected official with a new family," Swift says.

Swift and her husband, Chuck Hunt, a dairy farmer, lived on his family farm three hours away from Boston in the Berkshires. Commuting for Swift meant traversing the entire Massachusetts turnpike, each way, twice a day. Swift says many people were horrified that she would consider working three hours away from where her newborn daughter lived. So she packed up her family and rented a one-bedroom apartment in Boston to be closer to her office. But Swift's husband, the primary caretaker of their daughter, and an outdoorsy kind of guy, was miserable. Swift worked long hours, and Hunt had no childcare relief.

He sometimes brought their daughter, Elizabeth, to Swift's office so he could get a break and take a run. But if Swift was being yanked into meetings and couldn't watch her daughter, she would occasionally ask staffers if they could help babysit. This landed her in major hot water with the State Ethics Commission, who fined Swift for inappropriately using her staff. The babysitting brouhaha was then followed by another scandal when Swift used a state helicopter to chopper home after Hunt left an urgent message saying their daughter was sick and her fever had spiked to 104 degrees. The media was merciless in lambasting Swift, and her core base, the female voters, were also getting fed up with their sister in the State House who seemed to do things that smacked of executive privilege.

Then fate and fertility intervened again. When President George W. Bush named her boss Governor Cellucci ambassador to Canada, Swift got a promotion. On April 10, 2001, Swift, then eight months pregnant with twins, was sworn in as governor of Massachusetts. But as if to combat her critics who publicly wondered if she was up to the job, Swift worked extra hard to prove that the bulge in her belly wouldn't slow her down. Looking back now, she thinks that was probably a mistake.

"It wasn't always easy being eight months pregnant with twins and projecting an image of not missing a beat and not doing less than anybody else; that's not reality," Swift says. "There were many, many, many days when I was absolutely exhausted. In public life, in particular political life, you need to project a degree of certainty about everything that you are doing and that not only at times was difficult, but perhaps a disservice to the issue [of women]."

But eventually her body gave in. A few weeks after being sworn in as acting governor, Swift was hospitalized with premature labor contractions and was forced to run the government from the maternity ward, signing legislation and running meetings by teleconference. Some Democrats were not pleased. They wanted to go to the State Supreme Court to challenge Swift's right to govern. But the public rallied behind their very pregnant governor, fueling support for her to retain full control of the governor's office. While other expectant moms at Boston's Brigham and Women's hospital read magazines to pass the time, Swift ran the commonwealth, literally until minutes before she delivered.

It was while on a conference call with Vice President Dick Cheney that Swift's contractions began. As the pain increased, she quietly hung up the phone. She was prepped for a C-section and an hour later gave birth to twin girls, Lauren and Sarah Hunt.

Almost a year later, facing a formidable Democratic opponent, dismal poll numbers, and a cloud of controversy she couldn't shake, but hoping to preserve a potential political future, Swift announced to the surprise of her staff and supporters that she would not run for reelection.

At an emotional press conference, her eyes brimming with tears, Swift said, "Something had to give. I am sure there isn't a working parent in

America that hasn't faced it, that when the demands of the two tasks you take on both increase substantially, something has to give."

Swift's decision not to run for reelection generated almost as much publicity as her pregnancies. She was at once a role model and a cautionary tale. The media quickly turned her into a case study for all working women—did her dropping out mean that women couldn't have it all? NBC's *Today* co-anchor Katie Couric asked Swift the day after she withdrew from the race.

When I first met Swift, six weeks after she announced her withdrawal from the gubernatorial race, she was still exploring the answer to that question and considering her options and her future after politics. After all of the media whippings she had received, I wondered how Swift was doing and where she wound up. Knowing that she was the primary breadwinner and a politician without a trust fund, I was pretty sure that Swift wouldn't be retiring to her Berkshires farm anytime soon, and I was right.

I easily located Swift at a Boston-based venture capital firm. Two years after our first interview, the blue, stodgy skirt suit and regulation bob are gone. Today, she's sporting a stylish, choppy haircut, a little bit lighter than the last time we met, as is her entire demeanor. She comes bounding down the hall to greet me with a smile and a strong handshake.

"My office is not as regal as the last time I saw you," Swift says with a laugh and apologizes that she needs to eat her lunch as we talk. It's true— her office is anything but glam. The setup is of the nondescript, office park variety. The walls are stark white and aside from a few political photos that lean haphazardly against the floorboard, there is no sign that Swift once inhabited a much swankier office and title. In fact, the only pictures on display are those of her small children, which she is excited to show me. But Swift is not the least bit unhappy about leaving public office. She says it wasn't until after she had left the spotlight that she realized just how uncomfortable it made her. She struggles to articulate how odd it is to be a relatively famous and public person.

"It's just really weird to have an interaction with normal people that's abnormal. I would go to a soccer game, and there were all of these moms there who thought they knew everything about me, what I had done that day, potentially what I had done *wrong* that day, how my marriage was, or whether I was pregnant. So you try to have a normal interaction, and people feel strange. There was always this barrier for them to get past and realize that you are a normal person."

Swift is now a partner at Arcadia Capital, a firm that invests in for-profit education and training industries. As the sole breadwinner of her family, Swift spent a long time figuring out what path would give her family the best financial prospects and what also would integrate well into her family life. A year into her new job, she is thrilled with how everything is working out. She is still working long hours and traveling about half of the week, but compared to her last job, she has much more flexibility and control over her schedule.

"Elizabeth played soccer this year, and over the ten-week soccer program there were actually two Tuesday nights when I was at the field at 5 o'clock," Swift says proudly. "I was never able to be home at 5 o'clock on a Tuesday when I was governor, maybe once a year or when I was on vacation. So my husband and I will tell you that my new schedule is great."

Swift's family still lives in the Berkshires, and her husband is an at-home dad. But one of the hardest things for Swift is that she is living in a community that runs at a slower pace than her own frenetic life. This, she says, is what's both seductive about her hometown and difficult about the lifestyle.

"I love where we live. It's good for my soul, it's good for my kids to live near my parents, and that helps me to manage. But not having my kids have peer groups where other parents, particularly mothers, are having a work schedule similar to mine creates hurdles at times," Swift says.

"Elizabeth played in an introductory Little League this year called Buddy Ball, and I had written on my schedule when the final game was scheduled. It was a big deal. They were going to play it on the Little League field and announce the kids' names over the loudspeaker. My daughter had asked me days before if I was going to go to Buddy Ball, and I said I wouldn't have missed it for the world. But at the last minute the coach changed the day of the game. And then I had to tell my 5½-year-old I couldn't be there. That sort of last minute pivot of plans probably didn't impact any of the other parents. But if you're three hours away or three plane rides away with a meeting that just can't change, you're just done.

If I lived in a community where I was part of the majority, it would have been over time ingrained into the program director that when you decide on the big event, you schedule it weeks out, and you don't change it because you'll have a revolt if half the parents had to have a conversation with their 5½-year-olds that I had to have with mine. My husband went to the game, my parents went, our daycare provider went, they ate tons of hot dogs, and Elizabeth was fine. But it was not a comfortable moment for me."

The day I meet with former Governor Swift the announcement that presidential candidate Senator John Kerry has picked Senator John Edwards to run on the ticket as vice president is front-page news. A picture of the boyish Edwards emerging from his Georgetown brownstone with his two tow-headed young children is what catches Swift's eye. It's impossible to ignore the parallels between Swift and Edwards, both at one point young, ambitious politicians with small children. But the double standard in our society that a dad with young children running for high office is more palatable than a mom running for the same position is not lost on Swift. I can't help but ask her what she thinks.

"I would be willing to bet that with all of the ink about John Edwards joining the ticket, not only is there nothing in the paper today, but we'll see nothing in the paper over the next several days that will question his ability to be a good parent. Guess what, my kids are just as cute, and guess what, if I used my kids as props, it would have a completely different impact on the psyche of the electorate. So we didn't do it. If his wife, Elizabeth Edwards, was on the ticket and people saw that picture, they would have a viscerally different reaction to it. It would have been oh, my gosh, you've got these two young kids, how in the world could she ever be vice president. Whereas with him it's, oh, how cute."

But Swift isn't bitter that she was judged differently. In fact she sees herself as a positive person and argues that perhaps it's a good thing that our society places so much value on motherhood. However, she thinks it's unfair that women find themselves struggling with their dual identities, having to prove that the two aren't mutually exclusive.

"I think there are still situations where if you're in a high-level profession or position, that talking a lot about how much you love being a mother can be used against you to undermine your seriousness and credibility. Therefore, lots of really accomplished women rightly choose not to publicly talk about the wonderful aspects of motherhood. Similarly, I think that I'm probably equally guilty when I'm with the mothers of my daughter's friends who don't work or don't work with the same intensity I do, I sort of downplay my work for fear that in their eyes they may assume that I'm not fully committed to being a good mother. There still are lots of stereotypes that sort of prohibit us from being candid about the dual nature of the roles that we're in and the lives that we live."

As Peggy Orenstein writes in her book *Flux: Women on Sex, Love, Kids & Life in a Half-Changed World*: "If working mothers feel compelled by the culture to prove their devotion to their children, they feel equally pressured at the workplace to do just the opposite. When a woman becomes pregnant, the onus is on her to prove that motherhood changes nothing—that it won't compromise her productivity or split her loyalty, although for both men and women, it both does and should."[2]

For all of the You-Go-Girlism that defines our generation, the reality is that ideology and biology often come head to head. On the one hand, we want to believe that having babies won't slow us down and it shouldn't make a difference because if guys can do it, well, then, girls can do it better. But as Jane Swift and any pregnant woman who has retched on her way to a business meeting knows, it *is* different for women. Moms, for better or worse, are held to a different standard than dads. Society expects more of us, and we have come to expect more of ourselves. The question is no longer how women will achieve equal status in the workplace, but rather how women will balance both of their identities—of career woman and mom. That is the ongoing conversation of the postfeminist Gen X/Y generations. The fact that Jane Swift was excited to say she made it to two out of the ten soccer games her daughter played in this year would probably make many at-home moms cringe. But if a dad could only get to a couple of his child's weekday 5:00 P.M. games, no one would fault him, and in fact they would think he was a great dad for being there at all.

"We really should be talking more about work/life integration rather than balance," Swift says. "Because balance implies that if you're doing a really good job at work, you're not doing a good job as a mom or that the ability to do both is nearly impossible, and you'll always be tilting one way or another. The challenge is, how do you do work that you love and is meaningful and integrate it into having a life that is full and rich? And for me that means not only having children but also being an active part of their lives. A great degree of my happiness right now is that my work situation allows for that integration. Now that doesn't mean that my profession allows for that every day. It doesn't mean if I'm with investors I'm gushing to them about going to soccer games. But tomorrow morning at 9:00 A.M., I have a meeting at the cooperative nursery school where my girls go to school. I have it on my schedule, and we all have access to each other's schedules. But I don't code that nursery school meeting. I don't call it something it's not. My partners know that I'm the treasurer of the twins' preschool next year. There's not an underlying assumption that we can't be good parents to our kids and high-quality investors."

From Madison Avenue to Sesame Street

No matter how hard we sweat it out, sometimes our supercharged careers just clash with our family lives. This is one of the secrets of motherhood that no one bothers to tell young, ambitious women. The overwhelming majority of moms I've interviewed say that they did not choose a career based on whether it would ultimately be compatible with having a family. It simply was never a factor until they were married or on the cusp of having children.

But 32-year-old New Yorker Amy Gould *was* thinking about how she would balance her family and career before she even graduated from college. While a senior at Cornell University, Amy says she networked with alumni and questioned them not only about their careers but also about their work-family situations. After doing her own research, Amy felt like she had it all figured out. First she would be wildly successful in business, making a bundle of money, and later, by her mid- to late-30s, she assumed she would get married, start a family, and then maybe even become a teacher.

She was on track. In college, Amy was recruited by one of the most prestigious advertising firms in the country. But the business world, as Amy experienced it, unfolded like the clichéd plot of a bad chic-lit novel.

"It was a really rude awakening. I worked for two of the most powerful women in advertising who were arch enemies. One was a queen bitch who had a manicurist come to her office to do her nails, and you would have to do meetings at her hair salon standing over her showing her stuff because she was not going to reorganize her schedule. This woman had a gorgeous husband who lived in England but she never saw him. And the other woman had a family with lots of kids but she stabbed backs when she needed to."

Amy worked hard and quickly moved up the ranks, and at 25 years old, she became a partner at a global advertising agency. By her late 20s she was making close to half a million dollars, jetting to Europe on a moment's notice and living out of a suitcase three days a week. She says she thrived from the jolt of her job, the applause that came with landing multimillion-dollar accounts, and the financial rewards of bringing in big business. Despite her manic schedule, Amy found time to date and got married about a decade earlier than her life plan estimated. By 30, Amy was pregnant with twins, and an extremely sick pregnancy forced her to start reevaluating the direction of her life.

"I was throwing up thirty times a day and went into labor at twenty weeks," Amy says. "The whole time I was really afraid that I was going to lose the babies, or I was going to hurt them from all of the drugs that I was using to stop the contractions. When that all started, I knew that I wouldn't go back to work until after the pregnancy."

Amy initially planned on returning to work three months after her babies were born, but as she hibernated at home laid up for months on bed rest before their arrival, a primal maternal instinct started to emerge, and she realized there was no way she would return to a job that had her on the road half the week.

"I didn't want to do that with my babies at home. I didn't miss the work. I missed the lifestyle, staying at five-star hotels, flying around and feeling important, going to fun restaurants, running big meetings, and shocking the hell out of 60-something-year-old CEOs by having a woman from New York come in and run a meeting. That was exciting."

But the idea of teaching school—which had been on her short list of family-friendly careers since college—still lingered in the back of her mind. So when she decided that she couldn't continue with the ad exec lifestyle, she started to investigate her teaching options and hooked up with an organization she found on the Internet that sent her into elementary schools to work with talented and gifted children. As of this writing, she is now in school getting her master's degree in teaching.

But not everyone in Amy's family believed she was making a smart decision by becoming a teacher.

"My grandmother begged me not to go into education. She was so hard-line about wanting me to be in business. She wanted to know every detail of every promotion I got," Amy says. "She would say, 'Why are you going into teaching? We had to do that, and now you have a choice.' It's so funny because you want what you can't have. With teaching, the hours are fabulous, you're doing something really valuable, and the kids are amazing. It's 5000 times better than working with a bunch of back-stabbing, nasty people who all want to be smarter than the next guy."

Even though Amy is once again doing something she relishes, the enormous loss in income has had both practical and psychological effects. She sometimes feels guilty and torn about giving up her lucrative advertising career.

"Our lifestyle has had to change dramatically because of my decision not to be in business anymore. We're leading a much more modest, sedentary lifestyle," Amy says. "I hope I didn't strap the whole family because I wanted to indulge myself in something that I adore and I believe in. Sometimes I get pissed off when I think I did this to myself. I made this pay cut, and now we're paying the price. But then I'll meet people who are really inspirational who have dedicated their lives to teaching, and they are so happy doing their thing, and I think, I don't care about the other stuff. But I definitely feel stuck between the two, there's no question."

By leaving the prestige and lifestyle of a Madison Avenue ad executive behind, Amy has also realized the strong grip that money and identity have on her self-esteem.

"I realize now that I used to use my job to define myself and to give me the kind of reaffirmation and acknowledgment that I needed because I didn't feel confident on my own. I had to be an overachiever. Now it's very hard for me because no one is telling me you did a great job in that meeting, no one is telling me you brought in a $200-million account, go Amy! So I have to derive it from myself, but that's the way it should be."

Although she sometimes misses her former life in the competitive business world, Amy doesn't regret her career switch.

"The teaching is helping me because now that I have dedicated myself to a more altruistic profession, when I get these kids to write well beyond their ability, it's so exciting, and I come home riding so high. And I know that is enough."

Many women today reassess their careers around the time that they become mothers. They want to feel as if they're doing something meaningful or at least creative and intellectually stimulating. Susan Lapinsky, editor-in-chief of *Working Mother* magazine, explains that it wasn't always this way.

"The first generation of working moms, the Baby Boomers were so focused on making their mark in new career fields, they were so excited about being there that they were more likely to follow the company game plan. But the second wave, the Gen X and Gen Y women see their careers more like a hike in the woods, they take detours, and occasional stops. They are not going with the program, they are saying they want to write their own ticket and so they are doing creative things to stay connected."[3]

Cutting Back, Regaining Control

Since starting her family ten years ago, *Dateline NBC* producer Soraya Gage keeps recalibrating her life-work scale to keep her worlds in balance. I first met Soraya in 1997, when I was assigned to be her associate producer on a story for *Dateline*. At the time, having children was the furthest thing from my mind, and she was a mom to two boys under 3. We needed to fly to Dallas for a shoot, and what I vividly recall were the vast differences of our work experiences on that trip. I flew to Dallas the night before the interviews to sleep soundly and wake up with room service in a fancy hotel. Soraya woke up at the crack of dawn to take a 6:00 A.M. flight from New York to Dallas. After a grueling shooting schedule that ended at 10:00 P.M. that night, she raced to the airport and hopped on the last plane back to New York. She got home at 2:30 A.M. When I asked Soraya why she was rushing home only to arrive in the middle of the night, she simply responded, "My boys do better when I'm there in the morning."

We were producing the story with an affable NBC correspondent in his mid-30s who also had two young boys. But while Soraya caught the red-eye back home, the reporter and I stayed put and hung out at a local sports bar drinking beer and eating buffalo wings. My male colleague didn't feel compelled to kill himself to be home to have breakfast with his boys the next morning, but Soraya did. I remember wondering if the difference between moms and dads was simply that moms demanded more of themselves. What else would have explained her excruciating travel plans? Now as a mom myself, I realize it's much more complicated.

Soraya was promoted to a senior producer position while she was taking a six-month maternity leave with her second child. But the pressure and burden of additional work combined with a newborn and a toddler were just too much to handle. Back then I was 25 years old and new to *Dateline.* I distinctly remember hearing about her promotion and marveling over how evolved my new workplace was to promote a woman who had just had a baby. When I tell Soraya my reaction to her promotion at the time, she smiles at the irony of it all.

"I think they were more progressive than I was. I really do. I think they thought you could do anything, and I quickly realized that I couldn't. It wasn't a regular job, you had to work nights, you had to work weekends, and I just found that something had to give," Soraya tells me over lunch in Rockefeller Center where she works.

"My kids were really young, they were 1 and 3, and then 2 and 4, and I just felt like my family was falling apart. I was working all of the time, and even when I came home, I was totally preoccupied with work.

"That was also a really hard news year. It was the Clinton impeachment, the whole Monica Lewinsky thing, Columbine, a lot of big news events, and I was working on all of them. I remember I got paged at home, and it was a Sunday morning. I cried on the way into the office and just said to myself, 'I can't do this anymore,' and I was just trying to reevaluate why am I doing this? I love my job; if I didn't have a family, I could give this kind of time and this kind of energy. I'm giving it, but at a sacrifice, at a huge sacrifice, and I'm lost."

Always stoic and unemotional at work, Soraya met with her boss and almost burst into tears. She was on the verge of quitting when her boss suggested that she give up the senior producer job, cut back her schedule, and work four days a week.

"I felt an enormous relief right after that. I felt like now I can get my family back on track. Everything had been stressed, the relationship with my husband, my relationship with my babysitter, and my relationship with my children.

"I was trying to be such a great employee. That's what was really hard. I probably did best on the work front. I didn't fail, but I was not doing well on the others."

Soraya says that since relinquishing the management position, her family life has improved, but she feels that her career temporarily suffered.

"I didn't commit career suicide, but I feel like I was derailed," she says as she pierces a piece of lettuce with her fork. "But you can't look back; you have to make choices."

For ambitious women like Soraya, slowing down and easing one's workload can be an agonizing decision, one that can feel forced upon them rather than chosen. For people who have spent years reaching for the promotion and are now reaching for the Pampers, the shift in priorities can be particularly jarring.

As we're saying goodbye and she heads back upstairs to work, Soraya says, "As I've gotten older what I have learned is that it doesn't have to be a race, it can be a marathon."

Perhaps Soraya was meant to run marathons and not just sprint to the finish line. She has learned that it doesn't all need to come so quickly and simultaneously. Soraya gave up management, but she still gets many plum assignments and is greatly respected for her work. She also has a rich family life that she refuses to compromise for her career.

But ambition, that powerful force that in the best circumstances drives one to push ahead, can morph into a fiercely personal demon, tormenting and gnawing at us that we should be achieving more, even if to the outside world we seem to be doing just fine.

And God Created Woman

When one becomes a mother, a new set of priorities and childcare responsibilities often skews the professional roadmap that had once so neatly outlined the straight path to career "success."

Twenty-nine-year-old Rabbi Laurie Rice felt this conflict before she even officially began her career. After five years of rabbinical graduate school, she and her husband, Phillip, who is also a rabbi, were eager to start a family. Laurie and Phillip were both in the midst of the competitive interview process for rabbinical positions at synagogues when they learned she was pregnant. She struggled with what to do—go after a prestigious pulpit position or take a smaller, community-type of job. Laurie ultimately turned down a couple of big-synagogue job offers because they were not conducive to having a young family. Instead she accepted a part-time job at a very small congregation. Phillip, it was decided, would take the more demanding, but more lucrative, position at a large synagogue. Laurie says it's ironic that a rabbi's lifestyle is actually incompatible with parenthood.

"Being a rabbi is really time consuming, and the hours are awkward. It's weekends, it's evenings. This year alone I'm only working 50 percent, and I'm still giving up three nights a week. That's the paradox of the whole thing. Rabbis themselves preach one thing and often do another. And family is so central to Judaism, and yet the family is so often neglected in a rabbi's life."

When I speak to Laurie, she's bouncing around her Seattle home with her 14-week-old son, Shai, strapped into a Baby Bjorn, desperately trying to get him to nap. She says that having a baby and putting her career on a slow track has been hard on her ego. A few months earlier her husband had his "installation" ceremony at the synagogue where he works and Laurie admits she felt uncomfortably jealous.

"There was this whole to-do, and our parents came out, and I was feeling really sorry for myself. And that night at the congregation, a woman who was the daughter of one of the rabbis I interviewed with came up to me, and she said, 'Oh, gosh, you're Laurie Rice, you interviewed with my father, and he said you were one of the most outstanding people he had ever interviewed, and he's sorry you didn't take the job.' I started to cry. I felt so bad for myself. I thought, what have I done? There are definitely times when I feel, did I pass it up?"

A year later I check back with Laurie to see how she's doing. She's pregnant again and expecting another boy. Laurie's grown to love motherhood more than she imagined she would, and for the most part she's feeling satisfied with her work and more peaceful about her choices. She believes that she will be able to step things up in the future when her boys are a little older, and she's no longer feeling as if she's squandered her career by having a family before she was better established professionally.

"I just feel like my priorities have really changed right now. I don't want to say that I'm less ambitious; it's just that I'm wanting different things. My kids are really important, and I want to be able to tuck them in at night. If I were at a bigger congregation with more responsibility, that just wouldn't be possible," Laurie says.

In *The Price of Motherhood: Why the Most Important Job in the World Is Still the Least Valued*, Ann Crittenden writes: "With the arrival of a child, a mother's definition of accomplishment becomes more complex, her workload goes up and her income and independence go down. For all of the changes of the last decades, one thing has stayed the same: it is still women who adjust their lives to accommodate the needs of their children; who do what is necessary to make a home; who forgo status, income, advancement, and independence. Nowhere is this more dramatically illustrated than in the experience of the nation's most educated women—the ones who had the best shot of having it all."[4]

From my interviews with dozens and dozens of women, I have found that Ann Crittenden is right. Many moms have quit, altered, or intentionally slowed down their careers after having children. Many were looking to make adjustments in their work schedules to better accommodate their growing families. But whereas some women felt anxious about taking a step back, many more felt empowered to be able to control their careers and integrate it with their home lives. They also saw the slow down as a temporary state and believed that they could amp up again when and if they wanted to.

NBC's *Today* news anchor Ann Curry says that she feels having children temporarily stalled her career, but when her children got older and started school, she was able to take a deep breath and do an even better job at work. She says that since becoming a mother, she feels even more ambitious and driven than before she had kids.

"I think I would have done much more, much more quickly if I had not become a mother. But what's interesting is that since becoming a mother, I'm better. It's almost like having a delayed reaction and coming back with a much stronger focus and force.

"What got me through those early years of motherhood was that I started to look at my job completely differently. I said to myself, 'Not only do I want to do important work, but I don't want to waste my time while I'm at work. If I'm going to be away from my children, damn it, I'm going to make this time count.' So the focus was stronger, the requirement that I do important, good work was greater. My requirements of myself to rise up and be a better, more efficient, better skilled person was stronger. If I'm going to be away from my children, I wasn't going to waste my time, and that completely focused me so that I could, I think, be where I am today."

Just Saying No or Taking Things More Slow

It's a Tuesday evening in Millburn, New Jersey, and thirty women from a working mom's group are gathered into the comfortable living room of a charming, Tudor-style house. The women range in age from early 30s to late 40s; their children span the spectrum too—from seven weeks old to middle-school age. Some of the women with older kids are talking about sleep-away camp. This is the first year of camp for many of the children, and the moms are anxiously awaiting their first letters. Other women are commiserating over nanny problems and miserable commutes. Many of the topics that float throughout the room seem specific to the age of their children, and I wonder how much commonality exists between the mother of a newborn and the mother of a teenager. But as I begin to probe the women about the issues Stay-at-Work moms face, the conversation keeps pivoting back to universal themes that strike a chord with all of the moms in the room regardless of age. The familiar issue of "setting boundaries" between work and home becomes one of the core topics of the night.

"I remember before I had kids I used to be so meek about setting boundaries," says Sheryl Steiner, 45, a public relations consultant, freelance writer, and mother of two. "If a client called and said to you, 'It's an emergency,' you would drop everything. Clients would call at 2:00 or 3:00 A.M. knowing you would come in at 9:00 A.M. and have all of these frantic messages. Everything is an emergency, and I bought into that," she says. "But after I had kids, I started questioning things, and I would say to my superiors and my clients, 'What if we did it this way? And I don't think it needs to be in tomorrow.' I would manipulate it in a good way so everyone was happy and the client got what they wanted. I was still able to go home at 5:30 or 6:00 and not stay all night. You just have to be able to define your boundaries."

There are nods all around the room.

"I agree," says public relations executive Ellie Turner, a woman with shoulder-length blonde hair and funky black glasses. "I work differently now. I have to be a lot more efficient. I don't have time for the minutiae. I used to have great friends where I worked. I don't necessarily have that anymore. I go in, and I do my job the best that I can, and then I want to come home. But it's the same thing, the, Oh my God, this has to get done. But I've learned there's another way to do that; you don't have to be at work until 3:00 A.M. When I first came back from maternity leave, my boss would sometimes drop subtle hints about me not being able to be there for meetings at 5:00, and so I switched departments, and now I work for a man with three kids, and he gets it."

Laura Silver, an animated woman with shoulder-length blonde hair and apple cheeks, chimes in. "Back in 1995, I had just had my son and was working at Anderson Consulting, and I was still nursing, and I was pumping and throwing it out at every hotel. I remember missing my plane at O'Hare Airport, and I was sitting on the floor crying and thought to myself, I just can't do this anymore. So the first thing I did was called my boss, and I said I'm resigning; I'm hereby giving you a month. And then I called my husband and told him what I did, and he was like, 'You did what?'" Laura says, imitating her husband's total shock and horror, as the room of women explodes into laughter. "He was like, 'Call him back!' But then I sat there with my Rolodex, and I made up a business card on my computer, and I started calling my clients and said, 'If you haven't finished your year-end goals, give me a call.' I started getting tons of work and working three days a week. And I really thought I was just doing this until I got my next full time opportunity. It was really interesting because I had a lot of friends who were on the career track, and they said, 'What are you doing to your career?' I remember really wrestling with that for the first two years. But I had so much flow that I really stayed on my own for nine years. People ask what I want to do now, and I'm not sure. It all depends on flexibility. I also think about what will I do for retirement because I don't have a 401k now, but there are balances in life. I think it served me well. But it was a tough time. If you say you're a consultant, people think you're between gigs. But I really worked for nine years."

Setting limits, switching companies, managers or divisions, and empowering oneself at work is perhaps a more accepted phenomenon today than even a decade ago. Another mom in the room, a lean woman with short gray hair who at one time worked in the telecommunications industry, is amazed by the assertiveness and confidence of the women in the room, those who entered motherhood about five to seven years after she did.

"When my son was born, I didn't skip a beat. I was never home," says Judy Summers, 47. "Then my son got sick, and it was almost like a gift; it brought me home. Of course, thank God everything was okay, but it was very good for him to know that I cared enough to be home. It also helped my perspective on life so when I got fired from my job when the telecom bubble burst, I could handle it. But then I started my own business, and I work at home every day. My life has totally turned around. But it never even occurred to me to look for balance. I'm just impressed that so many people are making those choices so much earlier."

"You have pivotal moments," Jane Miller, 37, says quietly from the back of the room. "I had worked at Deutsche Bank, I got promoted, I went to another investment bank and went all the way up to managing director, which was very big. I had secondary infertility and got the promotion while I was going to Cornell Medical Center every morning at 6:30 A.M. so I could be the first to get my blood tested and be at work before my meetings. I found out that I was pregnant on the morning of September 11th. I found out because I peed on the stick, and I got to work at the World Trade Center for my 8 o'clock meeting. I called my doctor and said, 'I'm pregnant! I have to come in!' And then the planes hit the World Trade Center, and I was on the sixty-ninth floor. I walked down sixty-nine flights, and I could feel myself bleeding, and I didn't know what was happening. I didn't kiss my little daughter goodbye that morning (because I always left before she was up in the morning). And I remember I got outside, and I thought it was a war, and I thought I'm not, not kissing my kids goodbye in the morning ever again. I'm going to pray to God that the second baby is okay, and she was, thank God, and that was it. When it comes to opting out, I thought if it's full time or nothing, I'll take nothing. I'm now working part-time, and I've given up a lot of money. Everything is a trade-off, but now I get to see my kids in the morning."

Married to the Military and Mary Kay

It's naptime at Nicole Swanson's house on the military base of Ft. Polk, Louisiana, and while 3-year-old Katie Lee sleeps and Nicole's 6-year-old son, Graham, plays at a friend's house, Nicole is busy scurrying around. She's preparing welcome-home baskets for the unmarried soldiers who along with her husband are scheduled to return home from Iraq in the next week or so. "I've been up since 5:30 this morning," Nicole says cheerfully, in a lilting Eastern North Carolina drawl. "There's so much to do." Nicole's husband, Andrew, a First Sergeant in the Army, has been stationed in Iraq for the past fifteen months. He had been deployed for six months before that assignment. In fact, Andrew has been gone so much during Nicole's ten-year marriage that he's missed every single one of their daughter's birthdays. But Nicole doesn't like to complain.

"I'm not like some of these other military wives who sit around and whine and cry because their husbands are gone. I'm thinking you had to be aware of this, sister, when you married him, because he is in the Army."

Nicole is a high school English teacher, and four years ago she started selling Mary Kay cosmetics from home as a way to earn some extra income. She says that her husband's absence has been very hard on her son, and she felt she needed to make a change so she could spend more time with him. So in December 2003, after her husband had been gone almost a year, Nicole quit her teaching job to run her Mary Kay business full time.

She is now making double her teacher's salary and is about to find out if she wins a Grand Prix because of her high sales. She already won the Grand Am earlier this year.

"I've made the comment a lot recently that Mary Kay saved my life this year. It really gave me something to focus on when I wasn't in school and when I wasn't teaching. I could come home, and I could focus on my business and not be focused on, oh my gosh, there was another convoy attack, and oh my gosh, there was another explosion. Ignorance is bliss sometimes. Sometimes it's better not to know. If it doesn't affect me, and if it's not in my food chain, then I don't want to know."

Nicole's income has also given her the financial freedom to make last-minute decisions. Last Easter, Nicole and thousands of military families were expecting that their soldiers would be returning home. But a few days before the holiday they were told that the soldiers' deployment would be extended indefinitely. Nicole was crushed and decided that she needed to get home to her mother's house immediately.

"It was the Thursday before Easter. And I decided I'm going home. So I got on the phone and made plane reservations. It cost $1,100 dollars a plane ticket. My Mary Kay money paid for it. I didn't have to put that on my credit card. I didn't have to pay finance charges. It was really nice to know that now I have that option."

Options, choices, freedom, flexibility, this is the language of the Stay-at-Work mother. Although some women can feel stuck and trapped in professions that seem incompatible with having a family, many more have figured out how they can effectively transition their jobs, use their skills to change careers entirely, and venture off in a different direction. Former Governor Swift is still working in an intense job, and as the sole breadwinner she has the responsibility to bear the financial load of her family. Yet she feels that even though she travels and works hard, she now has better integrated her career and family life and has greater flexibility and satisfaction than she had while serving in public office.

Amy Gould has given up a hefty paycheck but has found a passion in teaching that gives her emotional and professional fulfillment and is extremely compatible with raising her twins. Rabbi Laurie Rice has discovered that she doesn't need the big job right now; it's more important to her that she has plenty of family time. And Nicole Swanson, who for the most part plays the role of single mother as her husband serves the United States military, feels liberated from leaving teaching, working from her home, and generating her own income through her Mary Kay business. These are different women, and they have made different choices, but the common theme among them is that they've not been afraid to re-create their work lives to accommodate their changing family lives. They are switching gears to make work, work for them, and they are succeeding.

Chapter 6

Moms at the Helm

A Business Boom Explosion

S*occer moms are so 1992.* Today, female entrepreneurs are the new "It" girls on the political radar. As their numbers have swelled in the last decade, women business owners have become a formidable political constituency and are also a dynamic and growing economic force.[1] For the past few years, women have been starting businesses at a rate double that of men. And today, women employ more people in this country than all of the Fortune 500 companies combined.[2] Although much has been made in the news recently about women opting out of the workforce, the business boom backed by women doesn't generate as many sexy headlines. But do a Google search on women entrepreneurs, and you get over one million hits. These links take you to entrepreneurial networking groups from Silicon Valley and Saskatoon to Stockholm.

Across the world, women-owned firms constitute between one-quarter and one-third of the business population. The number of women-owned enterprises is growing faster than the economy at large in many countries, and women are starting businesses in every industrial sector.[3] According to one global economic study, increasing the number of female entrepreneurs starting new businesses is critical to a country's long-term economic growth.[4] And despite the popular press saying that women today are exiting the workforce in droves and no longer are gunning for the corner office, a study by Catalyst, a nonprofit group that seeks to advance women in business, shows that women want a CEO job just as badly as men do—and most of these women are mothers.[5]

Why the surge in female-owned businesses? Many women dissatisfied or frustrated with their jobs and the lack of flexibility want to strike out on their own. They believe that having a business will not only give them the creative kick that they need, but also the ability to have a healthy home life too.

Makeup Mogul and Class Mom

Bobbi Brown had always wanted to become a mother—a CEO, however, is a job she never quite expected to have. But in 1990, Bobbi, who was working as a makeup artist and was pregnant with her first baby, was tired of toting around a heavy case of cosmetics to her jobs and she was frustrated with the lack of natural-looking lipsticks available. So she decided to create some of her own. Three babies and a little more than a decade later, and today Brown is the CEO of one of the most popular and successful makeup companies in the world, Bobbi Brown Cosmetics.

It's a particularly sticky and steamy summer day when I get ready to meet the woman behind the cosmetics empire. I don't usually wear more than a smudge of lipstick and a swipe of rouge, but in anticipation of my interview with this famous makeup mogul, I feel compelled to apply an expensive array of newly purchased cosmetics. A few sweaty hours and the entire length of the Long Island Expressway later, I meet Bobbi Brown at a coffee shop near her summer home in the Hamptons. She breezes in wearing gym clothes, a messy ponytail, and not a trace of her own signature makeup, and I immediately feel ridiculously over blushed. I want to run to the bathroom and strip my face before she sees me. But before I can even grab the ubiquitous baby wipe from my bag, Bobbi has folded herself Indian-style into a chair across from me. She is friendly and seems genuinely interested in talking about my book, but for several minutes as we speak all I can think about is how the humidity is probably melting my black eyeliner into my under eye creases, giving me that dreaded raccoon effect. I'm feeling mortified. When I confess to Bobbi that I felt pressured to be properly powdered and made up for our meeting, she laughs and says, "That's so funny; people always say that to me and look, I'm wearing nothing but lip balm."

So Bobbi is not exactly a walking advertisement for her own cosmetics line. But at 47, this surprisingly tiny titan (five feet tall) is such a naturally pretty woman she doesn't even need any of her own makeup.

Growing up in Chicago, where her favorite thing to do was to play at the makeup counter at Marshall Fields, Bobbi says she never envisioned herself as an entrepreneur because she wasn't at all career driven. She figured she would probably go into teaching, get married, and have babies. It wasn't until after Bobbi left Arizona State University and transferred to Emerson College where they let her major in theatrical makeup that she thought seriously about a career in makeup.

After graduating, Bobbi became a successful freelance makeup artist in New York City, doing magazine and advertising work. It was at 30 years old, recently married and newly pregnant, that she began thinking about launching her own cosmetics line.

"I was carrying all of these bags to work every day that just killed my back. I had too many things. But I realized when I did makeup lessons for women, I would recommend products to them from all of the different lines because someone had a good taupe and someone had a good blush. So I thought it would be a good idea to do an edited collection because I basically used the same things on most women. But when I sat down to think about it, I really started thinking about lipsticks because I hated what was out there. I hated the smell and the color."

Energized by a product she understood and a niche she saw clearly, she decided to create her own business and brand based on natural-color lipsticks.

"The first couple of years were tough," Bobbi says. "My husband was in real estate, and the market crashed during the early '90s. So my husband decided to go to law school. We moved to a house in New Jersey. Here I was with an infant, a husband in law school, not really sure how we were going to pay our mortgage every month. I did a lot of catalog work because that was the money job, and then I had this idea for lipsticks. We started with our own money, the last $5,000 we had. It's pretty amazing."

By chance, at a photo shoot, Bobbi met a chemist who helped her realize her goal of creating ten lipsticks that she hoped could mix and blend to come up with virtually any color a woman needed. At the same time she was launching her lipstick collection, Brown had recently given birth to her first son.

"I remember doing some early PR for the lipsticks because I had friends who were editors at the magazines. The big beauty editor at *Vogue* called to interview me, and I was really nervous. When she called, I was nursing Dylan, and he was crying, and then he threw up on me. And I was trying to have a conversation with this editor talking about what a new mom needs, and here I am covered in spit up, sitting at home wearing an old bathrobe. It was crazy."

But spit up and all, the public relations campaign paid off, and it immediately catapulted Bobbi into business. In 1991 her #4 lipstick, aptly called "Brown," transformed the lipstick industry.

"Magazines wrote about the lipsticks, and we got bombarded with orders, and I thought that I should just sell this in a department store," Bobbi says. "So I went to Bergdorf Goodman because I thought, that's a good store, and I met a buyer there, and she took a chance."

The chance paid off, and Bobbi's business exploded. But personally and professionally, as any entrepreneur knows, building a company is extremely demanding.

"It was really a struggle because I was traveling like crazy. The company was growing; we were adding products, and we launched in Paris, London, Tokyo, and Hong Kong. I traveled pregnant twice to Europe, and I was going to personal appearances all over. I hate flying. I always had this dreaded feeling that something was going to happen to me, and I would never see my kids again," she says.

"I also had a president [I was the CEO] who was running the company with me who thought no matter what I did, I wasn't doing enough. She didn't see my value. It was pretty miserable from day one. That was one of the reasons that we sold the company. I realized it was the biggest learning experience; I let things happen that I wouldn't now, I know more now. My husband used to say, 'Let them win the battle; we're going to win the war.' It was really tough, and you know what, they're not there anymore, and our business is really flourishing, and I'm really happy."

The Bobbi Brown brand has grown enormously since its debut more than a decade ago. In 1995, Bobbi sold her business to Estée Lauder, but she has stayed on as CEO and has creative control over the products. Bobbi has also written three books on beauty and regularly appears as a contributing beauty editor on NBC's *Today*. About a dozen years after the launch of her company, Bobbi feels extremely fortunate to have not only a thriving business but also a family-friendly schedule.

"It's evolved over the years. I've gone through three presidents, and I've finally found my soul mate; she's a working mom who has two kids. My first two presidents at the time didn't have kids, and they did not understand what it meant to be a mom. The first thing my personal assistant does with my schedule is put on school holidays, the half days, and then the birthdays. I don't put play dates on, but I put field trips or when I'm going to be somewhere, and she'll know not to book me an appointment on those days. My office really gets it. They were booking my book tour, and they said, 'Oh no, it's the first day of school; Bobbi can't do that.' They just don't even go there. I know I am so lucky."

Bobbi is the mother of three boys; ironically she has no daughters to whom to pass on the lip-gloss wand or whose eyelids long for a little shimmer, but that's okay with her. She gave birth to her first two boys, Dylan, now age 14, and Dakota, 12, in the chaotic early years of her business. But Bobbi always wanted a big family and as she approached 40, she started thinking about having more children and even adopting a baby girl.

"I turned 40, and I was like, oh my God, it's over, no more babies. And I thought it doesn't have to be over. I said, 'All right, let's see if I can get pregnant,' and it took me three or four months, and I got pregnant. I was lucky because when I was in high school, I had an ectopic pregnancy, and I only have one fallopian tube. I would have had a fourth [child] if I were younger," she says.

At 41 years old Bobbi gave birth to her third son, Duke, now 6. She says she's still shocked by the success of her business and being the name and face behind such an influential brand. She has a company that she's proud of and now has a flexible enough work schedule that lets her integrate her two lives as much as possible. And even though her job has many exciting moments, like doing makeup for the Oscars and making the faces of celebrities even more beautiful, Bobbi says she's most content just hanging out at home.

"My favorite thing in the world is to be home and make soup and have the kids hang around. I'm a homebody. I've gotten in demand in spite of myself."

From MBA to CEO

In Bobbi Brown's hometown of Chicago, two 30-something businesswomen find themselves in some ways following in Bobbi's footsteps. Like Bobbi Brown, they are infatuated with makeup and have discovered a void in the marketplace they are hoping to fill. But coming into cosmetics as a second career, they also have other needs.

"I wanted to do something that I felt passionate about and that gave me more flexibility," says Sandi Hwang Adam, co-founder and president of Maven Cosmetics.

I first met Sandi, a chic 32-year-old with shoulder-length black hair and dark twinkling eyes, when I was producing a series for CNN's *American Morning* show about dream jobs. We were looking to find inspirational stories about people who had left their careers to follow their passion. In my research, I stumbled across Maven Cosmetics, a fledgling makeup company founded by two women who were disenchanted with the grind of their high-flying careers in business consulting and were looking to do something more personally and professionally gratifying. Neither woman had children yet, but both already knew they needed to make a major life and career change.

Sandi met her business partner, Noreen Abbasi, in a Chicago coffee shop where a networking group of women called ChicWit were gathering to socialize and strategize about their careers. After a couple of chance meetings in 2000, Sandi and Noreen both discovered that they shared a guilty secret—their passion in life lay in makeup. And as ethnic women—Sandi is Chinese American, and Noreen is of Indian and

Pakistani descent—they also discovered that they both had a hard time finding foundation appropriate for their skin coloring. And so the germ of a business was born. The goal was to create a makeup line that worked for all women, not just white women.

"The more we talked about it, the more we felt, we had something here," Sandi says. "But we knew we needed to get some hands-on experience."

So the two women wrote a business plan and quit their lucrative consulting jobs, and for six months both women went to work in retail makeup. Noreen worked at the Bobbi Brown cosmetics counter at a Nordstrom's in Chicago, and Sandi took a job at Sephora, both of them earning about a quarter of what they were making before.

"I tell people it was the best job I ever had," Sandi says. "It was just so much fun, and we were able to identify some of the big gaps in the marketplace that allowed us to move in."

In November 2002, Sandi and Noreen launched Maven Cosmetics, and their products are now being sold in about thirty stores across the country, including Marshall Fields department store in Chicago and on-line at Sephora.

When I produced the story for CNN, Sandi was the mom of a 7-month-old; Noreen was not yet married and did not have children. When I check in with Sandi eight months later, she tells me that she is now four months pregnant with her second baby and has recently moved with her husband to San Diego. Noreen is still in Chicago and is getting married in spring 2005. The two continue to run Maven Cosmetics together but from separate cities. Sandi is now working out of her California home, and she's enjoying the freedom she has to integrate her business into her family life.

"I think I'm probably working as hard as I did in consulting, but now by having my own business and with a baby at home and a baby on the way, I'm working on my own terms. I try to block off between 5:00 and 8:00 P.M. each day so my daughter and I can have dinner and play together, and at 8 o'clock I start working again."

Having started her career on Wall Street and being accustomed to working in a predominantly male environment, Sandi was surprised to discover an undercurrent of prejudice toward pregnancy that still exists in business.

"I'm trying to close a deal right now, and I had met with some companies at an early enough stage in my pregnancy that it wasn't really clear to anyone if I was pregnant. I could tell some people were trying to probe, and I was afraid my pregnancy was going to impact the deal. I kept thinking, if I were a man it wouldn't be an issue. But on the other hand, I understood that if you're working with someone who is going to be a big player, you want to know if they're going to be able to deliver. So I had this dilemma: do I come forward and acknowledge that I'm expecting, or do I not tell them? I decided to tell them. But just because I'm expecting doesn't mean I wouldn't be able to deliver."

No pun intended. Having control over one's work life is what drives millions of women to go into business on their own. As I sat at a lecture in New York for a group of women all in their 20s to mid-30s, most of whom had MBAs and who worked in finance, I was amazed that the woman who leads the group, a sort of grande dame in the New York City investment banking community, was encouraging her much younger banking sisters to leave their jobs and start their own businesses. Her advice was simple and empowering. Create your own company or hedge fund and come back to the big banks as the client. "Then they'll roll out the red carpet and treat you like a queen. That's what happened for me, and that's the way to do it."

Having an MBA certainly can help you understand the financial piece of how to launch a business. But the majority of the 10.6 million women who own businesses in this country don't have MBAs. Whereas Sandi and Noreen did have business backgrounds, Bobbi Brown did not. What's more important is finding a niche in the marketplace combined with a passion for what you're creating.

"Anyone can learn the financial structure of a business," Sandi says. "But you have to really love what you're doing, and it has to give you the stamina to keep going because you're going to have good and bad days. Just when you think you're down to your last dollars, the next day can be great because you make a big sale. It's a rollercoaster."

Holding onto a Hard-Won Dream

Designer Vera Wang understands life on a rollercoaster. She'll be the first to tell you that the personal dips in her life have ironically helped her ascend to where she is today.

"I think everything I ever did I failed at," Vera says immediately after we sit down in her Seventh Avenue design room in New York City. It's a startling statement coming from one of the most successful designers in the world and the woman who single-handedly transformed the bridal industry from cream puffs to chic elegance. But Vera Wang, 55, has always been an overachiever, and her measure for success throughout her life is no doubt set to impossibly high standards. Vera has had many career incarnations. First she was an Olympic ice skating hopeful, then a *Vogue* fashion editor, followed by a move into design at Ralph Lauren before launching her own company, Vera Wang Bridal, Ltd., in 1990.

Vera's overachieving traits and hard-core work ethic are clearly inherited from her parents. Her father, Cheng Ching Wang, built multimillion-dollar oil and pharmaceutical companies after emigrating to the United States from China in the 1940s. Her mother, Florence Wu Wang, was a United Nations translator. When Vera was 7 years old, she received a pair of ice skates from her father for Christmas and instantly fell in love with the sport. Vera dedicated herself to skating, waking up at 6:00 A.M. to practice every day before school. As a teenager she competed in the U.S. National Championships in 1968 and 1969 and came in fifth. But perhaps the most devastating disappointment in Vera's life was not making the Olympics.

"It's still painful because I think at any given moment I could have qualified. I think part of what I realized about not making the team and not ever being in a history book was that I learned there was life after skating. I also had to learn to pick myself up and start a new life and find something else. In my case it was finishing college and going to *Vogue*," she says.

"I think that I always wanted to be a designer, and when I finished college and had given up skating competitively, my father didn't feel like paying for me to go to design school. He said, 'If you think that you're such a hot shot and you can have a fashion career, go and get a job,' which is what I did. I walked into *Vogue*, and I got a job, and I stayed there for sixteen years, and I was the youngest senior editor there probably in the history of *Vogue*."

But after spending almost two decades at *Vogue*, Vera's desire to move into design still beckoned.

"I was 38 years old, and I decided I wanted to be a designer again, and I asked my parents if they would back me in a design company, and my dad said, 'You're not a designer.' So I went to Ralph Lauren, and I got a job in design. I think I probably would still be at Ralph today if I hadn't wanted to get pregnant. I had to quit my job when I was going through infertility because I just couldn't work those hours."

It was at this same time when Vera was struggling with infertility and trying desperately to conceive that her father told her if she came up with a good business plan, he was ready to finance her design company.

"But by that time, after twenty years of begging my father, I didn't want to do it. I said, 'Listen, I'm 40 years old, and I worked all my life, and now I really didn't want my own business.' I think I was afraid of failure, and I was afraid of the responsibility. So I had a lot of doubts, and it was actually strangely enough my father who pushed me to do it at that point.

"I had not conceived, and my dad said, 'You're not a woman who is going to stay at home all day. That's never been you since you were 18 years old. So why would you think that you're just going to stay home and go to lunch and shop? You have to work for you and for your own sanity.' And I think it was his influence that really pushed me at that point even though it was he who was limiting me for the prior twenty years, isn't that funny? He said, 'Now that you don't want it, I think you actually could run a company.' I think all of the emotion was out of it," Vera says.

These days it's hard to imagine the bridal world without Vera Wang. But ironically enough, the birth of Vera Wang Bridal came from a woman who never wanted to get married.

"I was a real career girl. I never even thought I'd get married. I tell people if there's anyone who shouldn't have been in the wedding business, it was certainly me."

Vera launched her company the same year she and her husband, businessman Arthur Becker, adopted their first daughter, Cecelia, now 14. Three years later they adopted their second daughter, Josephine, 11. After several painful years enduring infertility, Vera says the adoptions of her daughters helped complete her life.

"For my husband and me, we realized that having children was really about parenting. We wanted to be someone's parents. And if we weren't going to do it biologically, we decided we wanted to adopt. I'll never forget when I was at the adoption agency, and we were coming to see our oldest daughter Cecelia for the first time, and there was this little plaque and it said that the birth mother gives life but the adoptive mother gives light. And that sort of said it all. We realized that this opportunity to parent was something that we felt so lucky and so blessed to have. Being a parent is probably the most challenging thing you can do. It isn't about you; it's about them. I think that's really quite amazing."

Vera had thought about adopting even more children, but the demands of her business and the reality of her age made her change her mind.

"I was hoping to have a boy at some point. At the time I had a new business, which was like a child unto itself. And my husband and I really got frightened about the sense of incredible responsibility, and knowing the hours we were both working, we just had to at some point say how much can we really take on. Whatever we thought parenthood would be like, it was ten times more. What really made it real for me was when I was 48 years old and I was at preschool with my second daughter, and I thought by the time she gets to kindergarten I'll be 50. So reality has a way of setting in, and I thought, would I really want now to still be going to preschool with a third child and dealing with potty training and all of the other things? So while I regret it to some extent, I can't believe I'm saying this, but I actually knew my own limitations."

Vera feels that raising her girls while simultaneously growing a business has been "a great adventure." "It takes tremendous dedication to be in fashion. It's not your job; it's your life," she says.

Today the Vera Wang brand includes not just bridal dresses but also couture, ready-to-wear, eyewear, fragrances, footwear, and even a home collection. Vera still has her toe on the ice rink by designing skating out-fits for Olympic ice skaters, including Michelle Kwan.

Vera credits her parents for instilling in her a hard work ethic and the confidence to become an entrepreneur. She hopes to teach similar values to her own daughters.

"For me confidence and self-esteem doesn't just happen one day. It's not something you can inherit; you have to earn it. And it isn't one partic-ular act; it's the journey and the process. It's all about the choices you make in life. To me the most important thing is to make your contribution."

Making Room for Baby

Three thousand miles away from Vera Wang's headquarters in New York City, another designer works amid mountains of fabric swatches. Except these pieces of gingham, percale, polka dots, and chenille are unlikely to find their way onto a bridal gown or to become part of a couture collec-tion. Instead, these funky fabrics, mixed and matched to create sophisti-cated, quirky, and beautiful designs, are at the heart of Wendy Bellissimo's wildly successful baby and kids bedding business. When we met Wendy earlier in the book, she was helping Brooke Shields register for her upcoming baby shower. Wendy is one of the premier baby nurs-ery decorators in the country and a favorite among celebrities. She's dec-orated the nurseries of Kelly Ripa, Catherine Bell, and Camryn Manheim in addition to Shields. Her swatches to riches success story really hap-pened the old fashioned way. She had a passion for design, she acciden-tally found a niche in the market, and she sewed her fingers to the bone.

"When I was 26 years old I was working in a furniture store in Mal-ibu, and they wanted me to throw away fabric samples that were dis-continued. But I thought they were so beautiful, and I didn't want to throw them away, so I just kept them, and I started making throw pil-lows for myself," Wendy tells me in her modest California office as the buzz of sewing machines from the manufacturing room behind us whirls in the background. "Everyone loved the pillows, and my friends said I should go to Santa Monica and try to sell them. So I borrowed a friend's old sewing machine, and I decided to go out and find some other fabrics that went with the ones I had. I combined the swatches of discontinued fabric with what I bought, and I made thirty pillows. I put the pillows in a trash bag, and my boyfriend Joe, who is now my husband, took me to Montana Avenue in Santa Monica. The first store I walked into, the owner bought twenty-nine of the pillows. From there I was just going around to specialty, boutique stores in the L.A. area and selling them and sewing all night. Sometimes I would sew for twenty-two hours straight.

"Then I did a trade show in San Francisco, and that was a success, and people were asking for duvet covers and bed shams and skirts to go with the pillows, so I started doing that."

From there Wendy's adult bedding business took off. She got orders from Strauds, a retail chain, Bloomingdales by Mail, Neiman Marcus, and Bed, Bath and Beyond. She also continued to sell in boutiques.

"It went really quickly, all of this within two years," Wendy says. "We were doing a lot of pretty big things. We actually started doing baby bedding by accident. I would see fabrics that I would think would be so cute for a baby or a little child, and so I ordered some rolls but never did anything with them. Then one day I was in the fabric center, and I saw a fabric roll sticking out that reminded me that I had all of these baby fabrics sitting around untouched. So two weeks before our big show in New York, something made me want to play with those fabrics. I didn't have kids yet, so I was coming from such a pure place. I wasn't influenced by anything out there. I just did what I thought was really beautiful from my experience of mixing adult fabrics. We went to the show and set up the booth, and all I brought was the baby and kids stuff. The next day I was swamped. I was doing slipcover bumpers and embroidery on the panels and sheer overlays. I was doing things that weren't out there.

"I was having so much fun with the baby and kids stuff that I made the decision to drop the adult line and completely focus on baby and kids, and that was the best decision I could have made. It's just so much fun.

Wendy went into business about two years before the first of her three daughters was born. Her husband Joe is her business partner. He does all of the marketing and public relations nd pops his head into our meeting room every so often as I interview Wendy.

Knowing now just how exhausting and time-consuming launching a company can be, Wendy's advice to new moms who are interested in starting their own business is to wait until their children are at least in school and to make sure that they really understand the market before they jump into something.

"It was just the right timing for us. We didn't have kids yet; we worked eighteen to twenty hours a day. I would cry every other day, and say, 'I can't do this anymore,' and Joe would say, 'Don't worry, it won't be like this forever, people love your things, keep going, keep going.' But it was so unbelievably hard."

Nearly a decade after starting her business and selling in hundreds of boutiques across the country, Wendy has recently signed an exclusive deal with Babies R Us. She still does all of the designing for her company, but she doesn't do any of the sewing anymore. She says she takes very few phone calls and really structures her days to focus on exactly what she needs to do to get her job done.

"I feel like I have achieved a good balance between my family and my business. I get to take Gracie and Cecilia to school, and I get to be with Willow in the morning. When this one comes, she'll be with me at work every day until she's about 6 months old; that's what I did with my other two. Everything is close by geographically, so I can run and pick Gracie up from school, I can eat lunch with them, and when they nap, I come back to work. Because it's my own business, I can do a lot of work at home at night. I do a lot of my creative stuff in bed. I don't have to be here all of the time. But sometimes I definitely feel overwhelmed. I have to have a good cry once a month. Before shows it gets really, really crazy, and all of the extra things that I do, like the celebrity nurseries or taping TV shows or the book that I'm working on, that's when it really gets grueling. I don't like to be away from the kids for a really long day."

Wendy says she can finally take a deep breath and realize just how fortunate she is to be in control of something that gives her such joy to create. "It's really just hitting me now, like, wow, we created this. I love getting emails from parents saying they are having fun planning their nurseries because they have this beautiful bedding to work with. I feel like I'm doing something that's making people happy, so it all feels good."

The Mother of Invention

Generations of toothless infant mouths would have never tasted Gerber baby food if it weren't for Stay-at-Home mom Dorothy Gerber. As the legend of Gerber goes, in the summer of 1927 at home in her kitchen, Dorothy was hand straining solid food to feed to her 7-month-old daughter Sally. Fed up with the chore, she asked her husband Daniel to give it a shot. As he struggled to strain the peas, Dorothy suggested that because he was already manufacturing a line of canned fruit and vegetables at the Fremont Canning Company in Fremont, Michigan, it would be relatively easy for him to start straining and jarring food for babies. Voilà, Gerber baby food was born.

Mothers as innovators are not new, but what is a recent phenomenon are the huge numbers of highly educated and professionally trained women who are able to take their skills and not only come up with a concept but successfully turn their idea into a business.

As was true for Dorothy Gerber, necessity is often the mother of invention, and motherhood these days is frequently the springboard for women who are starting their own ventures. Today there is even a term for these women who have created what is often a home-based company— "momtrepreneur." Interestingly, many of these women never intended on becoming entrepreneurs. Many had actually left their careers and planned on doing the stay-at-home routine until something inspired them to change their plans.

For Beth Besner, 43, her moment came in 1995 when she took her 6-month-old son to lunch, and he threw his plate of chicken strips Frisbee-style across the restaurant. She thought there must be something in the baby stores that could suction onto a table to avoid that messy and embarrassing situation from happening again. She couldn't find anything appropriate, so she designed one herself and created a company called

Neat Solutions, Inc. After Beth consulted with her sister, Randi, whom she calls a daring and innovative type, they came up with Table Toppers, the disposable plastic place mats that adhere to restaurant tables so toddlers can eat on a clean surface. After months of trial and error using various prototypes, the genius for the Table Topper invention came from a product that only a woman could appreciate—the sanitary pad.

"We spent months trying to figure out what kind of product would work," Beth, the mother of three boys, tells me from her home in Davie, Florida. "We even put it on hold for awhile because we weren't sure how to make it. Then one day my sister came over to my house with suction cups. And I said, wait a minute, and I ran into the bathroom and grabbed some sanitary pads and ripped off the backs and I said, 'This is it! This is the Table Topper.' The next step was to figure out who could manufacture this for us. I knew that Tampax couldn't make my Table Topper, so there was research we needed to do to get the product made and distributed."

Beth, who had practiced bankruptcy law for four years before having children, used her legal skills to negotiate deals and craft contracts for the manufacture and distribution of Table Toppers. Today, sales top $1 million a year, and the company has developed another product, the Potty Topper, a disposable sheet that sticks to public toilets. Table Topper is being sold nationwide in baby stores as well as at Target. A couple of years ago Beth sold the company, and she is now enjoying being a Stay-at-Home mom. Her boys are 9, 7, and 5 years old. Beth says she has ideas for other businesses but because of the enormous time commitment it takes to successfully launch and operate a company, she wants to wait a few years until her children are a little older.

"A lot of our success was getting the attention of the mommy story," Beth says. "I've found that a lot of women are interested in creating their own businesses. In fact, every time an article was written about Table Toppers, I would get phone calls from women who asked me for advice about launching something of their own. I think what we're seeing is that as women start families later, they have more confidence and sophistication to start their own businesses too."

Baby Einstein Grows Up

Julie Aigner-Clark is struggling to get back into the mode of writing press releases. She's agonizing about the wording on press material for her new product, Safe Side, that she's launching soon.

"The fun part for me is the creative part of writing and creating the video. Now the unfun part starts of getting press releases out and figuring out how we're going to launch," Julie, 38, says. "With Baby Einstein we never had press. We were just so fortunate that word of mouth was tremendous. We launched that first video at the Right Start store, and it was just moms telling moms, telling moms. It was unbelievable."

It's been three years since Julie and her husband Bill Clark sold their first brainchild, the Baby Einstein Company, which includes videos, books, and toys, to Disney for an undisclosed amount in the tens of millions of dollars. Now Julie and Bill have started a company called Safe Side, where using a combination of products starting, of course, with a video, they plan to teach elementary school children about how to stay safe in various situations.

"I think we've found a way to teach kids about safety in a really fun and cool way," Julie tells me enthusiastically from her home outside of Denver, Colorado.

Julie's daughters, Aspen and Sierra, those cute blonde toddlers, stars of the videos and forever frozen in digital time on DVD, have actually grown up. They are now 10 and 8 years old. Julie says the concept of her latest venture was born when she wanted to teach her daughters about safety.

"I was looking for safety videos for my own kids, and I thought they all sucked. They are all so boring. What's out there is a talking head saying, 'Don't go with strangers.' So what we're doing is completely different. We have a host who is hysterically funny and getting herself in all of these situations where goofy things are happening to her, and she's responding in a way that's really cool and safe."

In many ways this is like 1995 all over again for Julie. This former high school English teacher from Grosse Pointe, Michigan, and Stay-at-Home mom of an infant was looking for a video to stimulate her baby and couldn't find anything out there. As she floated the idea of creating her own video for babies, her friends, family, and even a pal at Nickelodeon thought she was crazy. She was warned that you couldn't market to babies because they can't turn around and demand a certain brand of rattle or formula. But Julie knew she was on to something. If a lava lamp or whirling object could mesmerize her baby and Mozart soothed her cranky toddler, then a video of these seemingly random objects together with puppets and poetry could entertain and comfort the rest of the world's babies as well.

So in 1995, with $18,000 in savings and borrowed camera and lighting equipment, Julie and her husband set up a makeshift studio in the basement of their then-Atlanta home and shot their first Baby Einstein video. The painfully low-tech video with disembodied hands floating in and out of the screen features images of toys with a backdrop of songs and rhymes spoken by mothers in seven different languages. After shooting the video and editing it on her desktop computer, Julie set out to find a store to sell it. She went to a toy trade show looking for representatives from the educational toy company the Right Start, a place she believed was a natural fit for her video. It took many phone calls and letters, but eventually Julie persuaded a buyer at the Right Start to sell Baby Einstein. When the video hit shelves in 1997, it became one of their best-selling items. Within five years Julie created nine other Einstein sibling videos and thirty books before she and her husband sold the company. Today, it's the number-one brand of videos for babies and toddlers, with nine out of ten infant developmental videos sold in the U.S. produced by Baby Einstein.

Julie's rise to "momtrepreneurial" superstar status was something she had never exactly planned. In fact, she had always wanted to be a Stay-at-Home mom. Her own mother had stayed home with her until she was 7, and Julie says she remembers fondly how amazing it was to have her mom always around. She also says that being an only child, she couldn't wait to have her own children and to create a blood connection to people other than her own parents.

"I was so ready to be a mommy. And when it happened, it was so meaningful and profound. I really didn't want to give it up, and I didn't want to go back to work," Julie says. "I don't want to say the whole Baby Einstein thing started by accident because I worked really hard at it. But I was able to do it around being a mom. It was and it continues to be the best of both worlds because I was able to work at home, and I was able to give my kids all of the time they needed, but then I was also able to have time for myself. So even when I say to you I really wanted to be a Stay-at-Home mom—and I did—I missed my professional life, and I missed having conversations that didn't have to do with baby formula and spit up. It was really important to me to be able to use my mind. And to have something that my own children were involved in was just an amazing opportunity. So while it wasn't accidental, because I worked really hard at it, it wasn't like I had set out to create this empire," she says with a laugh.

After taking a year off after the sale of Baby Einstein, Julie and her husband Bill teamed up with John Walsh, the host of *America's Most Wanted* and a spokesperson and advocate for missing children, and together they created Safe Side.

The company was supposed to launch their first video in the spring of 2004. But it was put on hold when Julie was suddenly diagnosed with breast cancer.

"I found it on my own, and it was smaller than a centimeter," Julie says. "I don't smoke. I'm not overweight. I'm fit. I breast-fed my kids. I did all the right things, and there I was with breast cancer at 37 years old. Fortunately I found it so early I was able to avoid chemo. But I decided to do a double mastectomy to get rid of all of the tissue. When it happened, it was such a complete shock. It was so devastating and frightening that I've compared it to feeling like a suicide bomber had gotten on my bus. I felt like here I was living my life and everything was lovely and great, and all of a sudden something was attacking me and wanted to kill me, and I didn't know it was there, and I hadn't had an opportunity to fight back. I thought I was fighting back by having such a healthy lifestyle. So for me it felt like the only way I could, excuse my French, say, 'Fuck you, you're out of here,' was to have a double mastectomy so there's no more breast tissue for you to go. While most women in my situation do choose a lumpectomy, this was just my way of dealing with it. And I am happy with my decision."

Six days after having her surgery, Julie was hiking in the hills near her home in Colorado. Physically she felt surprisingly strong, but emotionally she says she sort of "parked" the psychological loss of her breasts and the trauma of her illness aside. It wasn't until a few months ago that she started dealing with the emotional impact of her extreme surgery.

I speak to Julie about five months after her operation. She has now had reconstructive surgery and says she's feeling great and cancer-free. She has thrown herself into work on her new company.

"It sure makes you appreciate your life. It's been sort of healing to get back into this," Julie says.

When Julie, a pretty blonde with a stylish, shoulder-length cut, looks back on the woman with the long, platinum, poofy hair in the early days of Baby Einstein, she sees a woman unjaded and blissfully unaware of the aggressive side of business. She remembers that time as an incredibly pure experience.

"When I think about the start-up of Baby Einstein, which was all so unexpected in terms of how it grew and how successful it became, it was such a tremendous time. I was able to be really creative and stay home with my kids, and I worked with people who I loved. It was sort of an idyllic business. There are times when I miss it, and other times I'm so happy about not having to worry about Nickelodeon coming up with a competing product or someone suing me. But what a terrific ten years it's been."

Now 38 years old, a cancer survivor, mother of grade school girls, and a wildly accomplished businesswoman, in many ways Julie's in a very different place from where she was a decade ago. She's no longer shooting videos in her basement but flying to L.A. to cast actors and to hire professional camera crews. Her production budget has ballooned from less than $20,000 ten years ago to more than half a million dollars today. She has a proven track record in the industry and a vast personal fortune to single-handedly support any of her endeavors. But while you would think that after Julie's tremendous success with Baby Einstein no one would dare doubt her ability to create captivating and stimulating products for children, think again. Julie says there are still naysayers who don't quite get what she's trying to do.

"What's happened with Safe Side is similar to when I was telling people, including good friends, about my idea for Baby Einstein. They would all sort of roll their eyes and say, 'That English teacher thinks she can make poetry fun, oh please.' And it's the same thing with this topic. How could you possibly make the idea of strangers you don't know and safety fun. But I think you'll watch it and go, 'Oh, I get it!'"

The Power of Paper

In two tiny second-floor apartments at the edge of the ritzy downtown suburb of Westport, Connecticut, looking over what used to be a popular local restaurant here, Bonnie Marcus is eagerly waiting to give me a tour. Two years ago, Bonnie, 32, became an instant sensation in the stationery and invitation business with her fashionable line of wedding, holiday, and maternity cards, StylePress by Bonnie. I've come to Connecticut to observe the heart and soul of her home-based headquarters and get a sense of how this mommy of two babies under two is running her extraordinary business.

"We were so happy when the apartment next door opened up because, as you can see, there is no room in my apartment," Bonnie, a stylish woman with long dark hair and huge blue eyes, says as we walk single file through her galley kitchen and into her sunny home office. She's not exaggerating when she warns me that things are quite cramped these days. Next door where half of her six employees are working, a row of boxes filled to the brim lines the narrow hallway and towers above us as we squeeze by. First stop, Bonnie introduces me to her accountant, who works at a desk near a queen size bed in what was supposed to be the guest room. A few feet farther down the hall, a college student is sitting at a long card table tying pink ribbons onto a package of note cards that's headed to Bloomingdales. Another college student is tucked away in a small, unused kitchen sealing boxes for a UPS pickup later that day.

"So this is my crazy life," Bonnie says as our tour ends in her cozy living room where her 17-month-old son, Benjamin, is watching a video while his babysitter feeds his 4-month-old younger brother, Joshua, a bottle.

Bonnie has always worked hard and in positions that required insane hours and total commitment. Her first job in New York was helping designer

Diane Von Furstenberg get famous again with the relaunch of her 1970s creation, the wrap dress. Then for several years, Bonnie worked in event planning at a prestigious New York institution, the 92nd Street Y. She then worked as a wedding consultant at a start-up Internet stationery company.

"I was working with all of these brides, and they were not happy with the invitations available to them, so I would help them design their own invitations. Nothing was really cool and fun. The women wanted something a little trendier. So I worked with a fashion illustrator and would design custom invitations. People loved them, and I thought this could really be a business."

By then Bonnie had moved from New York City to Connecticut and was enduring a daily commute of nearly three hours roundtrip. She was newly pregnant and wanted to do something at home that would give her more flexibility. So she started "playing around" at home by creating sparkled invitations she made at her kitchen table. She sent out press releases to two publications, including a trendy, urban shopping Internet site called Daily Candy and *New York* magazine. Soon after, *New York* magazine included her in their "Best Bets" section. In the retail world, that is akin to winning the lottery or appearing on *Oprah*. Immediately after both *New York* magazine and Daily Candy featured Bonnie's line, hundreds of orders came in from around the country. So in the last trimester of her first pregnancy and "absolutely huge," Bonnie found herself in an envious but overwhelming situation. She had almost more orders than she could handle.

"One of the things that makes my cards special is that they are all hand sparkled. My husband is a dentist, so I sparkled the cards with his dental tools. It was a joke; I would call Andrew and say, 'Bring home more dental tools, we have another order!' The orders were coming in and then *Modern Bride* wanted to use them for their own stationery, and they ordered a thousand cards. I was sooo pregnant. I had my legs up. I was hand sparkling and hand packing all of the orders. It was crazy."

Bonnie's stationery has appeared in *O* (the Oprah magazine), *Modern Bride*, *New York* magazine, and *Better Homes & Gardens Decorating*.

Just a couple of years after designing her first invitation, Bonnie's stationery is now being sold in more than 700 stores around the world.

"I never imagined it would be this big this quickly. I really thought it was something that would keep me busy and close to home. But now as this grows I realize that I would really love to create my own brand."

Being a mom who works from home, Bonnie admits that she has changed the way in which she works.

"I always thought of myself as extremely efficient and organized when I worked in the city, but having children brings a whole new level to the phrase 'multitasking.' I used to spend long nights working on 'urgent' projects, but now I'm limited to my babysitter's schedule, and I don't have the luxury of endless evenings to finish projects. But surprisingly, I'm almost able to do the same amount of work in much less time. Also, I used to have numerous to-do lists on my computer and around my desk. Now when I think about a task, I try to conquer it immediately because if I decide to put it off for a few minutes, I never know what will happen. My child may wake up from his nap, or I may have to run out. Basically when I have quiet time to do work, I value every minute and make sure I get things done."

Interestingly, Bonnie's children are also now influencing the direction of her company. When she started her line of stationery, high-end weddings were her main focus, but today, her largest product selection, "Expecting in Style," can be found at Pea in the Pod and Mimi Maternity. Her best-selling items are fashionable "To-Do" lists for moms on the go, and maternity stationery and invitations are now the company's main focus.

"Now that my older son, Benjamin, is starting to write, my mind is racing with ideas for stationery for young boys," Bonnie says. "My sons and my new life as a mommy absolutely inspires me in my business."

Chapter 7

Making It Work for You

Life Goes in Cycles

If Hillary Clinton's infamous collegiate look of Coke-bottle glasses, unplucked brows, and stringy hair proudly defied good grooming and epitomized the trailblazing, liberated woman on the forefront of the feminist revolution, then Barbara Johnson represented the other woman on campus—the girl blissfully oblivious to the burgeoning battle cry who was perfectly happy wearing curlers and lipstick and getting pinned before graduation.

"It was still a time when girls went to college to get their MRS degrees and have babies," Barbara, a tall, wiry woman who looks a decade younger than her 58 years, says. "That's what most of us did."

If the goal of college was to snag a man, Barbara graduated with high honors. By her senior year she was married and pregnant with her first daughter. A couple of years later, she would have another baby. So while Hillary Clinton was breaking barriers and studying contracts at Yale Law School, Barbara was setting Jell-O molds and tending to her young family. But Barbara always saw herself in the workforce one day, and she knew she wanted to teach once her children were older. So when her daughters started school, she too went back to school part-time at a Midwestern community college to begin her long-awaited master's degree.

"When I started my program, I was surrounded by people who were all getting their PhDs, so I thought, well, I shouldn't stop at a master's; I'm quite capable of getting a PhD as well."

Soon after Barbara started graduate school, her marriage began to unravel. When she and her husband divorced in the mid-1970s, she was left on her own, simultaneously working toward a degree, single-handedly caring for her young children, and trying to get her life back on track.

"We ate a lot of macaroni and cheese in those days," she says with a laugh. "I remember when my car broke down, I couldn't afford to get it fixed, so for a month I had to ride my bike to class. I also remember how badly my daughters wanted those Lacoste alligator shirts that were popular then. But they were too expensive, so we would shop at JC Penney and get the knock-off ones. It's amazing that after all of these years those are the images that stand out."

It took eight years, but Barbara completed her PhD in history. At that time, she was recently remarried and eager to have more children with her new husband, who had no kids of his own. But now at 38 years old, armed with her degree and ready to take on a permanent teaching job, she was afraid of how pregnancy could affect her newly established career goals.

"I thought there was a prejudice that if I were pregnant, I would not get a full-time position. I didn't want to take the risk of getting pregnant because I knew positions in my field were opening up. But it was the classic 'the clock is ticking.' I had recovered from complications from an IUD infection, and I was told I could probably get pregnant again. But there was a sense that I had lost the good years, and now I was also really afraid of the prejudice of pregnancy."

Barbara decided that the most practical decision was to delay trying to conceive and instead get a full-time teaching job. But the desire to have more children never dimmed. It took nearly six years to get pregnant, and at 45 years old, and again at 48, Barbara defied the fertility odds and gave birth to two more girls. Today Barbara is a full-time history professor at a prestigious university on the West Coast. She intentionally put herself on a non-tenure track because she felt that pace would be better suited to raising a family.

"If anyone had said to me, you're going to move to the West Coast and work full time and have two more children, I would have never believed it. But we were so delighted when we found out that we could have kids it never crossed my mind that I wouldn't return to work and that I would be back home."

When Barbara gave birth the first time, Hillary Clinton was a junior in college. When she gave birth to her youngest daughter, Hillary was the first lady of the United States. Her experiences of motherhood have literally spanned two generations and have mirrored the times. In the early 1970s she happily stayed home with her girls, but when her youngest daughter was born in 1994, Barbara was back at work within weeks.

"I'm more relaxed and into having them, and I feel so blessed for having them," Barbara says. "And being older, you are so aware of how quickly everything happens; that's why it's so precious even when you're feeling exhausted."

Barbara's remarkably spaced fertile years have given her perspective. As a mother now to both a fifth and seventh grader, she is part of the swelling ranks of those older moms who are joining the PTA at the same time they are joining the AARP. Barbara's female students are understandably fascinated with her varied experiences and often seek advice when it comes to their own personal choices.

"I tell them you certainly can have a career and have a family, but I also tell them that life is very long and that's one of its virtues. I would think about trying to get into a career where you have flexibility and where you can take time off and then get back in or perhaps find something where you can you do part-time work so you can stay mentally alert."

Along with being the mom of two preteen daughters, Barbara is also a grandmother of three. Her oldest daughters recently started families of their own. Her daughter Lynn, an English professor at a university in the Northwest, is working part-time. Her daughter Jennifer left her career as a network news TV show producer to stay home with her son because she says her job combined with a brutal three-hour roundtrip commute to New York City was simply impossible to do.

"I'm very sympathetic to what my older daughters are both doing because I stayed home until they went to school, and I think the time when children are little is so precious," Barbara says. "I know with Lynn, who's teaching, that she can sort of find a balance between teaching and being a mother. You can do this if you're not working on a tenure track. In terms of Jennifer, I think she's doing the right thing to stay home but I just worry about her trying to get back into a television career. She stepped away from a big career she loved, but it's a gamble I really respect. My sister left her career to stay home, and when she went back, she did an entire career change. So who knows, Jennifer may also do something entirely different when her children are older."

Not My Mother's Life

A mother's life serves as a map for her daughter. She uses it as a guide to navigate her own course, sometimes following its path, other times avoiding its pitfalls. And for Barbara's daughter, Jennifer, who views her own mother's experiences through the naturally complicated perspective of the mother-daughter relationship, her road of choice is heading in the opposite direction of her mom's current path. Even though Jennifer appreciates and respects her mother's professional achievements, she sees the pressures of "trying to have it all" and isn't comfortable with what she sees.

"I think my mom is trying to take on so much between her job responsibilities and my sisters' activities; I constantly tell her to slow down. I worry about the impact of stress on her health, and often the pace at which she leads her life, and even her priorities sometimes. I have learned so much from her, but we are quite different and I think that has a lot to do with our ages when we got married.

"I married almost ten years later than she did and had already established a career and tired of it; I was ready for a break. I looked around the office and didn't want to be one of those people in senior positions doing the kind of work I was doing for the rest of my life. I'd done my share of traveling and had been living independently much longer than my mom did before she got married and had children. Before I got married, work was the focus of my life. But now family and friends are the center of my world, and that feels great. I often feel my mom spreads herself too thin, trying to do it all. I'm far more 'traditional' a wife and mother than my mom is or ever was . . . and I must admit, I missed that growing up."

This is the other side of the working mom story. Those kids of the first generation to let themselves into empty houses and plop down in front of the TV until a babysitter or their parents came home often say they admire their mothers for working but don't want to duplicate their lives. And so some are turning toward tradition, saying they want to stay home, at least temporarily.

As Jennifer puts it: "I don't see myself as a permanent Stay-at-Home mom, because I'd probably be bored out of my mind once my kids are in school. I also like working and contributing financially. That work ethic comes from both parents, but certainly my mom has set an example. I'll probably pursue something totally different—not go back into what I was doing before—but I have no idea what yet. For now, I believe I'm doing a better job than anyone else could do. It's the most rewarding and demanding thing I've ever done. When it comes down to it, my child means so much more than any news story I ever worked on."

Jennifer could be the poster girl for what *The New York Times* in October 2003 coined the "Opt-Out Revolution," a so-called backlash to the "Have It All Generation." Like Jennifer, these 30- and 40-something career women are "stepping out" or "opting out" of the workforce to take a mid-career sabbatical in the name of motherhood. Opting out, of course, is the luxury that most women can't afford to make, yet it's the red-hot topic that spawns passionate debate and endless conversation from those who are deemed to have some "choice" about working. To work or not to work, this is the question that seems to cause a whole host of Gen X women tremendous angst. What's happening? Are women truly being seduced by tradition and heading home like Jennifer, or is the so-called choice to stay home really not a choice at all?

Jane Buckingham is the founder and president of Youth Intelligence, a market research, consulting, and trend forecasting company that focuses on Gen X and Gen Y, and she's also a contributing editor at *Cosmopolitan* magazine. She has polled more than a thousand women about their thoughts on work, marriage, and motherhood and says she's not surprised women today are feeling conflicted.

"I think Gen X women really feel misled. I think we thought that we were going to be these Superwomen who have these great jobs and great families and we could do it better than everybody else could, and suddenly we got there and said, 'You know what, our mothers worked and they didn't seem happy, and our grandmothers didn't work and they felt pressure, so what the heck are we supposed to do?' I think Gen X is feeling really conflicted, and that's why you've got this core group of women who just don't know what to do. They are trying to work and take their kids to preschool and trying to juggle it all, and I think that the younger generation is sort of looking at us and saying, 'Okay, forget it. It's impossible.' I think you also see this in Gen X too; you see a lot of women who say, 'It's not worth it. I would much rather be a successful mom than a mediocre vice president at the widget company.'

"This was the generation who was bred to believe that you're the best, you're the brightest, you will change the world, and then they are at work Xeroxing or doing other meaningless work that doesn't feel so good. So they would rather be at home where there is some fulfillment even if it's only temporary."

Taking Time Off

Jessica Spira, 34, shakes her wet, wavy, blazing red hair and escorts me into her New York City apartment to talk. She apologizes for still being damp and smelling like leave-in conditioner. It's 3:00 P.M., her kids are napping, and it's the first time she's had all day to shower. She's feeling much better now that she's clean.

Jessica never exactly planned on staying home after having kids. As she describes it, it could have gone either way, but while she was on maternity leave terrorists attacked the World Trade Center, and everything changed. As the smoke engulfed downtown Manhattan and Americans painfully accepted a new national vulnerability, Jessica reassessed her own priorities and decided she wouldn't return to work; she would stay home with her then-four-month-old son Zachary. But three years later, as the poignancy of 9/11 recedes and life continues as usual, Jessica's resolve to be home has been replaced by ambivalence. That's because Jessica truly relished her career, first in publishing, and then working in the marketing and sales side of the financial media world. Like most professional women, Jessica's career helped shape her identity, and her six-figure paycheck gave her financial freedom and confidence. In fact, confidence was something Jessica never lacked. She graduated at the top of her high school class in Cleveland, Ohio, and after majoring in history at Barnard College in New York City, Jessica spent two years abroad teaching English in a rural Japanese village.

Ask Jessica if she is happy at home full time, and she'll say yes. But dig a little deeper, and you'll discover a raw layer of anxiety and angst. It's easy to ignore those feelings when she hangs out with her tribe of other at-home moms who are all sharing in the same daily rituals as she. But Jessica's insecurity creeps to the surface when she runs into old classmates who are decked for work, racing to the subway for a business meeting, and she's sporting play clothes pushing her double stroller down Broadway to buy diapers. She also gets a bit depressed when she receives her alumni magazine and learns about the seemingly more rich lives her old friends are leading.

"I think what I'm doing by being home is good for my kids. And I feel really fortunate and enjoy spending so much time with them. But a few weeks ago I was reading about a former high school classmate of mine, someone who didn't do as well academically and whom I didn't think much of, and she's now a radiologist in Atlanta with three kids and her own practice. That's when I think to myself, why am I not doing more with my life? And that's when I feel a little insecure."

Now that her son is starting preschool, Jessica has also realized that the community of at-home moms is shifting. Her mommy and kids play group, while still cohesive and an essential part of her support system, is splitting up for school. Jessica says she was surprised when the class list arrived, and she discovered that she was the only Stay-at-Home mother in Zachary's class. On a practical level, she was disappointed that the other moms wouldn't be home to readily become her new friends, and on a personal level it pinched at the tender nerve that is her anxiety about not working outside the home.

For a while Jessica was doing some part-time freelance work, and it boosted her self-esteem to be contributing to the household income and staying professionally connected. But now with another new baby at home, she has no time or energy for that.

Jessica ruminates regularly about what she will do next—whether it's going to graduate school or switching careers entirely. She also thinks about how she'll pitch herself to prospective employers when the time comes. But she's clear that she wants to wait until her children are older before she commits to another career again.

"I'm confident that if I want to do something, I'll somehow be able to do it. I have a dozen different interests, and I'd be happy doing lots of things. But I do worry about how I'm going to get back in."

Off Ramps and On Ramps

According to economist and author Sylvia Ann Hewlett, Jessica has good reason to worry. In concert with about two dozen private sector companies and law firms, including Ernst and Young, Unilever, GE, and Johnson & Johnson, Hewlett has launched a task force to investigate the "Hidden Brain Drain" of female talent happening in corporate America today. She is working with these companies to try to figure out ways to retain their female employees over a lifespan. Her research shows that many women do opt out primarily because of the increasingly long work week, which actually make it less possible these days to combine family and work than was true even ten years ago. But Hewlett says two-thirds of these women want to get back in full time after they've taken five years off. Her research shows that five years is apparently the "magical number" many women want to stay home.

"By that stage they are 37 or 41 years old, and there are all types of productive decades that are possible, and I think companies understand that life isn't over at 37."[1]

Hewlett feels that the problem with all of the talk of the so-called "Opt-Out Revolution" of women happily leaving the workforce in droves is that it represents a very static portrayal of a very select group of women.

"Those women who are so very passionate about their new priorities as moms, a little way down the road they will be passionately trying to get back in."

And getting back in is harder than most women thought it would be. But Hewlett believes women can protect themselves in various ways.

"Two things I'm beginning to learn are that if you can find a slow lane as opposed to getting off-ramped completely, that's probably good. It's much easier to accelerate into a faster lane than to reattach from nowhere. So slow lanes are good. I absolutely understand that a lot of folks really can't handle fifty-five-hour weeks and two small children because that is very difficult. So for those who can't find slow lanes and really need to take some time out, absolutely do it. Kids are really important, and those early years are extraordinarily powerful in lots of ways we now understand, and we have research to prove it.

"But I think you have to be very careful. I think you absolutely should arm yourself with some knowledge as to which companies might welcome your energies down the road and plan on keeping your networks very alive, and if there's some way you could do some significant volunteer work or activism, then you should find something with some leadership potential. Don't volunteer in five different contexts which involve licking envelopes; this is not what you should be doing. Try and do something that will enhance or keep your network alive because that is very powerful in terms of enabling you to get back in," Hewlett says.

My research has also found that many at-home moms are having a hard time reestablishing themselves, especially if they have taken many years out of the workforce. And now they regret it. Julie Robinson, 40, a former accountant with just a hint of a melodic Jamaican accent, tells me she's just finished her daily Monster.com job search and feels defeated. Twelve years ago, Julie decided to leave her job at one of the Big Four accounting firms to stay home with her new baby largely because she believed she couldn't find adequate childcare.

"It was at that time when the media was doing all of those exposés on abusive nannies beating kids over the head with spoons. I thought to myself, I just don't want to risk leaving my son with anyone. I felt like I couldn't find anyone good enough."

Two years later Julie had her second son, and when he started kindergarten, she says she was ready to resume her career—that is, until she discovered she was pregnant again. Her kids are now 12, 10, and 5 years old, and Julie says when she looks back at her choices, she has regrets.

"I think maybe I could've found a better balance instead of giving up my career entirely to be a Stay-at-Home mom. I feel like I did well in school, I'm a CPA, I did the Big Four thing to be what, to end up being a domestic? I hate to put it that way, but sometimes I see it like that. And now I see college coming down the road for my sons, and I worry about our financial position because I stopped working."

Opting In

"Fifteen years ago I thought I would be famous," Allison Busch tells me in a dead-on tone that I'm not sure is joking or serious. But she's serious. Allison, 35, a laid-back brunette with a self-deprecating sense of humor, was the kind of girl who always dreamed big. She won class president from elementary to high school and was voted Most Likely to Succeed. Her senior year, she gave her high school commencement speech to a roaring crowd of 2,000 people, where she dramatically thrust out her arm and declared, "We're the generation that can have it all!"

After graduating from college, Allison went to work in Washington, D.C., and became an organizer for the National Organization for Women (NOW). She led grassroots organizing around the country, and as a public face often representing NOW, she made frequent TV appearances. Today, Allison is an attorney who specializes in elder law at a small boutique firm in New York City. She descends from a long dynasty of attorneys; she is number thirty-four and the first female in the family chain. Allison is also the mother of a 3-year-old boy and a 6-month-old girl. Although today she's not a household name, except, of course, within her own home, Allison swears she's fine without the fame she once expected.

Juggling two kids and a job where she works three days a week is enough for now.

"People look at me longingly when I tell them I'm a lawyer who works three days a week," Allison says while home on maternity leave with her second child. "I know I have an amazing arrangement, and I'm really happy to have this flexibility and to be working."

As I write this chapter, a few months have passed since I first spoke to Allison about her dreamy, part-time schedule. She's now been back to work for about two months and shoots me a surprise email in the middle of the day saying she's terribly sorry, but she doesn't think she fits into my book anymore. She writes that she's quitting her law firm—just as soon as she can get the courage to go do it.

What's happened? Well, a bunch of things, she tells me when I call her. A few weeks before having her second child, Allison moved from New York City to the suburbs. Instead of the twenty-minute subway ride she used to have to work, she now faces a two-hour commute each day. With her baby not yet sleeping through the night, Allison's feeling dangerously exhausted, bordering on psychotic. She's so tense and tired at work that she's finding it tough to make her billable hours. She's stressed out because preschool has started for her older child and her nanny doesn't drive. The driver who Allison hired fell through at the last minute, on top of which her current nanny just announced that she's pregnant and not only can't she drive, but she can't do the fifteen-minute walk to and from school either. It's the combination of factors that has put Allison over the edge. Perhaps if she weren't so drained she could handle the stress at work better or have the energy to hunt for a new nanny. But the whole package together just isn't working, and Allison, a woman who says she doesn't like change, is ready for a huge one.

"I really think a working mother's life is like building and maintaining a house of cards. One weak card, like a sick nanny, and it still can be maintained as long as the rest is strong. Pull another card out, whether its bad childcare, a sick kid, exhaustion from kids keeping you up at night, or too much stress at work, and unless there's some serious intervention, like a husband who can be near home, or grandparents who can step in, the whole house will fall all at once, and it's hard to pick up the pieces. How some women hold it together even under the most pressured of circumstances is admirable, but that can be a little intimidating for those of us who can only take so much sleep deprivation and stress," Allison says.

"I really feel like a failure. But I just feel like I couldn't hold it together anymore, and I was starting a downward spiral. I think a lot has to do with exhaustion. But after five years of my firm loving me, I almost want to cut the tie before things get worse and they say, 'Well she was great until she had two kids.'"

Allison has decided that the best course of action for her is to work for herself from home. She thinks with the help of her uncle, an attorney nearby, she can cobble together a list of clients and make as much money as she is making at her firm while also having greater flexibility over her life. However, quitting the firm where she's been practicing for five years is a sudden announcement from a woman who admits mixing up her routine makes her nervous. But she feels she has no other choice. What she's doing now simply isn't working.

"I feel like I have to quit. But does that mean I'm opting out? I'm not comfortable with the idea of quitting," she says.

Allison is not opting out, she's opting to stay in, but she has to figure something out for herself and her family that makes sense. With her childcare situation unsettled and inadequate, she's feeling pressure to go home. On top of which, she simply wasn't making enough money to offset the stress on her life. In fact, after taxes and childcare costs, she's only netting $100 a week. She also says she's no longer feeling particularly jazzed about her job.

What Allison is experiencing is what millions of other mothers face at the intersection of career and motherhood. The house of cards Allison describes is a precarious structure. A sturdy foundation is based on great childcare, happy parents, and healthy kids. But Allison is choosing to do what Sylvia Hewlett recommends and that is to stay in the game as best you can even if that means slowing down.

A few weeks later Allison calls to tell me that she has given her firm notice. It was emotional. She felt like she had let herself down. But then on the train to work later that week she met a couple taking their 2-year-old to daycare. They started talking and Allison told them about her plans to open up her own practice. They told Allison they wanted to be her first clients and have even called to set up an appointment to meet.

"It pays to be friendly on the train," Allison happily tells me, sounding much more confident and less angst-ridden with her decision.

For Allison, as for many moms, she found that the fragile net holding it all together can easily be frayed. But she's figuring out a way to keep the net intact on her own terms. There are many times, however, when even our best-laid plans are out of our control, and life wreaks havoc in unexpected ways. And it's then, I've found, that women reach deep inside and rally in ways they never thought imaginable, and in turn they emerge changed and even stronger than before.

A Stitch in Time

It's a little breezy but otherwise the perfect sunny, summer day for a game of tennis in Westport, Connecticut, and that's just what Gayle Greenberger has been doing for the past hour. Gayle, 33, is a perpetually put-together woman with an electric energy and a soulful center. She is warm and engaged and has the rare gift, when lost in conversation, of making you feel like you're the only person in the world. She's also one of those casually confident women who has the courage to chop off her hair on a whim and never regret it.

Today she's on a typically tight schedule because in an hour she has to pick up her son from school, take him to therapy, and then race home to finish the dozen or so scarves she's hand knitting for a store in Connecticut. Recently Gayle and her sister Heather created La Folie, a small knitting business making chic hats, scarves, and accessories for high-end boutiques. Gayle says that since starting her business nine months ago, she is now straddling two worlds between Stay-at-Home mom and Stay-at-Work mom. The entrepreneurial part of her is a recent development, a conscious desire to fill an emptiness that motherhood alone did not satisfy.

Gayle grew up believing in white knights and Happily Ever After. After all, that's the fairy tale she saw her mother leading. Raised in a neotraditional family in an idyllic New Jersey suburb where her mother stayed home and her father, a prominent OB/GYN and the centrifugal force of her universe, pushed his daughters to conquer the world, Gayle says there was pressure "to not just have a job but to have a profession." Academically, Gayle did not disappoint. She excelled in high school and was easily accepted into a doctoral program in psychology before graduating from Northwestern University. But even before graduating, Gayle felt conflicted about what she really wanted out of her life.

"There was a real need to wow and please myself and my parents and be something big," Gayle says. "But truthfully I also think I was trying to stall having to get a job because secretly I never thought I wanted to work. And even though I was going for the PhD, I never thought of myself as a breadwinner. My quest was to land the guy to support me. That's what my mom did, and I saw a career as a bonus, not a necessity. But as I got closer to finishing my PhD program, my anxiety levels were rising. I put off getting an internship. I kept stalling. I started putting my efforts into getting married and then I *got* married. And so I delayed my internship again. And then I put my energy into getting pregnant. I replaced my career drive with my maternal drive and then gave myself an out when the fertility issues began."

A couple years after marrying, Gayle and her husband Harris tried to start a family. She imagined it would take a few months and then she would invite her parents and in-laws over for a fabulous dinner and announce in some dramatic, shock-inducing way, "We're pregnant!" There would be hugging and kissing and tears of joy, and her family would be falling over themselves with excitement as they toasted their expectant children. She played out this scenario dozens of times in her head and dreamed of that *Father of the Bride Part 2* kind of moment. But after six months when she wasn't pregnant, Gayle met with an infertility specialist who discovered some massive medical issues that were preventing her from conceiving. Nearly two years after her first attempt to conceive, and after major fertility intervention, Gayle was finally pregnant—with twins.

From the get-go, having two babies was more intense and exhausting than she ever anticipated. Her feelings about motherhood swung between elation and depression, often landing somewhere in that vast murky gray area in between. She had always envisioned motherhood as providing the ultimate satisfaction and was troubled when somehow her lifelong dream left her feeling strangely unsettled. But as her babies graduated from infancy to toddlerhood and the rhythm of life eased, Gayle picked up her doctoral work and started researching her long-delayed dissertation. The work was as much to feed her brain as to reassure her own ego that she was more than just a mother; she was still a doctoral candidate.

It seemed that Gayle's life was finally settling down, and she looked forward to the intellectual stimulation that finishing her PhD would give her. On a trip home from the beach one day during that period, Gayle looked in her rearview mirror as her two children slept and whispered to Harris that she couldn't imagine a more beautiful life. But something had been nagging at Gayle. She had shoved it to the back of her mind because her gut churned whenever she thought about it. A few weeks earlier she had her monthly check-in with her baby bible, *What to Expect the First Year*, and realized that her son had missed some major milestones. She had discussed her concerns with Harris and her mother, both of whom told her she was crazy and shouldn't worry; she would be seeing the pediatrician soon for the twins' one-year visit, and everything would be fine.

But two days after that blissful ride home from the beach, Gayle saw their doctor, who confirmed that there could be a serious problem with her son. He told her to contact the state's Birth to Three Program that evaluates and provides services to infants and toddlers with special needs.

"I expected the doctor to say, 'Gayle, don't worry about it. He's a boy, he's a twin, he'll catch up; it's nothing.' But instead he believed something was wrong. That day I called Birth to Three. They told me I'd have to wait two weeks for an evaluation. I insisted I needed someone immediately. They came two days later and evaluated Levi. I was defensive and in denial, and I didn't want to believe what they told me. So the next day I rushed Levi into New York City for a private evaluation. After hearing the developmental pediatrician's news, I went home and sobbed. I didn't get out of my pajamas for five days. I didn't leave the house. I just wept and felt sorry for myself. And then on the sixth day, I woke up and got on the phone with more therapists and begged for help and services."

Now nearly 3½-years-old, Levi has the official diagnosis of PDD or per-vasive developmental disorder—a disorder that in recent years some be-lieve has bizarrely taken on almost epidemic proportions in the United States. PDD is on the mild end of the autism spectrum, and a child's ul-timate fate, experts say, can be influenced by the quality and quantity of early intervention. Since that doctor's visit three years ago, Gayle has thrown her energy into fiercely advocating for her son—flooding him with the best services available, all the while also taking care of her daughter Raya, who does not have the disorder.

"I really feel like I'm pioneering Levi's life, fighting for his every sec-ond. I spend my days coordinating materials for him and for his thera-pists and teachers. I feel like the CEO of Levi. I want feedback. I demand results. I want to know what's happening at all times. I can't stand by; I have to be moving forward. I can't deny what's going on al-though I'm tempted to deny it because I would be happier if I were in denial. But every day I pull back from that denial. Ninety percent of my day, I do stuff for Levi. At his school, the teachers say they've never seen parents like Harris and me. I know I am a thorn in their side and they sometimes hate me, but I don't care. I never want to look back and think I could've done more for him."

Gayle officially gave up on her dissertation and degree about a year ago when she "timed out" of her program at Fordham University. The total drain of time and energy required to get Levi thirty-five hours worth of therapy a week and also tend to her daughter made it impossible for her to continue.

"Every time I turn my address book to the "F" pages and I see the Fordham numbers, I get sick to my stomach. I have such anxiety about not finishing. I just feel like I needed the degree to feel whole, to feel ac-complished. So there is a tremendous loss now, a loss of self-worth and a loss of self-esteem, and that void is profound."

At first glance, Gayle may seem like an anachronism, a throwback to Barbara Johnson's era. She thought she was the type who wouldn't want to work after having kids. But for Gayle, life has thrown her a cruel curve ball, one that requires her not just to be a mom but to be a mom of superhuman proportions, one who must practically lose herself to save her son. But what's interesting for Gayle is that in becoming Supermom, she's discovered her own need for a professional self.

The Happily Ever After picture that Gayle had always imagined has blurred into an abstraction that's difficult for her to articulate. In her affluent Connecticut town, fifty miles northeast of New York City where most mommies neither work nor take care of their children full time, but rather have nannies to help ease the monotony of childcare, Gayle usually doesn't discuss her complicated and heartbreaking story. Few women know of her dashed plans to become a psychologist, and few understand her inner angst to do more than merely join the morning tennis match or kaffeeklatsches after preschool drop off. Even though Gayle always thought she wanted to be a mother and a career was simply a sidebar—a good cocktail introduction and a fancy title next to her name—she now grapples with the missed chance of a professional identity.

"I guess in the deep recesses of my brain I always thought I was going to be big; it's only in not feeling big that I realize how badly I wanted to be big at something. And I think the parts of me that thought I could just be a mom seemed okay, but once I was just a mom it didn't seem okay any more. I do feel good when I see the progress Levi is making, and I know that I laid that foundation for him. But I also know that I need something for me too, something for my own self-worth. It's funny because I always sort of envisioned myself as a Stay-at-Home mom who plays tennis and does lunch. Of course in caring for Levi I know I do more than that now, but it's in tasting that world when I realize that kind of life doesn't feel good to me. I'm not satisfied with only that."

Gayle says her knitting business is giving her the self-esteem and purpose she's been missing. It's helping nourish the void that has been empty since she left her doctoral program. But on the other hand, she feels embarrassed and sometimes defensive because "it's only knitting."

"The struggle that I have is that I feel like I should and could be doing more with my life. I feel like I'm not fulfilling my potential. It's like I feel I slipped down a notch."

Sex and the City Revised

Heather Borden Hervé was living Carrie Bradshaw's *Sex and the City* life years before the TV character ever tripped over her first pair of Manolos. Heather is the other half of La Folie, the knitting business that she and her sister Gayle Greenberger own. After Heather graduated from Cornell, where she was a Cornell National Scholar, she held a series of glamorous jobs that at first blush would make any *InStyle* magazine devotee envious. She made her New York City debut in public relations at one of the world's largest agencies and then moved into magazine publicity before landing a high-profile segment producing job at *Entertainment Tonight*.

Heather was hip, happening, and oh so New York. She always carried the perfect handbag and wore the latest hairstyle. A striking woman, with a je ne sais quoi sparkle, she literally lived in that coveted HBO fantasy world where attending movie premieres, parties, and fashion shows and sitting at VIP tables at nightclubs were her regular diet. She even had her own Mr. Big experiences, dating some of the most successful, single, eligible men New York City had to offer, including NBC's *Today* co-anchor Matt Lauer and comedian and talk show host Jon Stewart. But the seemingly glamorous world of entertainment news took its toll. At 29 years old, stressed out and exhausted, Heather knew she needed to make a change.

"I had developed a strange eye twitch," Heather says. "I saw a doctor who didn't know what it was, and then I went on vacation to Club Med and it suddenly disappeared. But I got back on a Saturday night, and Sunday morning I popped in the VCR tape of the week's worth of *ET* shows I had missed while I was away. The first show started, the theme music began, and all of a sudden my eye started to twitch—just from the music. In that moment it became very clear to me that there were more important things in life than risking bodily injury and sickness. I know it was just an eye twitch, but still it was a sign of stress and anxiety and that I needed to make some sort of change."

If Heather were like one of the celebrities she covered for *Entertainment Tonight*, she probably would have checked herself into an Arizona spa for a few months to decompress. Instead, she decided she needed a major career change. Having just come back from Club Med where the eye twitch had temporarily disappeared, she figured if Club Med was the cure, than maybe she should work there.

As an *ET* producer whose contract was up, Heather was on the cusp of negotiating a new deal for nearly $100,000 a year; instead she fled to Florida for a gig that paid $540 a month. Her parents were aghast; upon hearing the news, her mother had a nosebleed. But Heather left New York behind and happily settled into a routine first at Club Med in Florida and then in the Bahamas, where she did everything from check guests in to perform in the resort's musicals, sporting feathered head-dresses and sequined bikinis.

While at Club Med, Heather fell in love with a handsome French man who also worked at the resort. They married and moved to Chicago. Having left the beach life behind, Heather got another job in TV production. Before she knew it, she had returned to the grind that had made her leave TV in the first place. Not long after Heather became a mother—her son Maden is now 2—she again began reevaluating her life. Her husband was working full time and going to business school at night, leaving Heather with full childcare and house responsibilities after her own long, stressful day at work. She was grocery shopping at 11:00 P.M., had little time for her son, on top of which she was working in an environment that she describes as borderline hostile when it came to respecting one's time for family. So when Maden was 1 year old, Heather quit her job.

"It was a financial sacrifice to stop working, but I felt I really needed to. It just wasn't at all working for me and my family."

After a few months of being home, Heather got restless. She was craving a creative outlet in which to throw her energy. She and her sister Gayle began knitting scarves and selling them at holiday shows in Connecticut when Heather would visit. The scarves were an instant hit, and voilà, La Folie was born.

"I think my grandmother must be rolling in her grave to think that my sister and I are knitting. She was a real hard-core businesswoman and wanted both of us to have serious careers. I think she would be horrified," Heather says.

A former college scholar, PR maven, and TV producer, Heather was on a fast track, leading a lightning-speed life. With La Folie as her creative outlet, she's now moving at a different, lighter pace. In both large and small ways, the marked change has her grappling with her identity just as much as her sister wrestles with hers.

"I was telling my therapist that shoe shopping is very anxiety ridden for me these days. I was addicted to shoes. I used to wear Manolo Blahniks. I once spent $400 at a charity auction for a pair of boots. So now I can't go into a shoe store without panicking. First of all I'm not making enough money to afford Manolos anymore, and what kind of mommy shoes am I going to buy anyway? I'm not wearing heels to the playground."

Heather also dreads having to define exactly who and what she is these days. She cringes every time she has to fill in the "occupation" spot on school and medical forms.

"What am I? I'm a mother, yes, but I feel like I'm more than that. So am I now an accessories business owner? I'm really never sure what to write. Nothing seems to feel completely appropriate."

For many women of our generation who graduated from school and came charging out of the gates galloping toward a promising future, the letdown of motherhood and only motherhood can be hard to swallow. Like Heather, many moms who have chosen the at-home route soon start itching for something more, another area in which to engage. For Heather, she is now eager to grow her new business and sees La Folie as yet another chapter in her life.

"Sometimes I wonder how my life would be different if instead of leaving *ET* permanently, I had just taken a few months off. One night I was cleaning my toilets, and I looked up and saw Jon Stewart hosting the Emmys, and I thought, wow, that could have been my life. In comparison, life now is hardly glamorous. The only parties I go to are the birthday parties of Maden's friends. I don't work out. I haven't seen more than five movies this year. But then I look at Maden and realize that old life doesn't even seem to come close. Even with the real stresses of today, of paying bills, making a mortgage, and caring for my son, when I compare that to the fact that the most significant and stressful thing used to be whether or not I was going to get the 'exclusive interview' with Howard

Stern or Caroline Bessette Kennedy's hair colorist, it all becomes crystal clear how worth it my decision was."

Gayle and Heather, two sisters who started from two very different places with vastly divergent professional goals and expectations for themselves, now want the same thing. Even though they are both struggling with a sense that they could or should be doing something perhaps more significant than knitting, they are thrilled to have ownership of a young business and control over their own lives.

"Who knows where this could go?" Heather says enthusiastically. "We're just starting to figure it all out."

○ ⁰ ○

Chapter 8

○ ○ ○
 ○

Finding the Holy Grail

What Moms Really Want

*O*n *a dreary fall afternoon,* perched thirty stories above Times Square, in the midst of the neon heart of America, 150 women are milling about helping themselves to a buffet lunch of pasta, broiled fish, and mesclun greens.

From a whole host of different industries, these women mingle throughout the room; they sport two name tags, one with their name and occupation on it and another with their kids' names and ages. They've turned out for the annual fall luncheon of Executive Moms, the New York City–based organization for professional working mothers. On the agenda today: "How to Be a Class Mom from the Office."

The moms have come to hear award-winning journalist Deborah Norville—the perky blonde who has been the longtime host of *Inside Edition*, and mother of three—moderate a discussion with a panel of experts about how they can stay involved in their child's classroom and participate in school even while they work.

"My day started with this," Deborah begins, waving her BlackBerry in front of us, "The CrackBerry, as my husband calls it. My first email came at 7:47 A.M. from the teacher," says Deborah, starting to read from her BlackBerry: 'Your son and I are getting to know each other and like each other. I think. At least that's the case from my side. The only surprise is his dismal performance in Latin. He seems to have forgotten what he knew over the summer . . . ' and it goes on."

"I want to go uptown and commit murder," Deborah says dryly, unmasking another side to her sunny, public persona that sounds defiantly more Mama-on-the-Warpath than Girl-Next-Door.

"Ladies, it's not easy because we feel responsible for everything," she continues. "We're kind of like the Pigpen of the working world. Remember Charlie Brown's Pigpen character and how the dirt just glommed on to him? Guilt just gloms on to us. I feel guilty about my son's dismal performance in Latin. He should have remembered everything because I should have been quizzing him all summer. But the fact is I didn't and as moms we *can't* do everything. But what we *can do* is find ways to integrate the family responsibilities that are so important and the work responsibilities which are equally important not only to our financial livelihood but to our own personal sense of self and position in this world."

Deborah is preaching to the choir. What she is suggesting cuts to the core of the ongoing struggle Stay-at-Work mothers have, integrating all of our worlds: self, family, children, and career. But the topic today is school. And with many polls showing education as one of the top concerns of parents today, it's perhaps no wonder why so many moms have turned out en masse for this lunch, even those whose children are too young for school.

"Don't do behind-the-scenes fundraiser types of volunteering," warns one of the panel members. "Spend your time in the classroom where your child can see you. Come in and read a book, help with a project. Be visible."

Good advice, I think, making a mental note to immediately take myself off of the holiday fundraising committee at my son's preschool and offer to come in and read a story instead.

Shuffling around the room before the lunch begins, I meet two attorneys, friends from the same firm who tell me that they've never been to an Executive Mom event but they're here because they're eager for a network of other working moms with whom to bond. Sharon Mercer, whose generous dose of freckles makes her look much younger than her 37 years, is a partner in a medium-sized employment law firm. She has a 3-year-old and an 18-month-old and routinely works eleven-hour days. Her husband, a former professional chef, stays home with the kids and takes care of all of the cooking and some of the housework. Sharon fits a relatively new pattern of female breadwinners whose husbands stay home. In fact, according to the U.S. Census Bureau's March 2002 Current Population Survey, among two-parent households, 189,000 children were cared for by Stay-at-Home dads. Although the figure is small compared to Stay-at-Home moms, who care for 11 million children, the number of Stay-at-Home dads has risen 18 percent since 1994. (The number of children living with Stay-at-Home moms has risen 13 percent.) It's an arrangement that often makes sense, and for Sharon it alleviates some of the guilt knowing that her children's father and not a nanny or daycare is their primary caretaker. But when I ask Sharon if she's happy with her work-life arrangement, she shrugs.

"Well, I'm not miserable, but I can't say that I'm really happy. I find my life right now to be a big grind. I have little time during the week for my children, my husband, or me. I typically don't get home from work until 8:00 P.M. My days are really long, and I think it's actually gotten harder since I became partner three years ago," she says. "But I keep thinking it won't last forever. I'll figure something else out. But you should talk to Catherine because she has a very different life than I do, a better life."

Catherine Riley, 43, a pretty woman with shoulder-length blonde hair and a warm smile, nods her head as she picks at her fruit salad.

"I'm on a three-fifths schedule, and I love it," she says enthusiastically. "I'm not on partner track because you can't be part-time and become partner, but that's okay. I don't know if I will ever want to go back to full time in order to pursue partnership because I really prize having the extra time to be with my family."

The mother of a 2-year-old and a 5-year-old, Catherine works Monday through Friday, 9:00 to 5:00. Her forty-hour week is considered part-time, and for that she feels lucky. Only in the insane world of law firms (and perhaps the equally insane world of investment banking) would three-fifths employment mean forty hours a week. I can't even mask my shock when I hear her satisfaction with that situation. But then again I'm not a lawyer, and my life doesn't revolve around making more than 2,000 billable hours a year. In comparison to lives her colleagues lead, I agree that Catherine truly does have good reason to feel fortunate.

"I'm able to be home and have dinner every night with my kids and do homework with them," she says earnestly.

Sharon and Catherine, two lawyers practicing the same specialty at the same firm, are leading vastly different lives both because they have to and because they've chosen different directions. Sharon took the partner route, a more lucrative but decidedly less family-friendly option, and Catherine took the slower path, less money but more family time. Catherine earns more than her husband, so her financial contribution to her family is significant. She's staying in her career, working forty hours a week, but will never make partner if she continues to work part-time, and that for her is okay. But Sharon doesn't have the "choice" to work part-time. She's the family breadwinner, and her income as a partner gives her family a secure and comfortable financial future. It seems that "choice," even between working moms and how they structure their careers, isn't necessarily such a choice at all.

Searching for the Holy Grail

In the two years that I have been researching this book, I've struggled to find some neat and tidy answers for how mothers can do it all. I've posed surveys and questions to more than a hundred professional women. But the more I've probed, prodded, and dug, the more I've realized it's impossible to paint this complicated picture using broad strokes. It's all in the shading and detail and even how the picture is framed. The support and infrastructure that keeps a working mom's life running is critical. Who is watching the kids, how comfortable are you with your caregiver, and ultimately how deep is your well of childcare coverage? Do you have a partner, and if so, what type of career does he/she have? How much does your partner share in childcare and household responsibilities? Who is the breadwinner and how important is your income to your family? Do you enjoy your career and does it allow you any flexibility? Is it an extreme job with extreme hours or is it a nine-to-five gig that doesn't require travel, homework, and extra curricular activities and events? And perhaps even more important, how much do you feel you *need* to be with your children on a daily basis? At what point does your gut wrench, if ever, from leaving your kids? What's your personal tipping point?

Every woman has a different answer to each of these questions. Still, the common theme that I have discovered is the universal desire for flexibility. And this, of course, is not just a woman's issue. In a 2000 Harris poll, more than four-fifths of men in their 20s and 30s said that a work schedule that allowed for family time was more important to them than a challenging or high-paying job.[1] That said, even though men and women both view flexibility as one of the most important factors in their job satisfaction, fewer men are taking flexible work schedules even if their companies allow them. As one male lawyer who works on Wall Street put it to me, "Asking for flexibility still makes you look like you're not very serious about your career, and I don't feel it's a smart career move to even inquire about it."

Perhaps not surprisingly, European attitudes toward flexibility in the workplace are more progressive than in the United States. In fact, in the 1980s in the Netherlands, the government began encouraging part-time work as a way to tackle unemployment. Part-timers were given the same benefits and access to education as full-time workers. Now 20 percent of Dutch men and 73 percent of Dutch women work part-time, compared with the United States, where only 17 percent of mothers with children under 18 work part-time (49.6 percent of mothers in the United States with children under 18 work full-time[2]). And 10 percent of Dutch parents of young children choose to work four days a week.[3] But America has never quite embraced the joie de vivre of Europe, and we're usually a few steps behind them on progressive social issues. So even though most American men still feel too squeamish to explore flexible work schedules, for women, particularly mothers, flexibility is often seen these days as a necessity for not only maintaining their sanity but also for keeping them in the workforce at all.

The Bar Rises

When Deborah Epstein Henry was 27 years old, she did something most recent law school grads and federal district judge clerks weren't doing. She had a baby. This fresh-faced, pregnant redhead was such an anomaly within the dark paneled confines of the judge's chambers on New York's Long Island, New York, that when lawyers visited, they almost always assumed that Deborah was the secretary.

"They couldn't believe I was a law clerk," she says.

A couple of years later, after having worked as a full-time associate in a New York City law firm, Deborah and her husband, a marketing executive, moved to Philadelphia for her husband's job. She was then pregnant with her second son and landed a position at a large law firm, locking in something that was rather unusual at the time—a 75 percent schedule—working three long days in the office and doing other work from home. Deborah says she was satisfied with her arrangement but felt like a social misfit. She wasn't quite accepted into the world of full-time attorneys and she didn't fit into the Stay-at-Home mother crowd either. Feeling isolated, Deborah began meeting with the three other part-time litigators at her firm for an occasional lunch to discuss the issues part-timers faced and how they were coping.

"I was really struggling. And I was looking for some people to talk to about balancing career and family. And I found that whenever I spoke to other lawyers who were doing what I was doing, they were experiencing the same thing I did. They felt isolated, and they were struggling. And I thought, where can we get together and talk about this on a monthly basis and start comparing notes?"

In 1999, Deborah emailed six part-time attorneys in Philadelphia, asking them to meet at her firm for a support-type group. Word quickly spread about her meeting, and 150 lawyers emailed her back.

"It was such an affirmation to get this overwhelming response. Immediately, I realized two things: I struck a nerve, and I'm not alone. At the time there was such a silence about this issue of work-family balance, and this was an opportunity to breathe life into that silence."

Deborah seized this opportunity by creating Flex-Time Lawyers LLC that same year. Cut to September 2004 and Deborah, now 36 and mother of three boys, 8, 6, and 3 years old, is smiling and shaking hands as she greets a stream of attorneys on the fiftieth floor of a midtown Manhattan office building. In five and a half years, Deborah's email list has grown from 6 lawyers to 1,300. The meetings are no longer just casual brown bag lunch affairs but organized events with guest speakers. A couple of years ago, her group expanded to New York, and today a large New York City law firm is hosting her monthly meeting with a lavish, catered lunch. The meetings don't discriminate against men; in fact, a couple of men show up and file to the back of the room. But this is clearly a predominantly female gathering, and about 100 lawyers wearing the conservative-suit-and-pumps uniform of the legal profession are here. One woman, a new mom on maternity leave, pushes her 8-week-old baby in a stroller and parks in the front row. She's here because she says she's feeling anxious about asking for flexibility at her firm and wants to learn about the best approach to negotiate a part-time schedule.

The guest speaker today is Judy Clark, a British attorney who is a partner in one of the world's largest commercial law firms. She is the mother of two teenage boys, and she's been working in the United Kingdom on a four-day week for many years. Judy doesn't as much give advice to these women who are looking to better control their schedules as she does give reasons why flexibility makes financial sense.

"I come here today and it's my law firm's position that the whole issue of flexibility is a business-driven issue. It's not a political issue. It's not a woman's issue. Flexibility should be for everybody. That said, there is a major business reason to have flexibility for women," she says. "In the U.K. the statistics show that in the last ten years the number of women applying for jobs in law has gone up 128 percent compared to men that has gone up 26 percent."

The rise in female lawyers in the past decade may not be as dramatic as it is for our sisters across the Atlantic, but since the early days of modern feminism, the number of female lawyers has skyrocketed. In 1972 only 12 percent of all law school graduates were women. Thirty years later, 49 percent of all law school graduates are female.[4] But whereas half of new lawyers joining the biggest firms each year are female, only about 16 percent of women make partner. Judy says that the desire to retain the best talent is what has motivated law firms in the United Kingdom to better accommodate its employees, particularly women.

"In London the recruitment of female talent has become a battle ground. That's why there has been a lot of significant change to insure that this massive group of female talent is harnessed and used, and women are the principle beneficiaries of this."

Most people in the legal industry agree that the reason there are still so few female partners in U.S. firms is because women often leave their legal careers after they have children. Studies show that inflexible work schedules, combined with brutal hours and insane workloads, make a legal career, particularly in a big firm, incompatible with having a family. But Flex-Time Lawyers founder Deborah Epstein Henry believes that law firms are going to have to start addressing appropriate ways in which to retain women because it's simply too expensive for them not to. With law firms investing on average between $200,000 to $500,000 per associate, Deborah sees economics as the most compelling reason why firms can no longer resist better accommodating their employees, particularly women.

"Law firm life has become so grueling that a lot of women and minorities are gravitating more toward in-house counsel jobs and then they are saying, we want the law firms we hire to reflect who we are. So as the complexion of in-house legal departments changes, they then want the firms they hire to look like them. So that's a strict business issue and that's the biggest way to change priorities for law firms. Another compelling issue is that with women now 50 percent or more of graduating law school classes, law firms can't afford to operate without half the legal talent available, and once they get them it costs a lot to lose them. And as lawyers start comparing notes and getting more public about the issue of work-life balance, employers will need to pay more attention in order to stay competitive," Deborah says.

The need for work-life balance in the legal profession is not a new development, according to a 2001 study done by the American Bar Association, "Balanced Lives: Changing the Culture of the Legal Practice." It writes that Leila Robinson, who in 1882 became the first woman admitted to the Massachusetts State Bar, posed this question to an organization of female lawyers and law students: "Is it practical for a woman to successfully fulfill the duties of wife, mother and lawyer at the same time?"[5] The pop cultural consensus at the end of the nineteenth century was that combining these disparate roles was not just inappropriate for women but also impractical. Although cultural norms have evolved over the last century, many of life's practicalities apparently haven't. Because when the ABA recently asked the same question, approximately a third of female lawyers responded that it was *not* realistic to combine the roles of wife, mother, and lawyer.

But as the ABA study concludes, this timeless dilemma among lawyers now has new urgency. When Leila Robinson raised the question, she was one of only about 500 women practicing law in the entire country. Today there are close to 400,000 female attorneys in the United States (there are 600,000 men), most of whom will at some point have spouses or partners or children.

As many people already know, lawyers overwhelmingly are an unhappy bunch—and for good reason. Workplace hours have increased dramatically over the past two decades, and most lawyers in American law firms now must work a minimum of sixty-hour weeks to make their 2,000-plus billable hours. (In the United Kingdom lawyers on partner track average about 1,200 billable hours.) And that's a relatively moderate workload compared to life in most large American firms, where the work requirements are typically even higher. It's no wonder that this unrelenting lifestyle has created a whole crop of unbalanced attorneys. Almost three-quarters of lawyers with children report difficulty juggling both professional and personal demands, and the number of women who doubt the possibility of successfully combining both work and family has almost tripled over the past two decades.[6]

But Deborah Epstein Henry is convinced that work flexibility is the key to helping solve this century-old legal dilemma. Even though she says the female lawyers she meets want varying things—some are happy never to be on a partner track, others are gunning for partner but want to take longer to get there by working part-time—she believes that everyone is looking for a healthier, more family- and life-friendly schedule.

"I do think something overwhelming that's pervasive with lawyers who I deal with is that they want flexibility. They want control and predictability in their lives, and to the extent they can get predictability and control they are much happier."

Flexibility Feels Good

My research echoes Deborah's findings. I've found that the vast majority of mothers with small children who work in fields ranging from investment banking and marketing to medicine and public relations would happily trade title and income for a more flexible work schedule. And those women who are fortunate to work flexibly by telecommuting, taking Fridays off, or creating their own schedules tell me that they feel particularly loyal to their employers and they have no plans to leave their jobs. Women also say that they are comfortable with slowing down their careers if it could afford them more time with their children. In fact, nearly everyone I've polled who has children under seven years old says they would prefer to stay in their current position rather than be promoted. Most women don't want to take on the added responsibilities and stress of a bigger title, even if it means a larger paycheck, while their children are young.

I don't believe that these conclusions mean that women today aren't dedicated to their careers. Nearly all the women I met and interviewed told me that they work not only because they have to but also because they enjoy having a career. It helps define them. It makes them appreciate their children more. It gives them the mental and emotional stimulation that they crave and helps them to thrive outside of the home. In fact, almost every woman said that if financially she didn't have to work, she would work, perhaps not in her current position, but she would do something, either entrepreneurial, philanthropic, or in the nonprofit world. There were only a handful of women who thought Stay-at-Home motherhood appealed to them, but when they flirted with that idea, they worried that they would grow bored and weary of that lifestyle.

A Truce in the Mommy Wars

In October 2002, a *New York* magazine cover story ran the headline, "Who's the Better Mom? The Growing Conflict in the City Between Working and Stay-at-Home Mothers." The cover shows a snooty looking woman with her hair pulled back in a tight bun, wearing a business suit and carrying a briefcase while her tow-headed toddler gazes stealthily in the opposite direction of his mother. That image, of course, represented the "working mom." The Stay-at-Home mom was shown as a petite blonde with a Pilates body and sculpted arms. She wore a sleeveless athletic shirt and was carrying an expressionless toddler on her hip. Inside the magazine the banner screamed "Mom vs. Mom . . . Working and Non-working Mothers are Slugging It Out in the Schoolyard Over Who's the Better Parent—and Who Gets to have a Sex Life." Yikes! The article went on to say—among other incendiary and hair-raising things—that at-home moms were having more sex than working moms because they had more energy. Even still, yoga butts and all, they were hardly Zen about their lives. Apparently, it was tough being at home even with a nanny to lend a hand.

"Non-working mother is an oxymoron. I manage a household. You try raising two kids and staying fit," was the quote on the magazine's cover from the at-home mother.

Working moms, the article suggested, were so strung out that not only were they out-of-touch as far as their kids' schools and social lives, they were also too tired to have sex, and because they couldn't make it to the gym, they weren't thrilled with their mushy bodies either. The article was nauseating to read and tapped into such a narrow, privileged subset of society that had the audacity to declare: "working has become deeply ordinary, there's status to *not* working," I tried to disregard the article and characterized it as obnoxious hyperbole. But in New York circles the caricatures contrasting at-home moms and working moms created long-lasting controversy; women still refer to the article two years later.

Was this just another media-provoked catfight, or was this the real thing? Are moms really drawing dividing lines between themselves on the playground? One of the questions I asked women I surveyed across the country was whether they believe the "mommy wars" exist. The response I got was varied. Some women didn't sense it at all; others felt under siege.

"The mommy wars are alive and well even down here in Texas," an attorney and mother of a toddler wrote to me. She had recently left New York City to move back home to Houston. "In New York being a Stay-at-Home mom was a status item, like a Classic Six apartment or a three-stone engagement ring. There the at-home moms were so passionate about their views that they were not open to the possibility that working moms could have a work-family balance and could raise balanced, happy children. Now that I am in Houston there's a different kind of mommy war—the war from our parents' generation. Many men see it as a knock against their masculinity for their wives to work. And many women down here cannot understand why women want to work, but they are not as expressive of their opinions as Stay-at-Home moms in Manhattan."

The tension certainly cuts both ways. Some Stay-at-Work moms admitted to me—usually apologetically—that they sort of snubbed their noses at women who were at home full time.

"I hate to admit it and it sounds awful when it comes out of my mouth, but I actually feel like I do more than moms who stay at home full time," a rabbi in suburban Connecticut confessed to me.

There were women who told me that they believed at-home moms respected them for working. But the majority of mothers said they didn't feel "war" as much as a simmering resentment created by insecurity and frustration on both sides. "It's as if no one is satisfied with what they have exactly, and that's what feeds the fire," a publicist and mother of a 3-year-old said.

Is solving the mommy wars as difficult as solving the Mideast conflict? Are passionate feelings so entrenched on both sides, rooted both in tradition and fear, that's there's no plausible way to unite the sisterhood? Former Governor Jane Swift believes that women can come together. She feels that all of the attention given to this emotional battle is really a disservice to women because it ignores the underlying problem all mothers face.

"I think the reality of these sort of wars is that there are people who are frustrated that they don't have enough choices. So I get angry about this media fascination of the 'mommy wars' for two reasons. Number one, it forces women to answer questions that men don't have to. There's the fairness issue, what kind of advantage should a mother get? What you're really saying is, is it fair for women to take some time off. Nobody ever asks men that. Secondly, there is an underlying assumption in those articles that everybody has a choice, and the reality for most parents is that they both have to work. So all of the energy that we've spent fighting about, debating, and focusing on the choices that some women make is energy that I think would be better spent on the lack of choice that many parents have. Rather than trying to figure out who is right and who is wrong, we should try to figure out how more of us can have choices that we think are right for us."

As governor, Swift says that every step of the way she fell victim not only to the vicious energy of divisiveness that pits mom against mom and scrutinizes the "choices" women make, but also to the mythical image of what motherhood should look like. She says that when she left office, she realized just how deep those stereotypes still run.

"If a guy had shitty poll numbers and formidable opposition, and he decided to pull out of an election and he stood up on stage with his three young children and said that he decided not to run because it's better for the Party, it's better for the Commonwealth, because he needed to spend more time with his family, and because it's good for him personally, every single article would say, he dropped out because he couldn't win. I stood up and said the exact same thing, and every single article reported that I dropped out because I couldn't be a good mother or I couldn't 'Have It All.' It just gets back to gender stereotypes."

A Labor of Love

Deb Berman cringes at the idea of "having it all." She has a full, busy life, is proud of her career accomplishments, and treasures her family. But she, like most women I spoke to, doesn't like to say "she has it all" because it implies things are perfect, and when it comes to managing a full-time career and a young family, nothing she says is ever perfect. A friend told me about Deb, a brilliant OB/GYN in Ann Arbor, Michigan, who is actually leading a life many would call downright masochistic. We spoke at night after she had put her two toddlers to sleep. And after talking for nearly an hour, I hung up the phone feeling both awed and exhausted by her tales in the trenches of labor and delivery. But what struck me most was not just how adroitly she seemed to be juggling it all but also how cheerfully she was doing it.

Deb understands why people think she's nuts. After all, who would plan on having not one but two babies while enduring the crushing pressures and murderous hours of an OB/GYN residency? But in the second half of Deb's four-year residency program at the University of Michigan she felt prepared not just to deliver babies but also to have babies of her own. She had always wanted to practice medicine and to be a mother. She says she had wonderful role models as she watched both her parents negotiate successful full-time careers. Her father is a radiologist in Los Angeles and her mother is a psychosocial cancer researcher and professor at UCLA. Deb says her mother always managed to have hot meals on the table seven days a week and never missed any of her or her brother's events.

When Deb was plotting her motherhood and career path, she decided that starting her family while still a resident was a smarter professional move than waiting until she joined the hospital's teaching staff, a position that she hoped to achieve. In fact, she worried that people might think she's a slacker or take her less seriously if she became pregnant and took maternity leave as a brand new faculty member. She also says that a conversation with her mom influenced her decision to get pregnant when she did.

"My mom once said to me, no time will ever be a good time to have kids, and no time will ever be a bad time to have kids. Those words have forever resonated with me."

It's true there may never be a good time to have children, but there's usually a better time than when you're working a hundred-plus hours a week as Deb was. But she and her husband, Rich, a resident in psychiatry, who was also working a pounding schedule, were not deterred by their workloads and decided to go for it. It took more than a year for Deb to get pregnant. She had hoped to have her baby in her second year of residency but wound up giving birth in the second month of her fourth year. Then three and a half months after giving birth to her son, Deb discovered that she was pregnant again.

"Maybe it wasn't the savviest decision to have babies so close together. But I'm so glad we did it," Deb says.

Deb's children are thirteen-and-a-half months apart. An intense situation under the best of circumstances, it's even crazier considering the demands of Deb and Rich's jobs. But Deb had plenty of company during her pregnancies. In fact, she says that her class was truly an anomaly in the history of OB/GYN residencies. It's a specialty that ironically is not favorable for women who want to start families of their own. Nevertheless, remarkably each resident in Deb's all-female class had a baby during her residency. And three of her five classmates, including Deb, were even pregnant with their second baby during their fourth year.

Ask Deb about her brutal work schedule combined with the challenges of coping with difficult pregnancies and raising two babies, and only after major coaxing do you get any acknowledgement that things were tough. Deb's simply not the kind of girl who likes to complain. As a former competitive gymnastics champion who is used to achieving goals while fighting through pain, a steady focus and an iron will are as rudimentary to her as a back handspring. It is perhaps fitting that Deb, who attended the University of Michigan on a full gymnastics scholarship for her balance beam ability, is so masterful at balancing the demands of her two competing worlds.

"There's sort of a 'you signed up for this' mentality," Deb says. "You wouldn't complain about your pregnancy, your health, or the hours. That was tough because I wasn't very healthy. I had a full neuropathy, which meant that my hands and feet were numb, and I was operating twelve hours–plus a day. I could get the feeling back by wearing double-tight gloves to push the extra fluid out of my hands so that I could function. And because we were all having babies and taking maternity leaves, that was really hard because we had to cover for each other. But this is truly a job where things just can't wait."

The senior resident on the front lines of a hospital labor and delivery ward, it was business as usual for Deb even as she approached her own due date.

"It was three days before I had my son, and I was absolutely HUGE. I was sitting at one of the labor and delivery desks when all of a sudden I heard an enormous yell. When you hear a scream like that in the labor and delivery ward, you don't ask questions, you just run. So I stood up and grabbed a pair of gloves and quickly waddled down the hall following the noise. Lying down in the hallway a woman was yelling, 'It's coming!' I put the gloves on and gently lowered myself to the floor, sitting Indian-style with my big ass on the ground and my big-ass belly hanging over my legs. I softly said to her 'Push.' The head was already nearly out. I was very aware that there was an elevator behind me and there's a very busy hallway in front of me. All of a sudden while she's in mid-push and I'm delivering the baby's shoulders, I heard 'ding,' and the elevator door opened and out walked about ten people who were witness to what must have been a horrifying picture: me in all of my pregnant glory sitting on the floor in the middle of the hallway delivering this woman in all of her pregnant glory. I gently turned around and said, 'Can you just step back into the elevator and go back to the second floor and come up in a little bit?' The woman was getting anxious and had her feet pushing on my stomach for leverage. And I said, you have to take your feet off of my stomach. I'll take care of your baby, but you have to take care of mine."

A few days and dozens of deliveries later, Deb went into labor. She had been on her feet for fourteen hours and had done five C-sections that day. Deb says she was "beyond exhausted" and had just crawled into bed with her husband and had instantly fallen into a coma-like sleep when she awoke to discover that her bed was soaked. After assessing that her water had broken and she hadn't peed in her bed (even being an OB/GYN, she admits she wasn't quite clear about what had happened), she and her husband went to the same labor and delivery ward where she had just left. She wound up giving birth to her son five weeks early. Deb took eight weeks of maternity leave and her husband took two months of paternity leave from his residency program when Deb went back to work. A dedicated breast-feeder, Deb continued nursing her son straight through her second pregnancy and continues to nurse her second child who is now 10 months old.

"It's amazing what you make happen when you want it to happen. I was a fourth-year resident working 110 hours with a baby at home and pregnant with my second one, and I was pumping between surgeries," Deb says.

"My mom was in from L.A. and came to visit me at the hospital, and I was in the call room, also known among the women as the Boob Juice Room, sitting in my scrubs with my shirt off and a double breast pump on, and I'm answering a page and typing on the computer. She walked in, and I said, 'Hi, mom!' I think she was totally stunned and perhaps a bit worried at the sight of me."

Now that Deb is out of school and working and teaching full time, she actually has a better schedule than her husband, who is still in his residency program getting a degree in childhood and adolescent psychiatry.

"I use the term loosely that my schedule is better than my husband's now," Deb says with a laugh.

Now a full-time practicing OB/GYN and clinical assistant professor at the University of Michigan, Deb drops off her two children at a nearby daycare around 7:30 A.M. Then it's off to the hospital to teach, perform surgeries, see patients, or deliver babies. Deb and her husband together pick up their kids at daycare at 6:00 P.M. From 6:00 P.M. to 8:00 P.M. is concentrated family time—dinner, playtime, baths, and bedtime.

"People are sort of horrified by our lack of in-home childcare help and household help. I know that people think we're beyond crazy to have our kids in daycare because getting two babies off to daycare before I get to work every day can require an act of Congress, it can be that difficult. And I think there's a lot of judgment about our sending our kids to daycare. But we love and worship our daycare and consider them our family. We don't have any family around, so that's hard on lots of levels."

Deb says she knows that some at-home moms criticize her and her lifestyle. And she wouldn't dare advise other women about how to run their lives. But Deb says she is very satisfied with the way things are going.

"My mom always says you shouldn't give advice, and so I'm certainly not preaching what I practice. God knows we have stacks of laundry piled up, and we have a dog and fur balls are in the corner. So I don't know if what I'm doing is right or wrong, but it's working right now, and if it stops working, then we'll reassess."

Deb says that she and her husband cherish their evening routines with their children, and weekends with her family replenish her.

"When I am at work, I'm really at work, and when I'm home, I'm really home, and my husband is integral and crucial to my happiness and functioning. I think it's really important to not always try to be someplace else physically and mentally. I will sit and play with Matchbox cars for two hours on the floor with my son even though I know have I laundry to do, but I try to ignore the impulse to do the laundry then because I know my time with my kids is fleeting. The time goes by so quickly and in a few years my son won't want me to play cars with him on the floor."

Deb is now trying to get articles published, is considering a three-year fellowship in high-risk obstetrics, and is attempting to reclaim her body by exercising again and trying to drop the pregnancy weight she gained. She also swears that she will finally hire a babysitter so she and her husband can see a movie or go out for cocktails, something she says they haven't done in at least two years. Deb says for her the hardest thing is trying to slow down because there is always so much for her to be doing.

"I know I'll get into bed tonight and think I should have read an article for my case tomorrow, or I should have started the first draft of some research that I'm hoping to publish, or maybe I should have thrown in a load of laundry. That's sort of the ongoing cycle that I struggle with. But overall I feel really happy and blessed to have two healthy children and a career that I absolutely love," Deb says. "I don't know if we're doing it right, but I can't say we're doing it wrong."

The High Cost of Prescriptions

When I meet Samantha Goldman, 36, at a coffee shop, she's in the midst of an important call she's been waiting for all day. She's talking to her daughter's pediatrician, discussing her 3-year-old's regression in toilet training and debating strategies to get her to poop on the potty. It's ironic that Samantha needs to consult the pediatrician because until last year that's what she was in training to become. A tall redhead with a take-charge aura, Samantha didn't always dream about going into medicine, but she was someone who liked to give back and help people. At Stanford, where she went to college, she worked in a battered women's shelter, tutored children, and counseled peers. After college she worked on Wall Street and realized that a career with the purpose of simply making money didn't fulfill her. She wanted to do something to make a difference in the world, and pediatrics appealed to her. So Samantha went back to school to take her premed classes and then she applied to medical school. At 29 years old, a few years older than most medical students, and newly married, Samantha started medical school at one of the country's most prestigious programs.

"I remember talking to people along the way, saying how do you make it work with a family, and they said, 'You get pregnant during your third year of medical school because the fourth year you have a lot of free time and then you can do residency and then maybe have another kid during residency.' And I totally bought into it 100 percent, as if you can completely control all of the forces of pregnancy," Samantha says. "Then I hit my first bump when I had a miscarriage third year, and I thought this isn't going the way I thought it would."

Samantha got pregnant again and successfully gave birth during her fourth year in medical school. When her daughter was 3 months old, she was doing a psych rotation in the hospital when two planes crashed into the World Trade Center.

"I was on a locked floor with psychotic patients, and we're watching the TV, and we see the second building collapse. I'm looking at the TV thinking, what's reality here? The buildings are collapsing, which didn't seem remotely possible. And you look at these patients and you think, what's the world we're living in? We're almost now in their world; this is something they could imagine, terrorists blowing up the World Trade Center. I think that whole experience made me say, 'Okay, I want to step back a little bit. I have a baby who I'm not seeing at all. Maybe I should take a year off and figure out what I want to do.'"

But before Samantha's sabbatical began, she was pregnant again. On her last day of medical school and twenty-two weeks into her second pregnancy Samantha was working in the pediatric disease ward when she started hemorrhaging. She checked herself into the labor and maternity ward where she stayed bedridden for the next ten weeks with a very rare and life threatening condition.

"My life was in danger and the baby's life was in danger. And we didn't know how long I was going to stay pregnant. It wasn't, just stay on bed rest and you'll be okay. It was, you've got to pray to God every single day that this baby stays inside you, and you know what, if this baby comes out between 25 weeks and 30 weeks, you're not going to be happy.

"It was such a trauma for me and my older daughter because I wasn't home and my husband wasn't either. He was sleeping at the hospital with me every night. My in-laws came and stayed for three months. They told me when I went to deliver, 'You could die; we're just letting you know you could die during delivery because you could hemorrhage to death.' They didn't even call it my delivery. They called it my surgery."

Despite arriving two months early, Samantha's daughter surprised the doctors and defied the odds, emerging incredibly strong and perfectly healthy. Samantha had major gynecological surgery after she delivered, and both mother and daughter were miraculously able to go home two weeks after delivery.

"I definitely felt much worse than my baby did. I got out of the hospital, and I was completely traumatized. But when I came home, I said to all of my medical school mentors, 'I don't know what I should do about applying for residency,' and everyone said I should just apply. So I went on all of my interviews and put on a brave face, and everyone said, 'Don't talk about the fact that you have kids.' So I sort of marched along thinking everything is fine; this is all going to work out."

When Samantha started her residency program, her daughters were 2½ and not quite 1 year old. The first rotation Samantha was assigned to was the pediatric organ transplant ward. Having just been a patient for almost three months and nearly losing her own life, having two toddlers at home and working a punishing schedule in an emotionally draining hospital ward, Samantha quickly discovered her residency was simply too much to handle.

"I would get to the hospital at 6:30 in the morning and get home at 7:00 P.M. at night. My younger daughter's first birthday was two weeks into internship, and I had to beg them to let me out early enough so I could see her awake. I just thought this is crazy, I'm not taking care of my own kids, and I'm in the hospital taking care of other people's kids. I can't do this right now. I don't want to do this."

Samantha told her residency director that she was having a really tough time and didn't think she could continue in the program. He told her she must be crazy and referred her to speak to the hospital psychiatrist. The psychiatrist told Samantha that her feelings were completely justified and perhaps the residency director could make her hours more flexible. But they wouldn't budge. They gave her a few days to make up her mind about whether she would stay. A few weeks later Samantha left.

It's been a little over a year since Samantha quit her pediatric residency, and the feelings of guilt, anxiety and even shame still torture her. Although she has no regrets about leaving because she knows she did what was best for her family, she nonetheless continues to struggle with her own sense of self.

"I had this intense period, sort of my whole life about being career focused, and then an intense mommy period being a new mom with two kids so close in age. I don't think I've figured out a balance that feels okay, and that's why it's so hard. How come for some women it's not so hard? How come they don't care that they're away from their kids a lot? And how come there are other women who don't care that they don't have a career? How can they *not* care? I really have tremendous angst about quitting. For me it was very much my identity. I was going to be a pediatrician; it took care of a lot of things. I was going to feel good about myself about giving back in that way. That's very core to who I am. And now I feel like how am I giving to the world and who am I now that I'm not going to be a pediatrician?"

Samantha sounds a lot like Gayle Greenberger from Chapter 7, who never finished her PhD in psychology. Like Gayle, Samantha is searching for an identity, something to replace the pediatric career she spent six years of school working toward. For a woman who always saw herself as a superachiever, where anything was possible, she's having a particularly tough time accepting the fact that she didn't finish, and she blames herself.

"It took me a month to tell my mentors that I left because I was so ashamed that I couldn't do it. I just felt like, how come I can't do this? I should be able to do this. What's wrong with me that I can't make this work? It didn't even feel so much like a choice when I made it. I felt like I can't make this work, and I couldn't see how to make this work."

Kerry Rubin, author of *Midlife Crisis at 30: How the Stakes Have Changed for a New Generation and What to Do About It,* says that young women today are blaming themselves for what they see as personal failures rather than problems within the structure of the workforce and within certain careers that makes it often impossible to blend the competing worlds of career and motherhood. "Women in their twenties and thirties are twisting the 'Girl Power' message of their youth, the well-intentioned empowerment campaign that told girls that anything was possible and are, instead, silently blaming themselves for failing to overcome the very real obstacles that still exist, despite the unprecedented workplace opportunities they inherited. Hitting similar roadblocks at similar points in their lives, young women aren't rallying together to question what's wrong with 'the system,' as many Baby Boomer women did when they were the same age; instead, Gen X/Y women are asking themselves, 'What is wrong with *me*?'"[7]

Samantha is now trying to figure out her next step. She's an MD but she can't practice medicine. There's no path for her to follow, so she's trying to pave one for herself as she goes. Right now, she's working with a physician doing research and hopes to publish some papers soon. She's also exploring the idea of even going back to school in a few years to get her PhD in psychology. She's attracted to an area of medical psychology where she would work with hospital patients. Her interest comes from her own experience as a patient.

"People say, 'Would you go back in three years and finish your residency?' and I don't know. Maybe if there were shared residencies or part-time residencies, which actually used to exist in pediatrics. But my hope is that in three years I will have found something else where I will be okay with the fact that I'm not going to do residency and that I'm not going to be a pediatrician because I found this other thing that thrills me."

Samantha says she felt completely blindsided by the impact motherhood had on her. She expected she would have her babies and would follow the course others promised her would be easy to navigate. But life has a way of interrupting our plans sometimes. Samantha's dangerous second pregnancy followed by a premature baby, an unforgiving work schedule, and the tug she felt toward motherhood altered her direction, surprising and scaring her at the same time. She, like other women I met, wants to impart advice to her own daughters—advice she never heard.

"I want to teach my girls that they can work if they want, and I think it's very important to show them that they can have a gratifying career. But they don't have to be a physician or a lawyer who clerks for the Supreme Court. They have to figure out what makes sense for them and what's going to fit in with their life."

Samantha is still trying to make sense of her own life now. She says she doesn't want to dabble in different jobs as her husband suggests; she wants a career. She's just not quite sure what that looks like yet.

"I think women really want something that's their own. You just need to do it in a way that doesn't sacrifice being a mom. I think that's what we're all trying to figure out. How do we do it so that we can have the mom piece and still have the work piece?"

Deb and Samantha had very different experiences in figuring out the juggle of starting a medical career while raising two babies. Is one woman ultimately more successful than the other? Is one the better mother? It's impossible and unfair to compare lives. What I've learned from all of my discussions and from my own experiences is that how we do it is intensely personal. What works for one mother may not feel comfortable for another. The ratio of work-family balance is also a fluid one depending on your child's age, the intensity of your career, and your family and partner situation. We all love our children, but what we need from them and what we need from work and how much sleep we require to stay sane is highly individual. For Samantha, following the established route into medicine while being a new mother just didn't work. She says one of her goals now is to work with the American Medical Association to help make part-time residencies an option for more women and to fully accept and integrate them into medical training. At this time very few programs allow doctors to do residencies part-time.

"There are a lot of really able minds that are not being put to good use because the system is still run by the men who haven't quite figured out how to incorporate the women."

The Zig-Zag

Former Secretary of State Madeleine Albright told a *Time* magazine reporter in 1997, "Women's lives don't go in a straight line, they zig-zag all over the place."[8]

Perhaps no woman in modern American history better personifies how to zig-zag her career trajectory as elegantly and successfully as Secretary Albright has. The highest-ranking woman in the history of U.S. government, Albright didn't begin her paid career in academia or politics until her three children were in school and she was 39 years old.

"Basically I was at home trying to figure out what I wanted to do. A lot of people thought I was an odd duck because most people at that stage were at home full time with their children. To that extent it's kind of upside down from where we are today," Albright told *Mothering Magazine* in 2003. Interestingly, Albright's daughters are now mothers themselves and all have careers yet are structuring their schedules differently. Two daughters are lawyers, and one is a banker. One started a law firm with another woman in order to have more flexibility. Another works full time and travels, and another, after having taken maternity leave, works a flexible schedule.[9]

As *Dateline* NBC news producer Lynn Keller, 40—who works part-time and is also the mother of three—puts it, "Madeleine Albright takes the career pressure off. You don't have to achieve everything in your 20s and 30s, there *is* life after 40, and it can be any life that you choose. This is the first time in my career that I haven't been anxious to get to the next level," Lynn says. "I used to always know where I was going next, but now I'm perfectly happy with staying put."

Most women don't move in the same linear direction as men. Pregnancies, babies, and the practicalities of raising children often affect our careers in ways we never anticipated. For many women today that means zig-zagging between various careers, starting businesses, going back to school, and even staying home for a while. There is actually a new term for this called "sequencing" as women weave in and out of various careers and jobs as they simultaneously raise their children. Women today are reinventing the paradigm of Stay-at-Work motherhood, to help make it fit into their multidimensional lives.

Once again, I'm left to wonder what the ideal Stay-at-Work situation really is? I posed this question to everyone with whom I spoke. Every woman responded that they wanted some flexibility or a part-time work situation. Some suggested that the ideal set up would be working five days a week but from 9:00 A.M. to 2:00 P.M. or when their children were in school. Others said that they would prefer working three long days a week. My favorite response was from Vera Richman, a mother of two who is pregnant with her third child and who works full-time in New York as a pharmaceutical regional account manager. "Part-time work with full-time help and a driver, that's the best situation," she says with a smile.

Almost unanimously, no Stay-at-Work mother wanted to relinquish her career, but many said that they just wanted to work differently. Pulitzer prizewinning economics journalist and acclaimed author Ann Crittenden says that it makes sense that women want to and *have to,* in many cases, work differently after they have children. She believes that an increase in workplace flexibility will improve not only the quality of life for mothers but actually benefit the U.S. economy as well.

"A lot of people want a shorter work week. That would solve a lot of problems. They would be doing what they were trained to do, just not working those long, brutal hours, and that to me is very feasible," Ann says. "I just think employers don't want to go to the trouble. I think having shorter work weeks will have to be mandated. It would really raise women's income and raise family income. It would give women more choices and produce more cash dollars for the whole country. Now you either work brutal long hours or you don't work at all.

"It's such a paradox because we have all of this choice in a consumer economy, and we have no choice hardly in the most important thing. So we really need to widen our range of choice in how our work is structured. All these rules were written for people who were not doing the child-rearing. So the rules have to be rewritten for those who want to include raising children, unless we want to be a society that doesn't want to raise our kids. Because increasingly the better educated women have the fewest children because it's so hard on them. And that's just not true in other countries."

Life Goes in Cycles

Times were different when Nita Lowey graduated in 1959 from Mount Holyoke College in Massachusetts. Only three women in Lowey's class went to law school, and a handful went to medical school. She took a job in advertising only to quit a few years later after she got married and started having children. But Lowey did not just stay home and iron Oxfords. She became very friendly with her neighbor, who happened to be Mario Cuomo, and got busy in local Queens politics. Today at 67 years old, the former PTA president, mother of three, and grandmother of six, is one of the most powerful people in Washington. She is an eight-term congresswoman from New York who has served as a member of the Democratic leadership and chaired the Democratic Congressional Campaign Committee.

I meet Congresswoman Lowey in her modest district office in suburban New York during the summer recess. At five-foot-four, this smiley, pleasantly pear-shaped woman hardly looks like a force to be reckoned with. But as anyone in Washington knows, Lowey is a fiery legislator and fierce fundraiser and one of the most influential voices on Capitol Hill.

I'm fascinated with Congresswoman Lowey both because of where she is today as well as how she got there. There is no doubt that Lowey is a natural politician, but she didn't run for office until she was 50 years old. In fact, Lowey didn't do paid work of any kind until her youngest child was 9 years old.

"I think it's very difficult to have it all at the same time, but life is a cycle," Lowey says as we sit on the sofa in her small office surrounded by pictures and community awards. "For me raising children was very important. I think it would be very difficult to do this job while my children were young."

When I ask Lowey, clearly an ambitious, driven woman, if she felt content staying at home with her kids, she reflexively says yes, but then pauses and adds, "I think if I knew then that I'd be a congresswoman now, I would've been much more relaxed doing all the things that I was doing because I wasn't quite sure what I wanted to do when I grew up."

For months, those words have lingered with me. I think the angst many moms feel is wondering where we're going to end up, especially if we slow things down, change careers, or take ourselves out of the game entirely. If we could look into our futures and see that everything turned out the way we hoped, or in Lowey's case, that we became one of the most powerful members of Congress, then it might be easier to appreciate the ride, embrace the early years of our children's lives, and not worry that we're jeopardizing our own professional and economic futures. As Congresswoman Lowey's scheduler ends our interview and hustles in a stream of constituents for her next meeting, the country's most politically formidable grandmother turns to me, smiles sweetly, and says, "Enjoy your children; they are only babies once."

I know that is heart-felt, grandmotherly advice, but truthfully I hate when people say that to me. It makes me feel pressure to cherish the moments, and it gives me anxiety that I'm not treasuring them enough. I then feel guilty for working and sometimes even a little resentful that I have to work as much as I do.

But when I step back a bit, I realize that enjoying my children doesn't mean I can't enjoy my work too. I know I must continue growing and challenging myself. I'm tired of making excuses or feeling embarrassed for not feeling wholly fulfilled with motherhood. Like most of the women whom I've interviewed, I am a happier and better mom when my brain is getting some exercise. There are some women who feel completely satisfied with being at home full-time, but many more women I've found want a dynamic career—something that motivates and energizes them—something separate from their family lives. These women, like myself, want to stay at work while still being present, engaged mothers. This is not shameful, and it's not impossible to achieve. This is what having a little bit of it, all of the time, is all about.

Acknowledgments

Book acknowledgments always remind me of the Academy Award thank-you speeches, without any of the entertaining drama of the winner crying, falling out of her dress, or tripping on the way up to the stage. To the reader, this section is a boring, perfunctory part of a book. But now having actually *written* a book and realizing just how sadistic and reclusive the process can be, I know that if it weren't for my rather large team of supporters, I would have never seen this book through.

First of all, I am forever indebted to all of the women in the book who generously took the time to share their stories with me. Without you, this book would not exist. To my incredible agent, Jill Marsal, it is because of your enthusiasm and dedication that these stories have found their way into print. You saw the diamond-in-the-rough potential of my book proposal and hve been my champion ever since. I also want to thank my brilliant editor, Marnie Cochran, for giving me all of the latitude in writing the book that I desired and whose unwavering enthusiasm, energy, and vision for this project have made it what it is. It was also Marnie who invented the marvelous phrase "Stay-at-Work mom," giving working mothers a more empowering and positive identity.

I also want to thank my mother, Brenda Bengis, my first Stay-at-Work mom role model. My mom was "sequencing" her life decades before the term was ever invented. She had many incarnations: from teacher to Stay-at-Home mom before eventually going to law school. She graduated from law school when I was a junior in high school. My mom's sacrifices, endless confidence, love, and belief in me have guided me throughout my life, and she continues to be a constant source of inspiration. To my dad, Paul Levine, fellow writer, friend, supporter, reader, and copyeditor: you have been an amazing help to me from the inception of the book. Thank you for your love and support. Nikki Rosenson, my soulmate sister, lifelong best friend, alter ego and conscience, thank you for being even more thrilled for me than I was when I sold the book. I can still hear you screaming with excitement when I called you to tell you I got a book deal. I know that you're my number-one fan, and I smile whenever I think of you. Thank you, Gayle Greenberger, for cheering me on through this whole process, indulging me in picking apart my thesis, developing my ideas, and helping me find interviews. Also, thank you for your heartfelt participation in the book and for your amazing friendship and love for fifteen years. I know I am so fortunate to have you in my life.

To Sue Ernst and Jessica Spira, my first "mommy friends"—motherhood would not be the same without you. Jessica, you have been not only my friend but my "working mother book" radar for three years, informing me on new research you read, relevant *Today* show segments you watched, and career versus motherhood articles you thought may be useful. Thank you for being my eyes and ears throughout this process as well as finding me people to interview. I am truly grateful for your help and our friendship.

To Brooke Horman, Allison Busch Vogel, and Lauren Decker Lerman, my three muses who have patiently listened to me agonize, discuss, and dissect "the book" forever. Thank you for all of your stories, experiences, and ideas and for never telling me to shut up. I am also so grateful for having met each of you. Thanks for keeping me sane in the suburbs. To Kerry Rubin, the smartest booker in TV morning news and an amazing author, I am so grateful for your friendship and for your guiding me through the process of publishing a book. To Carolyn Goldman, Soraya Gage, Sharon Nevins, Jamie Bright, Laurie Rice, Sophia Faskianos, Adena Traub, and my sister Debra Feinberg, thank you for cheering me on each step of the way. To Marianne Haggerty, thank you for all of your help and enthusiasm in getting my book off the ground and helping me get the publicity it needed. To the incredible Kate Kazeniac at Da Capo

Press, thank you for all of your energy and dogged determination in making sure the world would hear about my book.

It would have been impossible to have completed this project without the unbelievable support of my children's loving babysitter Nickesha Reed. I am indebted to you Nicki for working early, working late, and caring for my children as if they were your own.

My tribe of cheerleaders is not only female. Matt Bromberg, thanks for patiently listening to my first-time-author anxieties, believing in this project, and being part of the book. You are not only a great neighbor but also a treasured friend. And Mike Salort, thank you for hiring me twice, encouraging me to write, reading my early drafts, cheering me on, and always keeping me positive.

But the most important man in my world and the person truly responsible for making this book a reality is my husband, Michael. You have heroically stood by, both supporting and indulging me in the luxury of writing a book, even though the process has been anything but luxurious. Thank you for always loving what I write, even when it's not always good and for giving me total confidence to pursue this book.

And to Jonah and Alexandra, my sweet, beautiful children—you are my inspiration for writing this book and in many ways I wrote this for you. I hope that the struggles all parents face will eventually give way to more choices for both of you when you have children of your own.

And finally, thank you to Starbucks in the metropolitan New York/New Jersey area. Thanks for the outlets to plug in my laptop and write this book and for letting me camp out for eight hours at a stretch. A special thanks to the South Orange, New Jersey, Starbucks, where the bulk of the book was written. Thanks for the tall lattes even though they were rarely free.

Notes

Chapter 1

1. Lisa Belkin, *New York Times Magazine*, October 26, 2003.

2. International Gallop Poll found that 48 percent of those polled thought this model was best. "Americans Support Traditional Sex Roles More Than Those in Most Other Countries," *About Women on Campus,* Summer 1996.

3. Susan Chira, *A Mother's Place* (HarperCollins, 1998).

4. National Committee on Pay Equity, 1997.

5. *Working Women* (Dec.-Jan. 1998): 22–27.

6. Martha M. Sanders, Mark L. Lengnick-Hall, Cynthia A. Lengnick-Hall, and Laura Steele-Clapp. "Love and Work: Career-Family Attitudes of New Entrants into the Labor Force," *Journal of Organizational Behavior* 19 (1998): 603–619.

7. Census bureau, 2000.

8. American Institute of CPAs, *CPA Client Bulletin* (Jan. 1, 2003).

9. *Parenting* Magazine (June/July 2001).

10. Ann Crittenden, *The Price of Motherhood: Why the Most Important Job in the World Is Still the Least Valued* (New York: Henry Holt, 2001).

Chapter 2

1. The Association to Advance Collegiate Schools of Business, Newsline (Winter 1997).

2. *American Demographics* 19 (August 1997): 22.

3. CNNMoney, March 3, 2003.

4. Elizabeth Warren and Amelia Warren Tyagi, *The Two-Income Trap: Why Middle Class Parents Are Going Broke* (New York: Basic Books, 2003).

5. Ann Crittenden, *The Price of Motherhood: Why the Most Important Job in the World Is Still the Least Valued* (New York: Henry Holt, 2001).

6. *Time* (May 10, 2004).

7. Ibid.

8. *The Wall Street Journal* (May 20, 2004).

9. *The Work, Family and Equity Index: Where Does the United States Stand Globally?* (Cambridge, Mass.: Harvard University, 2004).

10. *Time* (May 10, 2004).

Chapter 3

1. *State Breastfeeding Legislation* (issue paper) (Raleigh, N.C.: United States Breastfeeding Committee, 2003).

2. CDC National Immunization Data, 2003.

3. Peggy Orenstein, *Flux: Women on Sex, Work, Love, Kids & Life in a Half-Changed World* (New York: Anchor Books, 2000), 198.

4. U.S. Department of Labor, "Average Hours per Day Spent in Primary Activities, 2003 Annual Averages" (September 14, 2004).

5. Ann Crittenden, *If You've Raised Kids, You Can Manage Anything* (New York: Gotham Books, 2004).

Chapter 4

1. Sarah Blaffer Hrdy, *Mother Nature: Maternal Instincts and How They Shape the Human Species* (New York: Ballantine Books, 1999).

2. Telephone interview with Helen Fisher, PhD, August 2004.

3. Peggy Orenstein, *Flux: Women on Sex, Work, Love, Kids & Life in a Half-Changed World* (New York: Anchor Books, 2000), 105.

4. Naomi Wolf, *Misconceptions: Truth, Lies and the Unexpected on the Journey to Motherhood* (New York: Anchor Books, 2001), 7.

5. Executive Moms survey, December 2002 (160 women responding).

Chapter 5

1. Carey Goldberg, *The New York Times*, May 15, 1998.

2. Peggy Orenstein, *Flux: Women on Sex, Work, Love, Kids & Life in a Half-Changed World* (New York: Anchor Books, 2000), 113.

3. Telephone interview with Susan Lapinsky, October 2004.

4. Ann Crittenden, *The Price of Motherhood: Why the Most Important Job in the World Is Still the Least Valued* (New York: Henry Holt, 2001), 26, 27.

Chapter 6

1. Susan Abrahamson, *Dallas Business Journal*, October 15, 2004.

2. Bureau of Labor Statistics, 2003.

3. National Foundation for Women Business Owners.

4. Global Entrepreneurship Monitor, 2000 (a twenty-one-country study of global entrepreneurship and economic growth).

5. Catalyst news release, June 24, 2004.

Chapter 7

1. Telephone interview, Sylvia Ann Hewlett, June 2004.

Chapter 8

1. "Opting Out: The Press Discovers the Mommy Wars, Again," *Reason*, June 1, 2004.

2. U.S. Bureau of Labor Statistics.

3. *Time International*, May 10, 2004.

4. American Bar Association website, www.abanet.org.

5. Deborah L. Rhode, The Commission of Women in the Profession, ABA study, "Balanced Lives: Changing the Culture of Legal Practice," 2001.

6. Ibid.

7. Telephone interview, Kerry Rubin, November 2004.

8. *Time*, February 17, 1997.

9. *Mothering Magazine*, March/April 2003.

Index

Abbasi, Noreen, 120
acting
  motherhood and, 12–13
Aigner-Clark, Julie, 131–135
Albright, Madeleine, 184
ambition, 8
  Bobbi Brown and, 15–16
  happiness and, 11
American Academy of Pediatrics, 44
American Bar Association, 168
American Idol, 19
American Medical Association, 184
American Morning, 28, 87, 120
America's Most Wanted, 133
Angelou, Maya, 50
attachment theory, 75
Australia
  maternity leave in, 41

Baby Einstein, 131
balance
  with career, 30
  commute and, 66–67
  for entrepreneurs, 128
  identity and, 100
  in legal profession, 168–169
  with motherhood, 30
  of work, life, 168–169
  of working mothers, 48–49, 67,
    104–105, 111, 166, 175, 181, 183
"Balanced Lives: Changing the Culture of
  the Legal Practice," 169
Becker, Arthur, 125
Bellissimo, Wendy, 45–47, 126–127
Berger, Cindi, 55–60
Berman, Deb, 173–174
Besner, Beth, 129–130
Better Homes & Gardens Decorating, 136
Blaffer Hrdy, Sarah, 71–72
Bobbi Brown Cosmetics, 116
Borden Hervé, Heather, 156–159
boundaries
  creating limits and, 61
  emotional, 51
  for managing work, family, 59, 60
  setting of, 110
breast-feeding
  ceasing of, 43
  cost-benefit perspective of, 47
  dilemma of, 44
  employers' support of, 47
  lactation rooms for, 43, 46

(breast-feeding continued)
  rights for, 45–46
  state-mandated accommodations for, 44
Britain
  maternity leave in, 41–42
Bromberg, Matt, 52
Brown, Bobbi, 15–16, 67, 116–117
Buchdahl, Rabbi Angela, 84
Buckingham, Jane, 143–144
Bureau of Labor Statistics, 53
Busch, Allison, 148–149
Bush, George W., 96
business
  pregnancy prejudice in, 122
Business Week, 4

career
  after 40, 184–185
  baby and, 166
  balance with, 30
  change of, 156–157
  after children, 25, 108
  children and, 23, 24
  clash with, 101–104
  compromises with, 107–109
  confidence and, 34–35
  curse of, 37
  delayed motherhood and, 22–23
  derailment of, 106
  family-friendly, 103, 140, 164
  family incompatibility with, 107
  female lawyers and, 167–168
  financial handcuffs of, 37
  flexibility and, 111, 141, 165, 185
  generational differences in, 104
  having it all and, 20
  identity and, 181–182
  importance of, 34
  income from, 103
  late entry into, 184, 186–187
  making difference and, 83
  motherhood and, 4
  motivational, inspirational, 50
  need for, 187–188

personal identity and, 14
  reassessment of, 104
  "sequencing" of, 185
  switch of, 113
  track for, 27
  women entrepreneurs and, 115–116
  work-life balance in, 168–169
  zig-zagging of, 184–186
Cellucci, Paul, 94
Cheney, Dick, 96
ChicWit, 120
Child, 45
childcare
  comfort with, 51–52
  equal partnership with, 52, 53
  unusual arrangements for, 56–57, 60
children
  adjustment of, 95
  adoption of, 125
  being present with, 51
  birthdays and, 80
  childcare for, 51–52
  close together, 175
  daycare for, 177
  delay of, 28
  expenses for, 38
  fostering independence of, 82
  ideal time for, 28
  mothers' impact on, 75
  parenting and, 125
  with PDD, 154
  peer groups for, 98
  physical proximity with, 90–91
  prehistoric v. modern care for, 74
  priority of, 94
  reality for, 89
  returning to work after, 25, 27, 35, 39
  rituals with, 90
  of stay-at-home dads, 163
  staying connected to, 90–92
  time for, 91
  work after, 185
choice(s)
  curse of, 37

for mothers, 37–39
for women, 37–39, 87
working mothers and, 106, 113, 164, 173
Clark, Bill, 131
Clark, Judy, 167
Clinton, Hillary, 139
CNN, 28
commute
work, life balance and, 66–67
Cooper, Kimberly, 33–37, 44, 89
Cosmo Girl, 3
Cosmopolitan, 143
Couric, Katie, 97
Creating a Life: Professional Women and Their Quest for Children (Hewlett), 23
Crittenden, Ann, 17, 64, 185
Cuomo, Mario, 186
Curry, Ann, 5–9, 20, 47–51, 109
on motherhood, 6
Czech Republic
maternity leave in, 42

Daily Candy, 136
Dalton, Lynn, 60–61
Dateline NBC, 8, 14, 21, 23, 104, 184
Democratic Congressional Campaign Committee, 186
depression
maternity leave and, 40–41
Desperate Housewives, 79
Discovery Network, 47
divorce
financial protection and, 16–17

education
women v. men and, 2
Edwards, Elizabeth, 99
Edwards, John, 99
emotions
ping-ponging of, 36
employers
flexibility and, 168

England
work flexibility and, 167–168
Entertainment Tonight, 45, 156
entrepreneur(s)
balance for, 128
Bobbi Brown as, 116–117
control of, 122
demands of, 118, 128
family-friendly schedule for, 115, 119
flexibility for, 120
inspiration for, 117, 121, 124, 126–127, 129–130, 131, 136, 137
Liz Lange as, 9–11
motherhood and, 133
naiveté of, 134
number of, 115
rollercoaster for, 122
starting business for, 121
success of, 132
timing and, 128
women as, 115–116
Epstein Henry, Deborah, 166
Estée Lauder, 119
Europe
work flexibility and, 165
Executive Moms, 40, 161

Families and Work Institute, 39
family
career conflict with, 101–104, 107
emotional boundaries with, 51
juggling work and, 56–58
prehistoric v. modern, 74
rabbinical career and, 107
Family Medical Leave Act, 41
Father of the Bride Part 2, 152
The Feminine Mystique, 2, 4
femininity
motherhood and, 77
fertility
age and, 23
delayed motherhood and, 23
problems with, 152
Fisher, Dr. Laura, 15, 65–67

Fisher, Helen, 73
Flex-Time Lawyers LLC, 167, 168
flexibility
    demand for, 170
    employers and, 168
    in England, 167–168
    in Europe, 165
    financial reasons for, 167
    in legal career, 167, 168
Flux: Women on Sex, Work, Love, Kids &
    Life in a Half-Changed World
    (Ornstein), 53, 77, 100
Fortune, 4
Friedan, Betty, 4

Gage, Soraya, 8, 13–14, 76, 91, 92, 104
Gerber, Dorothy, 129
Gerber baby food, 129
Goldman, Samantha, 178–184
Gould, Amy, 101–104, 114
Greenberger, Gayle, 151–155, 181
guilt
    alleviation of, 90
    biological, cultural roots of, 74
    lack of, 88, 89
    letting go of, 89, 92
    motherhood and, 72–75
    predisposition to, 73
    of working mothers, 79–80, 87–88, 162

Hewlett, Sylvia Ann, 18, 23, 146, 150
Horman, Brooke, 51–52, 79
Hubbard, Christy, 67–68
Hunt, Chuck, 95
husband(s)
    equal partnership and, 53
    help from, 49, 52, 95
    reliance on, 60
    stay-at-home, 163
Hwang Adam, Sandi, 120

I Don't Know How She Does It, 4
identity
    balance of, 100

career and, 13–14, 181–182
dual struggle of, 99–100
maintenance of, 66
motherhood and, 19
professional, 13
self-esteem and, 103–104
women and, 13, 77
If You've Raised Kids, You Can Manage
    Anything (Crittenden), 64
In Style, 45
infants
    needs of, 75
    survival of, 72
infertility, 69
Irish American Magazine, 29
Israel
    family focused culture in, 62–63

jobs
    reentry to, 25
Johnson, Barbara, 139–142

Keller, Lynn, 184
Kerry, John, 99

La Folie, 151, 156, 157, 158
La Leche League, 43
lactation room
    for pumping, 43
Lange, Liz, 9–11, 67, 87, 92
Lapinsky, Susan, 104
Last Night of Ballyhoo, 12
Lauer, Matt, 156
legal profession
    flexibility and, 169–170
    work-life balance in, 168–169
Lerman, Laura, 3
"Life Works," 47
limits
    creating boundaries and, 60–61
    setting of, 110
    for working mothers, 54–55, 59,
        60
Lowey, Nita, 186–187

Manheim, Camryn, 45
Marcus, Bonnie, 135–137
marriage
  reality of, 18–19
Martinez, Michelle, 53–55
maternity fashion
  success of, 9–10
maternity leave
  compensation for, 41–42, 42
  depression and, 40–41
  length, quality of, 40–41, 42
  working on, 42
Maven Cosmetics, 120
MBA
  women with, 37
medicine
  career in, 178–184
Mercer, Sharon, 162–163
Midler, Bette, 57
*Midlife Crisis at 30: How the Stakes Have
  Changed for a New Generation and
  What to Do About It* (Rubin), 182
Miller, Jane, 111
Miller, Susan, 25–28
Mimi Maternity, 137
*Misconceptions: Truth, Lies and the
  Unexpected on the Journey to
  Motherhood* (Wolf), 78
Modern Bride, 136
Moore, Meredith, 38
Morris, Kimberly, 17–18
*Mother Nature: Maternal Instincts and
  How They Shape the Human Species*
  (Blaffer Hrdy), 72
motherhood
  balance with, 30
  bond of, 70
  career and, 4
  career focus and, 109
  as chic, 69
  as coming first, 56
  competition of, 80–81
  complications of, 37
  "crunch period" of, 49
  decision of, 158–159
  delay of, 22
  difficulty of, 71
  ease, naturalness of, 78
  femininity and, 77
  guilt and, 72–75
  having it all and, 20
  identity and, 19
  impact of, 183
  infertility and, 69, 86
  insecurity, ambivalence toward, 70
  letdown of, 158
  as life-altering, 19
  lifestyle maintenance and, 35–37
  look of, 2–3
  maintaining identity and, 65
  "momtrepreneurs" and, 129
  mother-child bond and, 73
  multitasking and, 64
  new priorities and, 144
  personal experience of, 183
  in popular culture, 2
  positive attitude and, 32
  poverty and, 17
  public persona and, 97–98
  reality of, 19
  sabbatical for, 143
  sacrifices for, 32–33
  scheduling and, 30–31
  surrendering to, 14
  truth about, 71
  unsettling feeling of, 153
Mothering Magazine, 184
mother(s). *See also* non-working mothers;
  working mother(s)
  accomplishment and, 108
  advice for, 50
  advice from, 183
  ambition and, 109
  angst of, 186
  business development of, 129
  career switch for, 113
  celebrity images of, 31
  choices for, 37–39

(mother(s) continued)
  common ground for, 40
  competition with, myth of, 83–85
  divisiveness of, 173
  dual identity struggle of, 99–100
  exiting workplace, 4
  as good-enough, 3–4
  "good" v. "bad," 76, 80
  guilt of, 10
  husband's help for, 49
  identity and, 13
  illness and, 133–134
  impact of, 75
  influence of, 85
  as innovators, 129
  insecurity of, 78
  judgment of, 99
  lactating rights for, 46
  lessons of, 142–143
  maternal instinct of, 72
  "mommy wars" and, 171–173
  as "momtrepreneurs," 129
  multitasking and, 64, 137, 177
  new priorities for, 107
  perception of, 77–78
  practicing medicine and, 174
  pressure, expectations for, 31
  primate, 71–72
  priorities of, 144
  quality of life for, 185
  returning to work, 16
  as role models, 14–16, 33
  self-esteem, purpose for, 155
  setting limits for, 59, 60
  shifting emotions of, 35, 36
  single, 17
  of special needs child, 154–155
  standards for, 100
  support system for, 32, 57–58
  time crunch for, 39
  trade-offs for, 112
  of twins, 152
  two worlds of, 151

National Association of Black Journalists, 29
National Association of Hispanic Journalists, 29
National Bureau of Economic Research, 41
National Geographic, 73
National Organization for Women (NOW), 148
NBC News at Sunrise, 48
Neat Solutions, Inc., 130
New York Magazine, 136, 137, 171
New York Times, 143
New York Times Magazine, 4
Nixon, Cynthia, 12–13, 15, 89, 91
non-working mothers
  anxiety, angst of, 145
  difficulties of, 171
  drive of, 77–78
  insecurities of, 172
  perception of, 77–78
  return to work of, 147
  shifting of, 145
  void of, 154, 155
  working mothers v., 39–40
  years off for, 146
Norville, Deborah, 161
nursery
  bedding for, 45
nursing. *See* breast-feeding

O Magazine, 136
O'Brien, Soledad, 28–33, 38–39, 89, 91
Olympic Moms, 80–81
  competition with, 82
"Opt-Out Revolution," 143
Orenstein, Peggy, 53, 77, 100

Palmer, Karen, 43, 46, 61
PDD. *See* pervasive developmental disorder
Pea in the Pod, 137
People, 29, 71

pervasive developmental disorder (PDD), 154
politics
    pregnancy and, 94
postpartum depression, 71
Potty Topper, 130
poverty
    motherhood and, 17
The Practice, 45
pregnancy
    as chic, 69
    clothing for, 9
    delayed, 140
    in political office, 93–101
    prejudice of, 140
    problems with, 180
    public life and, 95–96
    timing of, 179
    with twins, 96
The Price of Motherhood: Why the Most Important Job in the World Is Still the Least Valued (Crittenden), 17, 108
priorities
    change in, 108
publishing
    women in, 54

Raymond, Brad, 30
Reilly, Evelyn, 94
Rice, Laurie, 107–109, 114
Rice, Phillip, 107
Richman, Vera, 185
Riley, Catherine, 163
Robinson, Julie, 147–148
Robinson, Leila, 169
role models
    for working moms, 19–20
Ross, Brian, 49
Rubin, Kerry, 182
Russia
    maternity leave in, 41–42

Safe Side, 131, 133, 134–135
self-esteem

contribution and, 126
money, identity and, 103–104
of mothers, 155
of women, 11–12, 126
working and, 11–12
Sex and the City, 12, 156
Shields, Brooke, 45, 71
Silver, Laura, 110
single mothers
    working and, 17
Spira, Jessica, 144–145
Stay-at-Home mothers. *See* non-working mothers
Stay-at-Work mothers. *See* working mother(s)
Steiner, Sheryl, 110
Stern, Rebecca, 62–65
Stewart, John, 156
StylePress by Bonnie, 135
success
    new paradigm for, 36
Summers, Judy, 111
Swanson, Nicole, 89–90, 112–113, 114
Sweden
    maternity leave in, 41–42
Swift, Jane, 93–99, 100–101, 113–114, 172–173

Table Topper, 130
technology
    added work and, 59
    boundaries and, 61
Thalberg, Marisa, 39–42
Time, 4, 39, 184
Today, 5, 47–51, 109, 119
Turner, Ellie, 85, 110
twins, 152
    pregnancy with, 96
The Two-Income Trap: Why Middle Class Parents Are Going Broke (Warren), 38

United States
    maternity leave in, 41
    work flexibility in, 165

U.S. Census Bureau March 2002 Current
   Population Survey
   stay-at-home dads and, 163

Vogue, 9, 118, 124
Von Furstenberg, Diane, 136

Walsh, John, 133
Wang, Cheng Ching, 123
Wang, Florence Wu, 123
Wang, Vera, 81–83, 90, 123–126
Warren, Elizabeth, 38
Weekend Today, 30, 31
Well, Jordana, 47
What to Expect, the First Year, 3, 153
"Who's the Better Mom? The Growing
   Conflict in the City Between Working
   and Stay-at-Home Mothers," 171
Wickelgren, Ingrid, 89
Wolf, Naomi, 78
women
   adjustment of, 108
   ambition and, 8, 11, 16, 106–107
   assertiveness, confidence of, 111
   boundaries, limits for, 61
   choices for, 37–39, 87
   confidence, self-esteem for, 126
   conflicted feelings of, 144
   early family for, 139
   education of, 2
   as entrepreneurs, 115–116
   expectations, attitudes of, 2
   family-friendly career for, 103
   fertility issues for, 152
   financial protection for, 17
   financial support and, 34
   greed, guilt of, 8–9
   guilt of, 74–75
   "having it all" and, 32–33, 173
   "hidden brain drain" of, 146
   household, childcare responsibilities for,
      53
   identity and, 13, 77
   ideology v. biology for, 100

infertility and, 86
judgment from, 3
in legal industry, 167–168
"liberation" of, 4
life after 40 for, 184–185
"midlife crisis at 30" of, 24
multitasking of, 63–64
options of, 25
personal failures of, 182
plan of action for, 61–62
professional identity and, 13
in publishing, 54
purpose for, 5–9
self-esteem, fulfillment of, 11–12
"sequencing" of, 185
zig-zagging of, 184–186
work
   attitude at, 79
   delegation at, 57–58
   demanding schedule of, 174, 175
   efficiency at, 110
   emotional boundaries with, 51
   family-friendly environment and, 24–25
   importance of, 170
   juggling family and, 56–58
   managing time at, 60
   maternity leave from, 40–41
   negotiating demands of, 32
   part-time, 166
   perfection and, 66–68
   return to, 146, 147
   stress of, 156
   structure of, 186
   system of, 182
   workweek for, 38
workforce
   "opting out" of, 143
   reentering of, 17, 18, 147
working
   after absence, 17, 18
   ambition and, 8
   equality and, 11
   importance of, 5
   liberation of, 12

reasons for, 5, 8
returning to, 16, 17
role models for, 14–16, 19–20
self-esteem, fulfillment and, 11–12
single mothers and, 17
Working Mother, 104
working mother(s)
  balance of, 48–49, 67, 104–105, 111,
    166, 175, 181, 183
  boundaries, limits for, 54–55, 59, 60
  children of, 143
  choices of, 106, 164, 173
  classroom involvement of, 161
  commute for, 66–67
  conflict of, 4, 59, 85
  creativity of, 92
  dual identities of, 99–100
  empowerment of, 88
  equal partnership and, 53
  fairness issue and, 173
  flexibility and, 165, 185
  focus of, 178
  fostering independence and, 82
  "good mother" standard and, 76
  guilt of, 79–80, 87–88, 162
  from home, 137
  "house of cards" of, 149, 150
  husband's help for, 49
  ideal situation for, 185
  insecurities of, 76–77, 172
  integration of, 162
  issues of, 47, 171
  juggling responsibilities of, 63, 64, 65
  in legal profession, 169
  life compartmentalization for, 51

  limitations of, 125
  making difference and, 83
  medical residency on, 180–181
  networking of, 162
  non-working mothers v., 39–40
  opting in of, 149–151
  options, choices, flexibility for, 113
  organization for, 40, 58
  paving road for, 182
  peer groups for, 98
  perfection and, 66–68
  personal experience of, 183
  personal time and, 89, 93–94
  physical demands of, 48
  priority shift for, 106
  problems of, 109–110
  proving oneself and, 80
  as role models, 88
  scheduling conflicts for, 55–56
  "sequencing" of, 185
  setting boundaries for, 110
  shifting focus for, 63–64
  shortcuts for, 59
  slowing down and, 178
  stimulation for, 40
  stress, loneliness of, 40
  structure for, 52–53
  support system for, 57–58, 164
  switching gears for, 114
  time off for, 179
  work/life integration of, 100–101
  working dads v., 105
Working Women, 11

Youth Intelligence, 143